Land and Property: The English Land Tax 1692–1832

Edited by
Michael Turner and Dennis Mills

ST. MARTIN'S PRESS · New York
1986

First published in the United States of America in 1986
St. Martin's Press, Inc.,
175 Fifth Avenue,
New York, NY 10010

Library of Congress Cataloging in Publication Data
Main entry under title:

Land and property.

Includes bibliographical references and index.
1. Real property tax – Great Britain – History.
I. Turner, Michael Edward. II. Mills, Dennis R.
HJ4337.L24 1986 336.22'0941 84-40611

ISBN 0-312-46436-3

Printed in Great Britain

Contents

List of Tables and Figures

List of Figures

Introduction

This book originates from a conference held in London during September 1981, under the auspices of Portsmouth Polytechnic and The Open University,[1] which revealed that considerable amounts of work based on Land Tax Assessments had been completed since the last major debate on the subject in the 1960s. That debate had been concerned with the technical uses and accuracy of the Assessments and focussed particular attention on the conversion of a money tax, mainly on land and built property, into a quantity of land measured in acres. This conversion was commonly known as an 'acre' or 'acreage' equivalent.[2]

The 1981 conference refined much of the sixties' debate, but it also revealed that, as major users of the Assessments, rural and agrarian historians had been joined by urban and industrial historians, and those interested in the origins and subsequent administration of the Land Tax. A very recent publication was Soltow's article on using the Land Tax of 1798 to study wealth distribution in England and Wales. Although it was criticised at the conference and subsequently in print,[3] it acted as a timely reminder that we are still discovering new uses for, and pitfalls concerning the Land Tax. This book of essays is a response to the enthusiasm promoted by the conference and it includes contributions by all the conference speakers, though not their original papers in all cases, along with a number of specially commissioned essays.

The book divides into four parts, Part I comprising an introductory and historiographical chapter by Turner. After this general overview, the book contains three parts, each with its own particular focus. Thus, Part II has four chapters on the uses and abuses of the Assessments in rural areas, the familiar stamping ground of the Land Tax historian. The chapters by Banks and Turner test the reliability of the Assessments, respectively, against tithe awards in Norfolk and enclosure awards in Buckinghamshire. Broad tests how far the Land Tax mirrors the diversity of three rural communities in Buckinghamshire at the end of the eighteenth century, by carrying out a nominal linkage exercise between Assessments, enclosure awards, and a militia listing of 1798 known as the Posse Comitatus.

Crowther's essay is on the relationships between landownership, enclosure, and topography in Eastern Yorkshire in the late eighteenth century. For her, the Assessments are second in importance to enclosure awards as a source, but she uses them in a way which is very familiar to rural historians.

In Part III the scene shifts to urban and industrial topics. Noble's essay is a geographically wide-ranging analysis of urban morphological development, looking at six East Yorkshire towns, while Henstock presents a more intimate study of a single market town – Ashbourne in Derbyshire. To complete this part of the book, Unwin has used the Assessments as a supplementary aid in unravelling the course of industrial developments in parts of the West Riding.

The final part of the book looks at the origins and subsequent administration of the Land Tax, along with the closely related matter of what the much neglected early Assessments of c.1700 might be able to tell us. Drawing mainly on Cumbrian examples, Beckett is concerned both with the origins of the Land Tax and its administration during the eighteenth century, when powerful personalities fought over the tax at the local level. Ginter's essay is a preview of a book which he is preparing on, among other topics, the question whether the Land Tax of the 1690s was revalued regularly, or ever revalued over the subsequent hundred years and more. Mills and Grover, for parts of the East Midlands and South East England respectively, consider the extent to which Assessments of the period c.1690–c.1720 could be used in conjunction with later Assessments to chart some of the changes in landownership structures during the eighteenth century. Finally, in order to encourage more attempts of a similar kind, the book concludes with an Appendix indicating the distribution of the survival of early Assessments, ie, those for the period before 1780, throughout England and Wales.[4]

Although the 1981 conference gave a crucial impetus to the preparation of this book, the subsequent drafting and/or re-drafting of essays has gone forward with authors in isolation from each other. Consequently, part of Chapter 1 takes the form of editorial comment on the essays in the hope that this will give them greater unity of purpose, and will highlight the major issues emerging. In the last analysis this is only one historian's attempt to set the scene, but if it stimulates discussion it will have served its purpose.

The book could not have been prepared and published without the co-operation of many persons other than the authors. We are most grateful to the Council of Management of the Marc Fitch Fund for a generous grant towards publishing costs. We would like to acknowledge the encouragement given to us by Dr Joan Thirsk and Professors F.M.L. Thompson and Arthur Marwick when our spirits were in danger of flagging. The editors would like to thank Derek Waite of the Cartography Office, the University of Hull for preparing the illustrations in chapters 3, 5, and 7 and in the Appendix, and the Photographic Department of the University Library for preparing prints for publication. We are grateful to Wendy Munday of the Cartography Office, Humberside College of Higher Education for preparing the illustrations in chapter 6. We would also like to thank the Lincolnshire Archives Office and the Cambridgeshire Record Office for producing facsimile copies of Land Tax Assessments with which to illustrate the book.

Many archivists have given much ready help and advice to the authors in the preparation of their essays and both they and a large band of volunteers, including both full- and part-time historians, spent a great deal of time and energy in providing information on the whereabouts of Land Tax Assessments. We hope the book will be some recompense for their interest and will enhance the usefulness and status of the Land Tax Assessments themselves.

Michael Turner
Dennis Mills
August Bank Holiday, 1984.

NOTES

1 For a resumé of the conference see Mills, D.R., 'The Significance of the Land Tax Assessments', *Local Historian*, volume 15, 1982, pp. 161–5.

2 Davies, E., 'The Small Landowner, 1780–1832, in the Light of the Land Tax Assessments', *Economic History Review*, 1st series, volume I, 1927, seems to coin the phrase 'acre equivalent', p. 105. See also Grigg, D.B., 'The Land Tax Returns', *Agricultural History Review*, volume 11, 1963, pp. 82–94; Mingay, G.E., 'The Land Tax Assessments and the Small Landowner', *Economic History Review*, 2nd series, volume XVII, 1964, pp. 381–8; idem., Letter to the Editor, *Agricultural History Review*, volume 15, 1967, p. 18; and Martin, J.M., 'Landownership and the Land Tax Returns', *Agricultural History Review*', volume 14, 1966, pp. 96–103.

3 Soltow, L., 'Wealth Distribution in England and Wales in 1798', *Economic History Review*, 2nd series, volume XXXIV, 1981, pp. 60–70. This article led to a debate in volume XXXV, 1982. See Ginter, D.E., 'A Wealth of Problems with the Land Tax', pp. 416–21; Wilson, G.J., 'The Land Tax Problem', pp. 422–6, and Soltow, L., 'The Land Tax Redemption Records, 1798–1963', pp. 427–33.

4 Gibson, J., and Mills, D., *Land Tax Assessments c. 1690–c. 1950*, Stourbridge, Federation of Family History Societies, 1983, reprinted 1984.

PART I: SETTING THE SCENE

Chapter 1

The Land Tax, Land, and Property: Old Debates and New Horizons[1]

MICHAEL TURNER

Introduction

(i) *A Short History of the Land Tax*

The Land Tax was supposedly a new form of Government revenue introduced in the 1690s for England and Wales; but as is well known, it was descended from a long line of predecessors. In a local county, or regional context it was indistinguishable in some ways from earlier taxation. It arose from the financial strains of the wars against France under Louis XIV and was authorised by an Act of 1692 (1693 New Style). In its first year it raised a little over £1.92 million.[2] From 1697 (1698 New Style) it became a fixed tax with a quota of assessment applied to each county, with the responsibility to distribute the quota among townships and parishes residing with the county administration.

The tax was originally calculated at half a million pounds for each shilling in the pound of nominal taxation, giving an initial rate of four shillings in the pound, and despite its name it was not in fact purely a 'land' tax. It was a real estate and property tax (including buildings as well as land, and also moveable goods), and also a form of income tax on salaries from certain public offices and from tithes. From 1692 until 1798 the tax was voted annually, the rate varying from one to four shillings in the pound until fixed at the higher rate in 1776.[3] In the 1690s the assessment of nearly two million pounds represented about thirty five per cent of all public revenue, but as the eighteenth century proceeded, and as the accumulated national debt expanded, so the Land Tax, fixed as it was from 1697, became a smaller proportion of total public revenue. By the 1790s, along with other assessed taxes, it represented about seventeen per cent of public revenue, and by the 1820s it was eleven per cent.[4] Despite widespread complaints in the eighteenth century about the burden of the tax, it was, by the end of the century, a rather small fixed cost on most estates. In West Derby Hundred (Lancashire) in 1801, local taxation in the form of the poor rate was a far more significant burden of tax on taxpayers than the national Land Tax.[5]

In 1798 in the wake of the first French invasion scare, at a time of seemingly runaway inflation and general financial crisis which had culminated in the suspension of convertibility into gold the previous year, William Pitt's administration sought new ways to raise finances to wage the war, to pay off loans to allies, and to finance the steadily rising Sinking Fund of National Debt.[6] The government separated the land and property items of the Land Tax from the salaries when it introduced income tax proper in 1798/9. At the same time a redemption of the redefined Land Tax was offered at a price equivalent to fifteen years purchase of the current tax commitment. This may have been a device to raise a large sum of money quickly during the financial crisis; G.J. Wilson for example suggests that the money so raised was a way of reducing the National Debt,[7] though in the end the rate of redemption was disappointingly low.[8] Up to 1813 or thereabouts landowners may have made the correct choice in resisting this offer to redeem this particular tax; as a fixed cost during a time of high inflation the Land Tax became a much reduced burden on the outgoings of an estate.

The county quota system of distributing the Land Tax remained in force from 1798 (less the amounts thereafter redeemed) until 1949. The Finance Act of that year introduced compulsory redemption, for example at death or when property changed hands, and finally, the 1963 Finance Act abolished all remaining unredeemed tax.

(ii) *The Origins of the Tax*

The quota system of distributing the tax among the counties, which dated from 1697, was based on the Land Tax assessed in 1692, even though in the first place this was assigned somewhat arbitrarily, and therefore not necessarily equitably. These quotas remained in force for as long as the tax itself, fossilising for all time any inequalities present at its inception.[9] What started out as a four shilling rate was not only not a true representation of general land values at the end of the seventeenth century, but in cross-county terms as the eighteenth century proceeded it did not take into account the differential improvements in land through enclosure, urbanisation, industrialisation, or other developments. This is an important point to remember when the discussion later in this chapter and elsewhere in this book looks at historians' attempts over the years to make cross-county comparisons of landownership patterns.

Though there was a decisive break in taxation procedures with the introduction of income tax in 1799,[10] for historians it did not solve the main problem in using the Land Tax, that is to which date and to which land values did it originally refer. It is evident that county tax rating procedures which were already in operation in the 1690s were adopted by the Land Tax administrators because frequent and expensive revaluations of property could then be avoided.

> 'long established values, though meaningless in terms of true worth, generally represented an accepted division between neighbours'.[11]

Such divisions could be based on the poor rate until at least the turn of the eighteenth century. The consequence was that the Land Tax,

> 'was only as efficient and equitable as purely local circumstances directed. Another implication is that the evidence of inequalities in the assessment of the poor rate was likely to apply with equal force to the land tax.'[12]

The greatest problem is that the rates became fossilised during a century when urbanisation, industrialisation, and enclosure, among other circumstances, changed land values to an unprecedented degree and at an unprecedented rate.[13]

In the case of Westmorland, for example, local practice acted as the fossilising agent when the 'Book of Rates' was employed for many items of local taxation including the Land Tax. It was the prescription for assessment from at least 1617, and even at this or some other founding date it appears that the rate was a nominal one rather than a real valuation. Reassessments of the 'Book' occurred in 1635 and 1693 (not full revaluations but the ironing out of existing inequalities), the latter inspired by the Land Tax of four shillings in the pound in the same year, and remained unchanged thereafter until 1818.[14] A similar rating procedure of similar antiquity was employed in neighbouring Cumberland known as the 'Purvey'.[15] Similar assessments to the Land Tax which were based on local circumstances or similar 'Books of Rates' can be found in other places as well.[16]

If the temporal and geographical origins and assessments of the Land Tax were unequal, so also was there an inequality in the personal assessment of the tax on land and property owners. Allegedly there was double taxation of catholics though there is some debate about both its origins and its enforcement. The legislation implies that this was the case and it has been related to the period of militant anti-catholicism following the 'Glorious Revolution'.[17] It has been pointed out, however, that double taxation of catholics was not a new thing but can be dated to the Subsidy Act of 1625 as a device to equate them with aliens.[18] There are problems in interpreting the Land Tax Assessments when catholics or their descendants renounced the faith.[19] In Lancashire where 'it would have been hard to find an area with more Papists', the enforcement of the anti-catholic clause varied enormously from township to township,[20] and in Cumbria they rarely paid double in practice.[21] L. Soltow claimed that after 1798 when this inequality was rectified and deductions on existing assessments duly made, such deductions amounted to only £2,305 out of the nearly two million pounds national quota.[22] This is partially contradicted by claims that it remained in force until after Catholic Emancipation in 1829.[23] This adds up to a picture of some confusion and

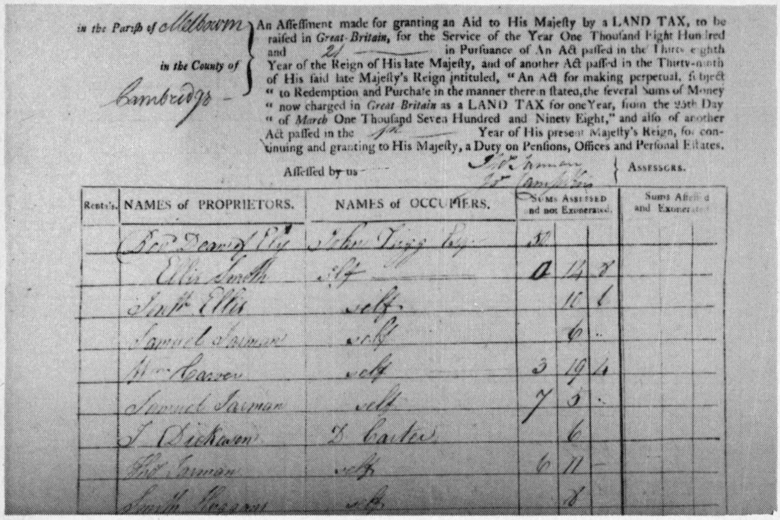

in the Parish of Melbourn in the County of Cambridge — An Affeffment made for granting an Aid to His Majefty by a LAND TAX, to be raifed in *Great-Britain*, for the Service of the Year One Thoufand Eight Hundred and 21 in Purfuance of An Act paffed in the Thirty-eighth Year of the Reign of His late Majefty, and of another Act paffed in the Thirty-ninth of His faid late Majefty's Reign intituled, "An Act for making perpetual, fubject "to Redemption and Purchafe in the manner therein ftated, the feveral Sums of Money "now charged in *Great Britain* as a LAND TAX for one Year, from the 25th Day "of *March* One Thoufand Seven Hundred and Ninety Eight," and alfo of another Act paffed in the 4th Year of His prefent Majefty's Reign, for continuing and granting to His Majefty, a Duty on Penfions, Offices and Perfonal Eftates.

Affeffed by us — [illegible] } ASSESSORS.

Rents's.	NAMES of PROPRIETORS.	NAMES of OCCUPIERS.	SUMS ASSESSED and not Exonerated.			Sums Affeffed and Exonerated
	[illegible] Dean of Ely	John [illegible]	30			
	Ellis Smith	self	0	14	8	
	Smith Ellis	self		10	6	
	Samuel [illegible]	self		6	..	
	Wm [illegible]	self	3	19	4	
	Samuel [illegible]	self	7	5	..	
	J. Dickason	D. Carter		6		
	[illegible]	self	6	11	–	
	Smith [illegible]	self		8		

Figure 1. Facsimile of part of Land Tax Assessment for Melbourne, Cambridgeshire, 1821.

shows that on some issues we are still a long way from a full understanding of the administration and history of the tax.

From 1780 to 1832 duplicates of the parish or township Land Tax Assessments recording the individual land and property assessments were kept by the county clerks of the peace as a check on the extent of the franchise, because the Land Tax became in essence an electoral register recording the property qualification to vote. Sometimes at first, and always by the early nineteenth century it was a register of occupiers as well. In addition it gave the sums assessed against the entries of land and property. These duplicate assessments have now descended to the county records and are held by the county record offices. Earlier and later Assessments do survive, and more will be said about this in later chapters and in the appendix to this book, but for the period when they are generally extant from 1780 to 1832 they have been most extensively used. There was always some difficulty in distinguishing the land from the built property, and so until recently it was the rural Land Tax, where it was more genuinely a 'land' tax, which was the proving ground for the source.

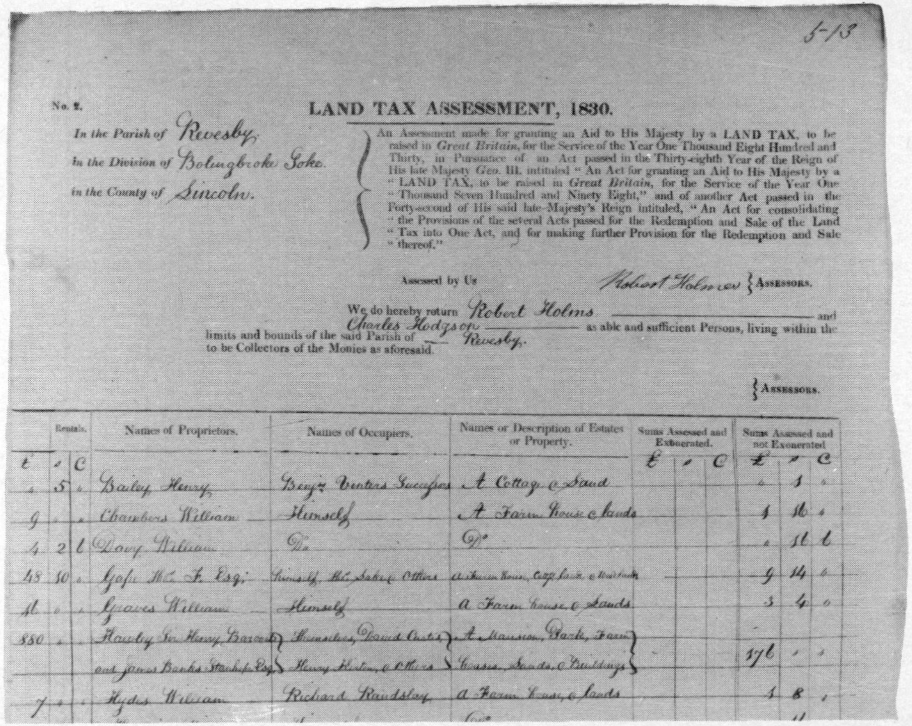

5-13

No. 2. **LAND TAX ASSESSMENT, 1830.**

In the Parish of Revesby
in the Division of Bolingbroke Soke.
in the County of Lincoln.

An Assessment made for granting an Aid to His Majesty by a LAND TAX, to be raised in *Great Britain*, for the Service of the Year One Thousand Eight Hundred and Thirty, in Pursuance of an Act passed in the Thirty-eighth Year of the Reign of His late Majesty *Geo. III.* intituled "An Act for granting an Aid to His Majesty by a "LAND TAX, to be raised in *Great Britain*, for the Service of the Year One "Thousand Seven Hundred and Ninety Eight," and of another Act passed in the Forty-second of His said late Majesty's Reign intituled, "An Act for consolidating "the Provisions of the several Acts passed for the Redemption and Sale of the Land "Tax into One Act, and for making further Provision for the Redemption and Sale "thereof."

Assessed by Us Robert Holmes } Assessors.

We do hereby return Robert Holms and Charles Hodgson as able and sufficient Persons, living within the limits and bounds of the said Parish of Revesby, to be Collectors of the Monies as aforesaid.

} Assessors.

Rentals. £	s	C	Names of Proprietors.	Names of Occupiers.	Names or Description of Estates or Property.	Sums Assessed and Exonerated. £	s	C	Sums Assessed and not Exonerated. £	s	C
,	5	,	Bailey Henry	Benjn Venters Successor	A Cottage & Land				,	1	,
9	,	,	Chambers William	Himself	A Farm House & Lands				1	16	,
4	2	6	Davy William	D^o	D^o				,	16	6
48	10	,	Gosse [illegible] Esq.	Himself, [illegible] & Others	A Farm House, Cottages, & [illegible]				9	14	,
16	,	,	Graves William	Himself	A Farm House & Lands				3	4	0
880	,		Hawley Sir Henry, Baronet and James Banks Stanhope Esq.	Themselves, David [illegible], Henry [illegible] & Others	A Mansion, Park, Farm Houses, Lands, & Buildings				176	,	,
7	,	,	Hydes William	Richard Raudsley	A Farm House & Lands				1	8	,
					D^o					11	

Figure 2. Facsimile of Part of Land Tax Assessment for Revesby, Lincolnshire, 1830.

(iii) *A Note on further reading*

W.R. Ward's *The English Land Tax in the Eighteenth Century* (1953) is still the primary study of the subject but the most useful general introduction is probably R.W. Unwin's *Search Guide to the English Land Tax* (1982). Using many transcripts or photographic examples from Yorkshire he gives a clear indication of the physical appearance of the township Land Tax Assessments and how they changed over time; what information they contained and how that changed over time; and then illustrates the types of local studies that can be carried out using Land Tax Assessments. In the context of general local taxation J.V. Beckett's pamphlet of the same name (1980) and his other numerous publications are invaluable. Finally we must note the county by county handlist of the English and Welsh Land Tax Assessments compiled by J. Gibson and D. Mills which reveals their survival rate under three broad period headings, before 1780, between 1780 and 1832, and after 1832, and which is prefaced by a very useful introduction to the Land Tax.[24]

Old Debates

(i) *The Controversial Use of the Rural Land Tax*

In the 1960s G.E. Mingay and J.M. Martin entered into a stimulating public debate over the usefulness of the Land Tax Assessments as a source for agrarian and economic historians. There had been two other notable land marks in Land Tax studies: the pioneering use made of the source by A.H. Johnson (1909) and H.L. Gray (1910), and the subsequent large scale investigations by E. Davies (1927) and J.D. Chambers (1940 and 1947).[25] These four all addressed the same great issue which concerned many historians from the end of the nineteenth century of whether there had been a decline in the previous two centuries in the numbers and collective landowning strength of the independent peasant farmer, yeoman farmer, owner-occupier or owner-farmer – as he was variously known – and was this decline attributable to enclosure. This was a political hot potato when Johnson and Gray were writing in view of the large amount of radical opinion in agrarian history writing, epitomised by the Hammonds.[26] By Davies' time it had become less political and more a phenomenon to be investigated, and his study was a tour de force on nearly 2,000 parishes in a broad swathe of Midland counties comprising Cheshire, Derbyshire, Lincolnshire (Lindsey), Nottinghamshire, Leicestershire, Warwickshire, Oxfordshire, and Northamptonshire. His was truly the first and possibly still the only spatially extensive use of the Land Tax.[27] Chambers in turn looked at a large selection of the same counties investigated by Davies, and, at the time, with the emergence of European Marxism in the 1930s he found himself as much as anything responding to a resurgence of writing in agrarian and economic history which pointed the finger at the damaging consequences of capitalism, and particularly enclosure, for the well-being of the small peasant farmer.

Thus these pioneers of Land Tax studies used the source because it was a record of owners and occupiers, and hence a record from which the various tenurial relationships of owner-occupiers, landlords, and tenants could be disentangled. In its extant form as a record held by the county clerks of the peace covering the period 1780 to 1832, it straddled the largest single enclosure movement of the eighteenth and nineteenth centuries in the 1790s and 1800s, and followed on from the second largest enclosure movement of the 1760s and 1770s.[28]

Johnson used the Land Tax both as a way of counting the aggregate numbers of owner-occupiers (and other tenurial groups) and as a means of converting what was a money tax into an indication of spatial size by converting the money into an equivalent acreage. He was aware that the quota of tax was unequally distributed among the counties[29] and therefore he based his analysis on the county unit and rarely indulged in direct cross-county comparisons. Even so, it seems that he may not have appreciated that within counties the distribution of the tax among parishes or townships was unequal as well. Gray in 1910 did appreciate this fact and made comparisons with enclosure awards. He demonstrated that in Oxfordshire the rate of parish tax assessment varied from an equivalent of one shilling and sixpence to two shillings per acre.[30] However, he eschewed such conversions and presented his findings from the Land Tax of 1785 for over three hundred townships in terms of the numbers of owner-occupiers and also in terms of the degree of concentration of those owner-occupiers. He devised five categories of concentration; where owner-occupiers paid collectively over twenty per cent of the Land Tax, where they paid ten to twenty per cent, five to ten per cent, less than five per cent, and where they paid nothing at all because there were no owner-occupiers. Townships could then be categorised into one or other of these groups and hence related to events such as the incidence of enclosure. Subsequently Gray made comparisons across time with the Land Tax of 1804 and 1832. An important observation that he made, and which will be touched upon several times in the course of this book, is that the very smallest sums of money assessed as tax may have been assessed on the property of landless cottagers or cottagers having a very small amount of land. He therefore included only those entries of owner-occupiers who were assessed six shillings or more,

'Cottagers paying less, who *may* have had an acre or two of land, will be pretty well counterbalanced by the unavoidable inclusion of some landless dwellings which pay six shillings or more'.[31]

He was therefore trying to capture *land* owners, but arguably because he inevitably included many very small ones in possession of only a few acres, he was stretching his definition of yeoman farmer somewhat. At the other end of the scale were those large owner-occupiers who may have been in occupation of a home farm as country squires,

'Often it is so large an item in the parish that to treat it as a yeoman's farm would give misleading results.'[32]

Thus arbitrarily he excluded all Land Tax entries of greater than twenty pounds. Thus based on his knowledge of the distribution of the tax among the townships and the way this could be used to convert a money tax into an acreage, he claimed that he was isolating the yeoman farmer in possession of from one to 300 acres. Thereafter, apart from two occasions when he does estimate gross acreage occupied by his owner-occupiers, he leaves his calculations and investigations in terms of numbers, in terms of the degree of concentration of tax assessed, and in terms of aggregates of tax assessed. This is an important point in view of the later debate over the calculation of acreage equivalents.

Davies and Chambers tackled more parish examples than both Gray and Johnson, and ultimately defined the distribution or concentration of owner-occupancy in terms of broad groups based on the amount of tax assessed. Thus Davies devised nine groups, those assessed at less than four shillings, those between four shillings and ten shillings, ten shillings and one pound, £1–2, £2–4, £4–5, £5–10, £10–20, and over £20. Chambers simplified these groups into five.[33] They both studied the broad distributions in cross sections in time, the way those distributions changed, and whether there was any discernible relationship with enclosure. Davies chose the early 1780s as his base with subsequent views in 1802 and 1832 and Chambers looked at 1790, 1800, 1812, 1822 and 1830. In addition, Davies, though he recognised that the quota system of distributing the tax among the counties was inequitable, appears to have made the assumption that within counties the quota was equitably distributed, even though Gray had indicated that this was not so.[34] He proceeded to convert the money tax into what has passed into legend in Land Tax historiography as the 'acre equivalent', and then made comparisons across counties, thus obscuring the variations that there were within counties.

This short historiographical note on the pioneering uses of the Land Tax is here used not to study the good or ill fortunes of owner-occupiers, but rather to give some background and firm base from which to review the subsequent debate which ensued in the 1960s, and which is still alive today.

Mingay's 1960s critique of the Land Tax as a source was based on a number of objections and ambiguities surrounding its use. He claimed that valuable though it was, it could not be used for detailed interpretation of landownership.[35] He asserted that since the tax was unequal across county boundaries because of differential county quotas, the investigations by Davies and Chambers in terms of cross-county comparisons were of doubtful use. This is a problem that we willingly concede and perhaps it is unshakeable, but it does not invalidate studies based on the proportions of tax assessed within a parish, along the lines of Gray's study for example. Mingay went on to say that the conversion of a money land tax into a unit of landownership by the calculation of Davies' 'acre equivalent' does not overcome this problem of cross-county inequality because such inequalities could easily reside across parishes even within the same county, and indeed within parishes. The critique proceeded to point out that in 1798 when there was the voluntary redemption of the tax at fifteen years purchase, the land so redeemed disappeared from the tax schedule or assessment, or was listed in such a way as to blur the distinction between owner-occupied land and other forms of ownership and occupancy. Consequently, the completeness and hence the usefulness of the Land Tax was in question for the period after 1798. In addition, from 1798, because of a change in the Annual Land Tax Act, all of the smallest owners the value of whose property was less than twenty shillings per annum were no longer chargeable to the Land Tax, making comparisons involving such small men before and after 1798 hazardous. There are now considerable doubts as to the extent to which this particular clause of the 1798 Act had effect.[36] G.J. Wilson has pointed out that Mingay's identification of this exclusion clause in 1798 is confusing since such a clause dates from 1692 and was a fairly standard provision in other seventeenth-century legislation like the Hearth Tax. In short,

> 'It is possible that the earlier provision had been overlooked or ignored in some parts of the country but this would have to be demonstrated before any 1798 vanishing act could be assumed'.[37]

There were a number of minor, and some other major objections to the use of the Land Tax.[38] Users of the Assessments have become accustomed to these problems and preferred to lose parishes from their studies rather than include them knowing that there were question marks surrounding interpretation. We can readily agree with Mingay therefore that,

> 'It is not suggested that individually these sources of error are very

important, but collectively they must compel caution in accepting the land tax figures at their face value'.[39]

His criticisms were cautionary rather than downright damning, but as he pointed out, a wrong interpretation of the problems could be crucial, as witness Davies and Chambers who used the same Land Tax documents in the same county of Nottingham but nevertheless arrived at different results.

Mingay's main criticism concerned Davies's assumption that county quotas were equitably distributed *within* each county. If this was acceptable then perhaps acreage equivalents were valid, but as long as it was in doubt the whole idea of acreage equivalents was brought into question. In addition, because it was thought that reassessments, or more strictly revaluations, of the tax were either not made or not made frequently after the 1690s acreage equivalents or any other interpretation of the tax could not take account of changing land values, whether across counties, within counties, or even within parishes. Thus in many respects there was a great suspicion that the tax by the late eighteenth and early nineteenth centuries was a fossilised later seventeenth century relic. Furthermore, from a few Nottinghamshire examples Mingay concluded that

'the small owners . . . in proportion to their holdings, . . . paid considerably more tax than did the large proprietors',[40]

so that even the use of an acreage equivalent within a single parish was open to doubt.

Mingay's attack on the Land Tax was foreshadowed by D.B. Grigg in 1963, and to some extent by H.G. Hunt and J. Thirsk before that.[41] Nevertheless this did not prevent Grigg from using the Land Tax, in particular to investigate the owner-occupier in south Lincolnshire between 1798 and 1812.[42] Grigg used the Land Tax in the way pioneered by Gray and Johnson, avoiding the controversial problem of acreage equivalents. He concentrated on the tenure rather than the conjectured size of the taxed properties and taxable proprietors. He did make measurements based on the size of individual's tax assessments, but he chose to do so in terms of broad frequency distributions.

It was J.M. Martin who principally came to the defence of the Land Tax.[43] Initially he brushed aside the minor problems in using the source, problems which with relatively little experience the researcher could easily overcome. More seriously he confronted the two main planks of Mingay's criticism: concerning the completeness of the Assessments, especially with the voluntary redemption in 1798; and concerning the use of acreage equivalents. He dismissed the first issue fairly easily from his Warwickshire study.[44] There is now general agreement that those who redeemed their tax in 1798 or thereafter were still entered on the Assessments. The calculation of acreage equivalents, however, was the most contentious issue. By the use of other contemporary sources it is possible to establish for individual estates or properties the relationship between estate or property size and tax paid. This can then be compared with the estimate of estate or property size which would be derived by using a parish acreage equivalent. The difference between the actual estate size and the estimated estate size would yield the margin of error. If one sampled extensively enough it might become possible to assess the probability that estimates of estate sizes from the Land Tax on the basis of parish acreage equivalents were acceptable reflections of true estate size. In Warwickshire Martin found that such margins of error were mainly very small or even negligible and that only in the estimation of the smallest holdings was the error as much as or more than twenty percent.[45] J.M. Neeson in her study of neighbouring Northamptonshire also found that where it was possible to check acreage estimates derived from the Land Tax with actual surveys, the biggest errors also occurred in estimating the smallest landownership groups, in her case particularly those below twenty acres.[46] If the object of the exercise was to measure the size of individual properties for their own sake then a twenty percent error, or anything remotely close to it, was a very large error to defend, but if the object of the exercise was to use the Land Tax to say something in broader, rather than precise terms about society, then it was useful to identify where the main errors of estimation were found on the socio-economic ladder. The Land Tax could then be used to say something about the remainder of the ladder. One explanation why errors of estimation are most problematic at the lower end of the landownership spectrum is that the Land Tax was a property tax and therefore the smaller the land element in the total property the larger was the landowners' dwelling house or other buildings in the tax assessed. Quite naturally therefore the tendency is to overestimate the amount of land owned by the smaller owners.

As long as parishes were compared with their peer groups in terms of parish acreage equivalents, or as long as differential parish acreage equivalents were adjusted appropriately, Martin's defence of the Land Tax through his defence of the parish acreage equivalent seemed perfectly sound.[47]

Wilson has looked at the issue of acreage equivalents from a different angle. For part of Lancashire from the Land Tax of 1798 he constructed a table of parish pound (£) equivalents, that is how many acres there were per £ of assessment. Such £ equivalents varied from 136.5 acres per £ assessment in a township situated in marsh and heath land to 6 acres per £ in a market town. Initially at least this established the distribution of the tax across a region according to imputed land values. Eighty percent of his townships fell within the narrower yet still broad range of 20–60 acres per £.[48] A point made by Grigg, however, is always present. Rent per acre within parishes varied so much, in south Lincolnshire at least, that parish acreage equivalents could hide enormous differences in values *within* parishes let alone between parishes, and therefore make the use of the Land Tax in this way always problematic. Ideally we should study only those parishes with fairly uniform rent per acre.[49] For this we require land to be of fairly uniform quality, a point which Martin also recognised. Within tolerable limits this is not an insurmountable barrier. In this sense Martin's riposte to Mingay was generally accepted.[50]

Historiographically in the 1960s and 70s agrarian historians have used the Land Tax with caution, but confident in the knowledge that as a general indicator of landownership in rural society it was the only wide scale source that could be used, but that it was ill advised to make precise measurements from it about individuals in society.[51] Traditionally it became a powerful tool to aid the study of enclosure. The fortunes, whether good or ill, of various socio-economic groups formed the framework for research and the Land Tax in its extant form from c. 1780 to 1832 in traversing the single most intensive phase of enclosure activity was the obvious source to use. As long as the study of enclosure was buoyant the use of the Land Tax was assured. After Chambers' studies of the 1940s and early 50s there followed Hunt's work on Leicestershire, which in turn was succeeded by Martin's work on Warwickshire. It was mainly Martin who revived a flagging interest in enclosure and who asked so many novel questions. But the study of enclosure was in competition from other issues; agrarian and economic historians were asking wider questions about agricultural change and productivity in the eighteenth century, and about dietary and output problems in the nineteenth. When geographers turned their attention to enclosure it was principally with reference to land use and spatial distributions rather than with the individuals or groups who were at the heart of the events. In the 1970s however there was a revival of interest in enclosure and therefore automatically in the use of the Land Tax. It was mainly used in its disaggregated form to identify or distinguish owners, occupiers, owner-occupiers, and therefore by implication absentee owners. The methodology had great antecedents but we might usefully mention Grigg, Martin, Yelling who reworked Hunt's Leicestershire material and presented a little fresh evidence from Wiltshire and Worcestershire, Turner, and Neeson, and most recently of all, Crowther.[52] The great conclusion to emerge was that enclosure was not the great despoiler of the small owner or any other owners, as Chambers and Mingay had said before. Nevertheless, the Land Tax revealed many hitherto unknown adjustments in the composition of landownership groups which the traditional Davies' and Chambers' approach of broad aggregation had hidden. In particular it threw back into the melting pot the issue of the social consequences of enclosure.[53] In addition, for the first time, the rural Land Tax was used in a form dissociated from enclosure. Arguably Grigg had done this in the 1960s, but unquestionably much of his work was strongly underpinned by enclosure. Most recently Broad as part of a wider study of Midland England used the 1798 Land Tax for northern Buckinghamshire to show very effectively the concentration of landownership in relatively few hands and Mills has used a large amount of Land Tax material for c. 1830 to 1832, especially for Leicestershire, underpinned in part by enclosure but mainly concerned in analysing social differentiation in the English village of the nineteenth century.[54]

(iii) *Avoiding the Controversy: The Land Tax as a Census of Owners and Occupiers*

The debate over acreage equivalents focussed attention upon the individuals of the past because it discussed attempts to assign acreages and hence comparative sizes to them. But then these individuals were consigned to broad landownership groups, and the debate lost sight of the fact that they were individuals with specific names, and they lived not simply in cross-sections of time, often separated by decades, but rather *through* cross-sections of time, and not necessarily in continuous occupation of their land and paying their tax. In other words it lost sight of the fact that people buy, sell, and exchange land; people die and leave land to others, and they also inherit land; and in terms of the occupation of the land some owners sell up and become tenants, others rise from the tenantry to become owners, and yet others and their forebears and ancestors remain in continuous occupation of their rented or customary held land. The Land Tax eventually records all of these changes. It is in that sense a census of owners and occupiers.

In the mid-1970s in a wide study of Buckinghamshire enclosures I used the Land Tax in a way which partly reflected this quality of the source. I looked at the effects of enclosure by using the Land Tax not for a few cross-sectional years between 1780 and 1830, in the Chambers mode – though I did this as well – but for a critical ten year period for sixty parishes incorporating for each parish the three or four years before an enclosure, the three or four years of the enclosure, and the three or four years after the enclosure was completed. As a control group, seven of the parishes were anciently enclosed. For these I took ten years of Land Tax spaced out over the 1780s and 90s. The study was therefore based on about 600 separate parish Land Tax Assessments – sixty parishes for about ten years each – including about 1,600 personal names for each of ten years. This was the novelty of the approach; looking not at broad socio-economic groups based on acreage equivalent conversions, but rather eschewing the Mingay/Martin controversy and looking at the individuals. The idea was to compare the total number of original names in the first year of study for each parish with the total number of surviving original owners in each subsequent year, to see who of those originally assessed, in a base year three or four years before an enclosure, had survived as owners up to ten years later.[55]

In comparison with the usual method of aggregated landownership structure the results of this different use of the Land Tax opened up once again the whole question of the social consequences of enclosure. Davies did hint at this possible methodology in 1927[56] but he did not follow it through to its natural conclusion, and the study of seven Derbyshire parishes by Chambers went no further than to analyse owner-occupiers and tenants for those crucial years, leaving the results as aggregates without isolating the individuals.[57] In his 1965 thesis Martin also hinted at this possible use of the Land Tax. He looked at the survival rate of family names between the time of enclosure and the Land Tax of 1825. He found two extremes of survival rates. In six parishes enclosed between 1760 and 1764 there were 80 different family names holding over ten acres of whom 27 survived to appear in the 1825 Land Tax, a survival rate of 33.8 per cent. In seven parishes enclosed between 1798 and 1812 of 74 family names holding over ten acres 52 survived to appear in the Land Tax of 1825, a survival rate of over 70 per cent.[58] The survival rate among the leading landowning families was the greatest. Unfortunately Martin did not relate his study of surviving family names to the precise moment of enclosure nor did he look at a control group of parishes which were not enclosed during his periods. My own results pointed to a close relation between the incidence of enclosure and the turnover of names in the Land Tax.

J. Walton investigated the relationship between the turnover of occupiers and the incidence of parliamentary enclosure for Oxfordshire. His study escaped from the traditional focus on the owner-occupiers because he considered the effects of enclosure on *all* kinds of farmers. In so doing he measured the residential mobility of farmers. As a check on the reliability and punctuality of parish Land Tax Assessors in recording changes in proprietorship and tenancy he cross-checked the Land Tax with auctioneer's advertisements in local newspapers. It appeared that,

> 'In all cases . . . the outgoing occupier's name was removed from the land tax list to be replaced by that of his successor at the assessment immediately following his departure'.[59]

His main findings were that enclosure was accompanied by an increase in the rate at which holdings of both owner-occupying farmers and tenant farmers changed hands; this also provided the opportunity for completely new occupiers and tenants to enter the county as well as a redistribution of existing ones. However, the social consequences of this residential mobility did not necessarily result in the dispossession of small owner-occupiers or the extinction of small tenancies.[60] These conclusions however were by no means consistent for all parishes.

Turnover studies gathered momentum. In an as yet unpublished thesis on Northamptonshire, Neeson found a rate of turnover of landowners directly related to enclosure which parallelled to a large extent the findings in Oxfordshire and Buckinghamshire.[61] The rate of turnover of landowners' names within two or three years of enclosure in Buckinghamshire was over 20 per cent with 40 or 50 per cent as the norm and 60 per cent as not unusual. For a control group of old enclosed parishes this rate of turnover over a ten year period was much lower at 18 per cent, and this was evenly spread over the ten years suggesting the operation of a normally active land market.[62] In Northamptonshire Neeson looked at 2,179 entries on 46 Land Tax Assessments to give evidence of owned and occupied land for 1,598 individuals. Three quarters of the owners owned land in parishes enclosed during the period of study and one quarter owned land in parishes which remained open until after 1815. Fifty-two per cent of the landowners no longer held land at the end of a ten year period of study during which their parishes were enclosed. The equivalent turnover rate over a ten year period for parishes which remained open was only 26 per cent. Neeson reworked the Buckinghamshire figures to allow a comparison with Northamptonshire. The mean parish turnover was 46 per cent in enclosing parishes in Northamptonshire compared to 39 per cent in Buckinghamshire, and 22 per cent in open parishes in Northamptonshire compared to 18 per cent in old enclosed parishes in Buckinghamshire.[63]

Most recently Martin has reinvestigated his Warwickshire material. There was an apparent enlargement of the principal gentry estates during the eighteenth century, but the small landowner was seen to decline as a class by up to 25 per cent within a decade of enclosure taking place. This was not merely by a system of transfer of ownership, but also by engrossment by landed families. In addition, in some places the bigger peasant families became even more substantial by the purchase of land from the smaller peasants.[64]

Thus for four closely gathered counties in the south Midlands of England, Northamptonshire, Oxfordshire, Warwickshire, and Buckinghamshire, it may be possible to say something forceful about the fortunes of the small owners and farmers as a result of late eighteenth-century enclosure. The only other rural study known to us which looks at turnover is Crowther's thesis on East Yorkshire. She found that the rate of turnover of landowners was at a much lower level than that found in the south Midlands but unfortunately she did not analyse a control group of parishes without any enclosure activity, and so it is not yet possible to make a true comparison with these other counties.[65]

To complete this section on using the Land Tax as a census we must note that turnover studies have crept into urban and industrial histories, as the papers by Noble, Henstock, and Unwin below indicate.[66] A word of warning is necessary however; it may be that historians have slipped rather too easily, in Wilson's words, from the term 'proprietor to owner', neglecting the distinctions between freeholder and copyholder, and lifeholder, that the term proprietor could hide, such that some of the so called disappearance in turnover studies related to enclosure may have been,

> 'part of a general movement of discontinuation of life-leases, which was paralleled in other parts of the country and had no necessary connexion with the process of enclosure'.[67]

(iv) *The Land Tax and the Distribution of Wealth.*

The most recent controversy surrounding the use of the Land Tax is whether it can be used to study the distribution of wealth on a large scale. Soltow has suggested this use for the 1798 Land Tax for England and Wales, by employing the recorded yearly values of property attached to the Returns which were transmitted to London. As Ginter makes plain in his chapter below, the values in question were appraised rents rather than actual rents. In addition, the county quota system which was introduced in the 1690s was not necessarily equitably distributed among the counties, so that by the 1790s the quotas were 'based on economic relationships existing [at least] a century earlier'.[68] Soltow seemingly understood all of this, nevertheless he proceeded with his study of wealth distribution. His calculations suggested that 20 per cent of all properties – that is individual line entries in the Land Tax[69] – were owner-occupied which in turn was about 11.5 per cent of all families. This was comprised of 12.5 per cent of farm families and 9.1 per cent of urban families.[70] The general feeling therefore was one of absentee ownership and an extensive landlord/tenant relationship.[71] To the extent that it is possible to disentangle the ownership of property of individuals on such a large scale where that property is scattered throughout the uncollated volumes of the English and Welsh Land Tax in the Public Record Office,[72] we find, for example, that the Duke of Bedford had 1,800 scattered properties in Bedfordshire, Devon, Southampton, Surrey, the Isle of Ely, and Middlesex. Wealthy as he undoubtedly was this was still only 0.17 per cent of all the properties and only 0.07 per cent of all property values.

This exercise sounds ideal in providing a bench mark c. 1800 to compare with the New Domesday of Landownership of 1873 and the various other attempts at discovering wealth distribution since Gregory King's day.[73] However, Soltow's interpretation and use of the Land Tax for this purpose was subject to substantial criticism. Ginter in particular suggested that if anything he was not measuring the wealth distribution of individuals, but rather the distribution of property bundles, in which case the total property of an individual was not necessarily entirely contained in one line entry in the Land Tax. The example of the Duke of Bedford mentioned above well illustrates this. In such cases, 'The data can only be useful if the property of individual proprietors (however that term is interpreted) can be aggregated.'[74] The Dukes can be picked out of the many volumes of the Land Tax but can all of the John Smiths be so readily separated? An equally serious problem according to Ginter is Soltow's attempt to convert assessed taxes into real property values (and hence to describe wealth and wealth distribution), by applying a fixed ratio of tax to appraised rents which assumes that 'the tax was 20 per cent of the rent assessed'.[75] This fixed ratio of tax to rent therefore works out at 5:1. In practice, Ginter found that no such ratio was fixed at this level or remotely close to it; in the North Riding of Yorkshire it varied from township to township from 13.4:1 to 49.6:1 with a mean of 25.6. Isolated examples in other places reached as high as 80:1.[76] Where he did find a ratio of 5:1, in parts of the East Riding of Yorkshire, it was equivalent to the four shillings in the pound tax which was the original rate of the 1690s and tantamount to saying that real land values, expressed through appraised rents, had not changed for 100 years. Ginter's conclusion seems inescapable, that in these cases appraised rents had become ossified for 100 years and were valuations akin to the 1690s rather than the 1790s. Unless it is possible to separate all the townships so ossified from those which had clearly undergone regular revaluations – as described by Ginter in his chapter below – then the 1798 Land Tax as a data base for national wealth distribution is spurious. The problem is that not all of the 1798 Land Tax line entries will give appraised rents. Where township revaluations have taken place then

> 'estimates of wealth distributions *within* townships may be safely made from land tax returns. Such estimates should be sufficiently precise to establish typological differences between towns in their landholding and wealth structures, for example. But any use of tax as a basis for estimating wealth distributions across township boundaries is surely doomed to failure'.[77]

Wilson offered further criticisms of Soltow's work. He suggested that he took too literally clauses in the 1798 Act which were not necessarily to be applied equally nationally and which anyway were 'legal fossils without significance' dating from 1692; and he misunderstood the extent and importance of the county and regional variation and unevenness of the fixed quotas. Under the former objection the Act repeated that the assessment was at four shillings in the £ – hence the 5:1 ratio – and under the latter Soltow concluded that

> 'These are probably not very serious within counties, and do not make a great difference even at county level'.[78]

As Wilson responds,

> 'land tax quotas became progressively much lighter the further north and west counties were from London. At the same time there is evidence of significant variation in its incidence within counties.'[79]

The arguments and evidence used by Ginter and Wilson in their criticism of Soltow were very powerful and persuasive, and perhaps best summarised by Wilson,

> 'These observations suggest that Soltow's calculations do not accommodate the considerable disparities that existed in land tax allocation'.[80]

In reply to his critics Soltow compared his wealth distribution derived from the 1798 Land Tax with the fresh valuations of 1803–15 constructed for the purpose of the recently introduced income tax. If anything the 1798 estimates overstated the degree of wealth inequality, which is what Ginter and Wilson implied anyway, but in truth most of their criticisms were unanswerable. Basically Soltow was left with the self-deception that since the land tax documents are the best of their kind available to the social scientist, they must be used. This is not a very satisfactory conclusion, but thankfully those who still work at the parish and county level will find a considerable ray of hope in Ginter's chapter below, that *within* townships the distribution of tax is representative of the distribution of wealth and with care, we may suppose that cross-township and cross-county comparisons are still possible. The lifeline which Ginter offers is the extent of eighteenth and nineteenth century township revaluation.

New Horizons

(i) *Introduction*

This summary history of the controversial uses of the Land Tax has suggested that with care, and without the need to make point specific measurements, the identifiable problems involved in using the Land Tax can be overcome by the careful researcher. Cross-county comparisons are hazardous because of the inequitable quota distribution of the tax, and parish by parish comparisons must be conducted with the utmost caution because even within counties the parish quota of tax was inequitable. Nevertheless such comparisons are possible and broad studies of society can be made in terms of the distribution of the tax. As a census of owners and occupiers the Land Tax seems to have had its greatest recent successes. This section, on New Horizons, is prepared as a guide to the remainder of the essays in this book. The intention is to show how new questions can be asked of the Land Tax and also how some of the old debates keep returning, especially the problematic issue of acreage equivalents. Since the authors of these essays have not enjoyed the luxury afforded to this editor of seeing the whole collection in one piece it is useful to make direct reference to the essays to draw out some of the similarities they share, the novel approaches they make, or the contentious disagreements which still exist.

(ii) *The Rural Land Tax – Old Problems Reappear and New Ones Emerge*

The assumption was made earlier that Martin's reply to Mingay in the 1960s was a successful one and allowed subsequent researchers to use the Land Tax with renewed confidence. In one area at least, the acceptability and accuracy of parish acreage equivalents, the issue may have been too summarily dealt with by Martin. I review the problem again and so does Sarah Banks. According to Banks,

> 'the most serious [problem] is the alleged inconsistency *even within a single parish* of the relationship between the individual assessments and the acreage of land upon which they were made'.[81]

Such inconsistencies arise because although the Assessments may have accurately reflected different land uses and values at the time they were initially constructed they did not subsequently record or take into account changes in comparative values as between properties when new Assessments were made. Banks is correct up to a point but revaluation was undertaken, as Ginter describes in his chapter. Nevertheless, if Martin did not take it into account then at best the reliability of acreage equivalents as a true reflection of actual distributions of individual or group landownership is a hit and miss affair, and at worst it is a non-starter.

There is no other document with comparable landownership details such as is found in the coverage of the Land Tax of 1780 to 1832, and with which to check systematically the accuracy of acreage equivalent conversions. On a random basis estate surveys or enclosure awards exist, the latter in some areas in large numbers. Martin used such material in attempting to establish the general accuracy of acreage equivalents.[82] I use enclosure awards as a check on acreage equivalent conversions and suggest that randomness is only a problem for the study of individual owners, but when the Assessments are taken as aggregates they reflect a very close resemblance to actual gross distributions. For her study area of West Norfolk Banks uses the tithe surveys of the late 1830s and early 1840s to check against the Land Tax of 1831. Her selection of 89 parishes is taken from a predominantly agricultural district with no great variations in soil type, perhaps as near as it is possible to fulfil Grigg's and Martin's requirement to study parishes with uniform quality. The tithe material clusters around 1840 some nine years after the 1831 Land Tax.[83]

One of her main conclusions is that compared with the tithe the Land Tax can be used with 'reasonable confidence' to compare the 'relative differences in concentration and dispersion of ownership between parishes', though in absolute acreage terms the distribution from the Land Tax generally underestimates the true size of properties. The distribution in terms of broad size categories – 1,000 acres or more, 500–999 acres, 100–499 acres, 10–99 acres, 1–9 acres, and less than one acre – however, produced a markedly different picture when comparing the Land Tax with the tithe. In particular, those parishes where the land or tax was distributed most unequally among taxpayers or landowners were subject to greater differences between the two sources than those parishes where greater equality prevailed.

The tax paid by small owners was assessed on land but bolstered disproportionately by the inclusion of a cottage or other buildings, a point noted long ago by H.L. Gray. The larger the land element in the tax payment, generally speaking, the more it is a land tax as distinct from a property tax. As Banks table 1b indicates under the 'sum' column, it is impossible to predict accurately the true number of owners of less than one acre by acreage equivalent conversion from the Land Tax, a view I endorse from Buckinghamshire. Banks found that there were over 700 fewer owners of less than one acre derived from the 1831 Land Tax compared with the tithe of c. 1840. Perhaps those in possession of property of less than twenty shillings annual value were omitted from the Land Tax as Mingay suggested they were. We can attempt to isolate the difficulty of identifying the smallest owners. From Banks' table 1b in the column marked 'sum', if we ignore all landowners reputedly with less than one acre under the assumption that they were underrecorded, the distribution which remains is remarkably similar from the two sources.[84] In broad terms the distributional description of landownership derived from the two sources is the same: of the revised total of landowners eight or nine per cent owned over 500 acres each and something under eighty per cent owned less than 100 acres each. The errors in using the Land Tax are not so great that in eighty nine West Norfolk parishes one could not confidently say that there was a large maldistribution of land c. 1830 which on average in each parish allowed ninety per cent of the land to be owned by just four landowners (Banks table 1a). Arguably, does it matter how the remaining ten per cent was distributed?

In general, my own chapter on Buckinghamshire suggests that even in specific landownership terms estimates from the Land Tax are an accurate reflection of actual landownership distributions. Furthermore, within a parish they portray an accurate rank order of landownership. As a guide to the precise landowning size of individuals the Land Tax is beset with problems of usage, but in terms of relative landownership size and distribution it can be used with considerable confidence.

But the Land Tax is not always accurate or up to date with changes in property ownership, and such problems may be particularly important in landownership turnover studies which depend so much on the ability to identify specific names in the source. Walton felt that the Land Tax assessors registered changes in ownership and occupancy shortly after such transactions took place, but not everyone shares that optimism. Unwin has noted that at the Yorkshire county election of 1807 there was inaccurate or partial entry of freeholders in the Land Tax. It was supposedly a register of electors but effectively it disfranchised 2,000 of them because of careless rating of estates to the Land Tax.[85] John Broad returns to this issue of registration and also asks the wider question of how representative was the Land Tax of general village community life, for example in terms of occupational (job) structures.

Broad points to two difficulties in the registration of names in the Land Tax: there could be delays in that registration; and the Land Tax is only a partial census of a village community, it captures landowners and heads of households but not sub-tenants nor non-household heads of families. On the other hand, no one has ever claimed that the Land Tax was a complete census. Broad's essay is an exercise in nominal linkage, that is tracing names, the same names and therefore hopefully the same people, in more than one source or as a check on the accuracy and completeness of sources. Noble, Henstock, and Unwin also use the method partially in their chapters. Broad cross-checks the personnel in three Buckinghamshire parishes using the Land Tax, contemporary enclosure awards, and the 1798 Posse Comitatus. This last source is a militia listing of all males aged between sixteen and sixty and who socially were inferior to the title of 'Gentlemen'. In addition the Posse gives in some detail the occupations of most people it lists. A disturbing feature of this exercise is that the names in the three sources do not always coincide, even though the sources are dated within a year of one another. It begs the question of whether there was an active land market, or alternatively whether one or other source was an inaccurate register of names. From enclosure historiography we might suppose that there was an active land market on or around enclosure, as turnover studies using the Land Tax have indicated.

Broad found a very high correlation between Land Tax assessed and acreage awarded at enclosure. This is not to pronounce renewed faith in the technique of converting the money tax into an acre equivalent, but rather that large landowners were assessed large taxes and vice versa. This part of Broad's chapter should be read in conjunction with my own study of neighbouring parishes in the same county of Buckinghamshire, especially Broad's measure of rank order correlation and my own demonstration of the same. It appears from both studies that the Land Tax is a good surrogate from which to construct rank order land differentiation.

But land is not the only measure of social and economic differentiation in the English countryside; most people were not property owners of any sort, and it is on this issue that the Posse highlights the amount of village life which is not represented in either the Land Tax or in enclosure awards. Broad also demonstrates the problem of tracing names using the Land Tax on its own, and the simple categorisation of people into owners, owner-occupiers, tenants, and landlords which belies a much more complex tenurial structure which actually existed, where landlords could also be owner-occupiers, and they could also be tenants renting land from other landlords.

Janice Crowther's chapter is the only one which uses the Land Tax in an historiographically traditional way. She is concerned with enclosure, with the patterns of ownership and owner-occupancy and their relationship with enclosure. Notwithstanding the complexity of the regional variations she finds within East Yorkshire, in more general terms what emerges are some similarities with existing enclosure studies, but also some fascinating dissimilarities. Familiarly, the East Yorkshire Land Tax reveals that in the 1780s there were fewer landowners per township in old enclosed townships compared with those in open or recently enclosed ones. Many of these old enclosed places were concentrated in the uplands thus giving fewer owners in those areas where poor soils worked against small scale ownership and farming. But the patterns are by no means always so clear cut. In some old enclosed townships there was very little evidence of the concentration of property so often found in the Midlands, and conversely there was some concentration of ownership in open-field townships which remained in open fields into the nineteenth century.

Compared with the Midlands the dissimilarities in landownership patterns in East Yorkshire are striking. In open-field townships in 1787 there were fewer landowners than in those which had been recently enclosed (that is enclosed between 1725–79), by my calculation twenty four per cent fewer per township. The common explanation for late enclosures is that there was strong, small or medium sized owner resistance, but this belief is clearly contradicted in East Yorkshire.[86] Crowther's interesting alternative hypothesis is that the restrictions and retarding qualities often associated with open-field farming could be more easily accommodated by communal co-operation where there were fewer owners. Thus in these townships expensive enclosure could be delayed, while in townships with many landowners co-operation was less easy to achieve and those frustrated progressive landowners and landlords could only relieve their frustrations by early enclosure.

In a number of ways the East Yorkshire Land Tax singles out the county in contrast to contemporary Midland counties, but this study by Crowther does fall into line in one important respect. Though owner-occupiers comprised upwards of forty per cent of all owners by number, by territorial strength collectively they were not very strong, and only marginally stronger in townships in 1787 which were recently enclosed or still open when compared with old enclosed ones. In all cases on average they contributed no more than fifteen per cent of all tax assessments. This was stronger than Gray and Davies discovered in various Midland counties, but clearly the addition of East Yorkshire to our historiography reinforces the fact that the owner-occupier (some may say peasant, some yeoman) was never very strong by the late eighteenth century over any great area.

(iii) *The Urban and Industrial Land Tax*

Thus far the Land Tax has not enjoyed extensive use in urban studies,[87] perhaps because of the vast number of individual tax assessment entries for even quite small towns. This compounds traditional problems of using the source so far encountered in rural studies. Adrian Henstock partially overcomes the problem of size by using a team of research workers, and other adult education tutors might also consider this methodology. In the six East Yorkshire towns in Margaret Noble's study, in the year 1832, the built property accounted for between sixty and ninety per cent of all Land Tax entries. From 1780 to 1820 the population increased threefold with much migration into the towns and a concomitant expansion of their service activities. This resulted in several hundred new dwelling units as well as more commercial and industrial premises. This took place by a process of demolition and reconstruction, infilling, and subdivision of existing properties. The Land Tax is invaluable in piecing together the morphological and chronological changes of this exciting period.

With the aid of tithe and enclosure plans Noble distinguishes between land and building property, which is of course one of the main problems which faces the rural user of the Land Tax. But an alternative hazard for her is the failure of the assessors to record separately all of the properties of a single owner, particularly after about 1800, preferring to group them in one entry into what Donald Ginter refers to as a 'property bundle'. This may obscure a more complex landownership and tenurial pattern which existed at the time.[88] This is borne out when comparisons with other sources reveal that the Assessments do not fully reflect the true increase in the number of individual properties over the course of the late eighteenth and early nineteenth centuries.[89] The complexity and individuality of each town is illuminated through the Land Tax and must encourage others to further research, but in general the Land Tax also reveals what may be urban history truths. The 1790s was a period of significant urban growth, a finding which also emerges from Henstock's study of Ashbourne in Derbyshire, and in both locations this was also the decade of highest property turnover rates.

One important conclusion which emerges from the East Yorkshire towns is that changes in property ownership involved small plots of land where small proprietors were encroached upon and their land divided to form new building plots, while the land of prosperous merchants, tradesman, the squirearchy and the gentry remained virtually intact.[90] Was the urban peasant under threat, or, was he threatening to encroach upon what little building land was still available? The numbers of the very smallest landowners paying less than four shillings land tax steadily increased; a case perhaps of the growth of the urban peasantry. They purchased building land released by taxpayers in the next highest tax bracket. It sounds like an example of urban cramming, and no doubt the agricultural margins of the towns, especially during the prosperous times for agriculture in the period 1790 to 1815, were jealously guarded against encroachment from builders, and yet this was also the period of largest rate of growth of the urban population. Infilling and cramming inevitably resulted.

These changes can be related to the general economic climate which prevailed at the time, as Adrian Henstock shows in his study. He also detects significant changes in urban form at the turn of the century, with rising population, and agricultural and industrial prosperity bringing forth urban expansion and rebuilding.[91] Both Noble and Henstock produce a measurement of contemporary property turnover rates. The 1790s emerges as the decade of greatest turnover, with nearly sixty per cent turnover in Ashbourne and fifty per cent in the East Yorkshire towns. In Ashbourne this is a rate nearly twice as great as in the other decades in the broader period 1780s to the 1820s, while in East Yorkshire the range was between twenty and seventy per cent depending on the town. Population pressure was the major contributing factor in building development, with the small man often initiating small building projects. As with the East Yorkshire towns so in Ashbourne as well where no new building land was available this pressure of population had to be accommodated by infilling and some division of properties; what I have termed urban cramming.

Henstock relates the peak in activity in the 1790s to the cyclical changes occurring in the national economy. There was a building boom in the late 1780s which peaked in 1792–3. The following outbreak of war with France which brought with it periodic financial crises, bankruptcies, and general inflation may have accounted for the peak in property turnover rates in the 1790s. The building trade recovered after 1801. Noble also identifies an intensity of activity from 1787–92, followed by a lull down to 1797, and then a resumption of activity up to 1802. The contemporary financial crises culminated in the suspension of cash payments in 1797, followed by a proliferation of country banks and paper money in circulation. We may speculate that this provided a new means of credit creation to fuel a new building boom.

If urban historians are now using the Land Tax then industrial historians, whose subject matter was practiced in town and country alike, can also gain from a wider dissemination of the source. Wilson used the 1781 Land Tax in Lancashire to demonstrate the contribution of colliery and other industrial owners to local taxation, and Grover indicates the industrial content of the Land Tax in his chapter below with reference to the old Wealden iron industry.[92] Robert Unwin's main concern in using the Land Tax is to reveal some hidden secrets of industrial development in the Barnsley coalfield from 1690–1830. This was an area of mixed industrial and farming activities which the Land Tax by itself is incapable of completely disentangling, but which is invaluable by processes of nominal linkage for separating individual colliery owners and their tenants from each other. In general terms it is possible to measure the extent and development of the coal industry over the eighteenth century, and in particular to reveal the process of industrial consolidation in the late eighteenth and early nineteenth century when an upsurge in demand for coal encouraged a combination of canal, colliery railway, and industrial investment. For example, the Barnsley Canal which was constructed from 1793 to 1802 brought in its wake the development of the colliery interests of the Spencer-Stanhopes in the township of Cawthorne. This was given a further boost in 1810 with the opening of a colliery railway. In contrast, the other estates of this family in Thurgoland did not develop over the period because of inadequate land and water communications. The Land Tax committments of the family bring out this contrast very well.

(iv) *Land Tax Administration and the Early Land Tax*

As John Beckett's introduction suggests there are still many questions to ask about the administration of the Land Tax. His answers are tentative and suggestive rather than definitive. In illustrating Cumbrian Land Tax administration he exposes some of the administrative follies enacted at the national level, in particular the unequal division of the tax among the different counties; with the heavy burden which was placed on London and the Home Counties and the relatively light burden on the Northern Counties.[93] In Cumbria, as elsewhere, this fixed, historically fossilised, Land Tax quota effectively held down land values and hence sale prices, such that any 'calls for an equal tax' would not have been 'relished by those who had recently purchased estates on the understanding that no change was likely.'[94]

Beckett cites much evidence showing that there was tax avoidance, delays in remitting the tax receipts to London, and losses of revenue to the government through arrears or because money which was collected was not eventually remitted to the Exchequer. In 1693 the receivers remitted forty five per cent of that year's assessment within six months and most of the rest went to London within eighteen months. By the early years of the eighteenth century less than five per cent was remitted within six months and the bulk found its way to London from six to eighteen months after the annual Act which ordered it.[95] The collection of land and assessed taxes has been described elsewhere as a 'notorious feature of eighteenth-century governmental administration', because in the time between collection and remittance the collectors found 'numerous pecuniary openings', such as the financing of the West Riding woollen industry,[96] or the floating capital which founded country banks.[97]

We have discovered that the Land Tax was unevenly distributed by county quota through the country, and from Beckett's work it would appear that there were strong moves to preserve this inequality. Furthermore, it was an inequality with historical antecedents. The quota system was employed in the Ship Money Valuation of the 1630s, the Commonwealth Monthly Assessments, as well as for the Land Tax from the 1690s. But this apparent standardisation of procedures could lead us into a false sense of historical security, because,

> 'Anyone reading the legislation could be forgiven for thinking that here was a smooth, well-oiled machine for efficient annual assessment and collection, but it was one thing for central government to lay down rules and regulations, and quite another for it to enforce them.'[98]

In a number of ways Beckett confirms, reinforces, or overturns many of the existing beliefs and mysteries surrounding the administration of the tax: the remittance procedures; the personal constituency of the tax; the patronage, bias, prejudice, and politicing associated with the tax; the personalities involved; the original basis of the tax; the discussion of periodic reassessment of the tax; and the thorny question of whose responsibility it was to pay the tax, landlord or tenant, a complication which was particularly evident in Cumbria where so much land was held by customary tenure such that at certain times and under certain conditions tenants rather than landlords were required to make tax contributions.

We are left therefore with a Land Tax based on land values loosely applicable to the 1690s, but possibly in some cases and definitely in others applicable to earlier periods. In 1697/8 the tax was transformed into a county based quota system and such local quotas, in Donald Ginter's language, became ossified until in 1798 the Redemption Act made them permanent. Thus the township or parish assessments basically never changed in the two and a half centuries that the Land Tax was administered. But, land values rose or diminished according to local and national trends, though not necessarily in the same positive or negative directions or by the same magnitudes in all places, such that by the eighteenth century it may be that,

> 'the proportional distribution of township quotas no longer bore any consistent relation to the distribution of real land values.'[99]

There simply was no revaluation at the county quota level, or any adjustment of the county distribution at the township level.[100] As a consequence Ginter suggests that there are serious problems when analysing the Land Tax Assessments for individuals after 1780 and comparing them *across* townships. But did reassessment or revaluation take place *within* townships? This is the vital question which Ginter investigates. If revaluation took place at reasonable intervals then at the township level the redistribution of a fixed township assessment among all of the properties in that township may have reflected changing land values. In such circumstances it may yet be possible to construct cross-township comparisons. Ginter's study district is Gilling East Wapentake in North Yorkshire, a district which was relatively isolated from urbanisation, industrialisation, and enclosure, three of the most important eighteenth century events which changed land values. He identifies four different methods of revaluation, and, significantly for historians, he suggests that there was a direct relationship between revaluation, the land market, and the movement in rent.[101] Thus from the mid-eighteenth century to the close of the Napoleonic Wars, a time of rising prices reflected in rising rents reflected in rising land tax valuational rents, the fixed Land Tax became a progressively smaller burden in real terms on the outgoings of estates.

If revaluation was a universal practice can we say we have come full circle in the debate of whether the Land Tax Assessments at the township level accurately reflected the true distribution of land? Notwithstanding the ever present problem of the original, possibly inequitable distribution of the tax, does Ginter's work which shows that tax entries *within* townships were revised on a regular basis, and to a degree which followed the land market, allow us to use acre equivalents with renewed confidence? Unfortunately not, because as his closing remarks remind us there is still the inescapable issue of incomparability *between* townships. Equally important, though there was revaluation it did not necessarily result in a more equitable distribution of the tax within the township. It *may* have maintained the inequitable distribution which *may* have existed from the earliest days of the tax. The door is not closed by any means, but also it is not yet wide open.

We turn finally to a discussion of the uses which can be made of the early Land Tax. Even if the distribution of the county quotas among local townships was not perfectly equitable in the late 1690s, we may suppose that on a rational understanding of the principles of raising a tax it was closer to equitability than at any other time. The discovery of early Assessments on a large scale may open up the eighteenth century to new speculation, amongst other things, on the course of landownership change, especially in the period before parliamentary enclosures became dominant in some areas. The analysis of early Assessments may allow new insights into discovering the mixed fortunes of that most illusive Englishman, the 'peasant'. Dennis Mills and Richard Grover address these issues and lay the seed bed for such investigations by their discoveries of early Land Tax Assessments.

The survival rate of the earlier Assessments is probably greater than historians have previously appreciated. Mills indicates this in his appendix. The first survivals for the majority of parishes occur at either pole of the period 1690s to the 1770s; the first incidence simply related to the origin of the tax and the second to the suggestion that from 1745 perhaps, and definitely from 1780, the duplicate Assessments were required as an electoral register. Grover is fortunate because for his study area there seems to be an almost continuous run of Assessments from the 1710s onwards. We may yet discover a more general, healthier survival rate since these early Assessments are likely to turn up in private muniments rather than in county records.

Mills embraces the peasant debate and addresses the question of the disappearance of the small landowner in the eighteenth century. In Comberton in Cambridgeshire from the Land Tax of 1707 and 1829 it appears that there had been little or no change in landownership structure. This is taken as support for A.H. Johnson's assertion that of all periods the end of the seventeenth and the beginning of the eighteenth century was the most critical for the small landowner. This stretches the data somewhat because all manner of positive and negative changes may have occurred in the twelve decades which separate the sources, though it remains true to observe that in 1707 small owners were dominant in numbers but certainly not in collective landownership strength; this was concentrated in very few hands. In contrast, over the period 1699 to 1815 in the parish of Meldreth, a middle range of peasants had acquired land produced by a filter from the two poles of the landownership spectrum and converging on the middle.

> 'In terms of capitalist agriculture very little had happened, but in a period of rapidly rising population the chances of owning a cottage and a modest few acres had receded considerably.'[102]

From several Lincolnshire examples – in the period 1709–80 – unconnected with enclosure incidentally – Mills then challenges Johnson's thesis and places the crisis for the small landowner firmly in the eighteenth century. Here there is confirmatory independent evidence to show the existence of a filter up the agricultural ladder to strengthen the hand of the large landowners with the concomitant disappearance of the small ones. In six parishes in 1709 there were 244 landowners in the Land Tax, but by 1780 there were only 148. If Assessments survive for the period of the agricultural depression of the second quarter of the eighteenth century they may more precisely locate the main period of change and suggest possible reasons for the change; certainly independent evidence puts the main crisis point sometime before 1747.

The counties in Mills' study are part of the general Midland group, the traditional debating chamber of the mixed fortunes of the small landowner. In contrast, Grover's study area is Kent and Sussex, not counties well endowed with contentious enclosures, but conversely counties with contemporary histories of proto-industrialisation, albeit in the process of deindustrialising by 1700. For the sake of continuity Grover follows similar procedures adopted by Mills, that is using an early Assessment, in his case 1702 or 1705, and comparing with a later one, 1780 or 1781. Over that period, here in an area quite unlike Mills' Midland counties, there were similar adjustments in landownership strength. In broad terms the largest units prospered and those which could have been worked on a part-time basis using only family labour also survived. In consequence the observed decline in landownership was concentrated on holdings which were too large to be worked part-time but also too small to enjoy economies of scale. This is a reminder of Chambers' discussion of the social effects of parliamentary enclosure. He observed that any declines in ownership were mainly in a group of middle sized owners.[103] In Grover's examples of course there was no such influence from enclosure; other forces must have been at work.

> 'The picture which emerges is one of a polarisation in the size distribution of estates and farms, with the larger and smaller units increasing and the medium sized ones declining.'[104]

Conclusion

The way ahead seems clear, and the message which emerges from this collection of essays is encouraging. The Land Tax remains an invaluable source to use, and one in which we can grow in confidence in that use. Our increasing understanding of the origins and subsequent history of the Land Tax and its local administration allows us to reinvestigate the period 1780–1832 with greater understanding of what we are using and greater awareness of the problems of usage. Coupled with a new understanding of the revaluation of the tax at the township level, the Land Tax need hold few fears for the careful researcher. There is an important proviso however; we must beware of making precise measurement both of distributions of urban and rural ownership and occupancy patterns and the way those changed over time, and of the personal constitution of those owners and occupiers in the Assessments. As an indication of broad changes and trends in social distributions of land and possibly wealth, the Land Tax is invaluable, but it must be used wisely.

Perhaps the most exciting future for the Land Tax is the use of the relatively recently discovered early Land Tax Assessments. This opens up the eighteenth century to the possibility of fresh speculation, certainly in rural agrarian and industrial studies, and possibly in urban studies. The still unresolved 'peasant' debate can be reinvestigated with a new source material and the fortunes of various socio-economic groups analysed afresh. Recently it has been suggested that the seventeenth and not the eighteenth was *the* century of English enclosures.[105] That may or may not prove to be the case, but whatever late seventeenth or early eighteenth century enclosure there was, or may yet be discovered, may usefully be investigated with contemporary early Land Tax Assessments, and the social effects of enclosure isolated. The Mills/Grover approach points in some respects in this direction, but suggests more general agrarian changes on or after 1700. It may have been unwise to distill their studies so prematurely because above all others in this volume they are exploring the Land Tax at the frontier, but in the future we must identify the changing tide of events between the poles of c. 1700 and 1780 and perhaps isolate the consequences of the agricultural depression of the second quarter of the eighteenth century. Tentatively it seems that there was a general filter of landownership strength towards large scale ownership and occupancy and hence the emergence of a growing degree of landlessness, or at least greatly reduced powers for small landowners, but that this occurred in areas quite unconnected with enclosures. Perhaps enclosures have undeservedly earned a harsh reputation in the past. In any event, it seems fitting that the rural Land Tax should have the final say in this volume.

NOTES

1 My thanks to Dennis Mills and John Beckett for their valuable comments on the first draft of this chapter.
2 This history and subsequent events are well outlined in the items collected in note 24 below.
3 See the table in Chapter 11 below, note 12.
4 Calculated from Mathias, P., *The First Industrial Nation*, London, 1967, p. 462.
5 Wilson, G.J., 'The Land Tax and West Derby Hundred 1780–1831', *Transactions of the Historical Society of Lancashire and Cheshire*, volume 129, 1980, p. 73.
6 In general on this background see Cooper, R., 'William Pitt, Taxation, and the Needs of War', *Journal of British Studies*, volume XXII, 1982, pp. 94–103.
7 Wilson, loc. cit., pp. 70–3; Cooper, loc. cit., pp. 101–2. There is some confusion over the rate of redemption, some or even most historians say it was at 15 years purchase, but Cooper says it was at 20 years.
8 Wilson, loc. cit., p. 70.
9 This point is expanded upon by Beckett and Ginter in their chapters below.
10 As outlined in Cooper, loc. cit; see also Beckett, J.V., 'Local Rating: Customary Practice and Government Inertia', *Bulletin of Local History: East Midland Region*, volume XV, 1980, p. 4.
11 Beckett, ibid., p. 5.
12 Wilson, loc. cit., p. 75.
13 Beckett, loc. cit., p. 5; idem., *Local Taxation*, London, 1980, especially pp. 22–4.
14 Beckett J.V., 'Westmorland's "Book of Rates"', *Transactions of the Cumberland and Westmorland Antiquarian and Archaeological Society*, volume LXXVII, 1977, pp. 127–37.
15 Beckett, J.V., 'Local Custom and the 'New Taxation' in the Seventeenth and Eighteenth Centuries: the Example of Cumberland', *Northern History*, volume XII, 1976, pp. 105–26: for more examples see idem., *Local Taxation*.
16 Unwin, R.W., *Search Guide to the English Land Tax*, West Yorkshire County Record Office, Wakefield and Leeds, 1982, p. 6.
17 Wilson, loc. cit., pp. 64–6.
18 Aveling, H., 'Catholic Recusants of the West Riding of Yorkshire, 1558–1790', *Proceedings of the Leeds Philosophical and Literary Society*, volume 10, 1963, p. 258.
19 For which see chapter 12 below p. 207–8.
20 Wilson, loc. cit., p. 64.
21 See chapter 9 below, p. 166.
22 Soltow, L., 'The Land Tax Redemption Records, 1798–1963', *Economic History Review*, 2nd series, volume XXXV, 1982, pp. 431–2.
23 Aveling, loc. cit., p. 258.
24 Ward, W.R., *The English Land Tax in the Eighteenth Century*, Oxford, 1953; Unwin,

op. cit; Beckett, op. cit; idem., 'Westmorland's Book of Rates', 'Local Custom', 'Local Rating', and 'Local Taxation in England from the Sixteenth Century to the Nineteenth', *The Local Historian*, volume 12, 1976, pp. 7–12; Gibson, J., and Mills, D. (eds), *Land Tax Assessments c. 1690–c. 1950*, Federation of Family History Societies, 1983 reprinted 1984, available from the Society at 4, Churchill Drive, Amblecote, Stourbridge DY8 4JS, and direct from J. Gibson at Harts Cottage, Church Hanborough, Oxford OX7 2AB: see also Hunt, H.G., 'Short Guides to Records, No. 16, Land Tax Assessments', *History*, volume 51, 1966, pp. 283–6; see also Brooks, C., 'Public Finance and Political Stability: the Administration of the Land Tax', *The Historical Journal*, volume XVII, 1974, pp. 281–300.

25 Johnson, A.H., *The Disappearance of the Small Landowner*, Oxford, 1909; Gray, H.L., 'Yeoman Farming in Oxfordshire from the Sixteenth Century to the Nineteenth', *Quarterly Journal of Economics*, volume XXIV, 1910, pp. 293–326; Davies, E., 'The Small Landowner, 1780–1832, in the Light of the Land Tax Assessments', *Ec. H.R.*, 1st series, volume 1, 1927, pp. 87–113; Chambers, J.D., 'Enclosure and the Small Landowner', *Ec. H.R.*, 1st series, volume 10, 1940, pp. 118–27; idem., 'Enclosure and the Small Landowner in Lindsey', *The Lincolnshire Historian*, volume 1, 1947, pp. 15–20.

26 Hammond, J.L. and B., *The Village Labourer*, London, 1911, Levy H., *Large and Small Holdings : a Study in English Agricultural Economics*, Cambridge, 1911; Hasbach, W., *History of the English Agricultural Labourer*, London, 1908, among a large and similar literature.

27 Gray looked at over 300 Oxfordshire parishes and Johnson had earlier looked at over 500 parishes from a variety of counties, though a number of these he found he could not use, Johnson, op. cit., p. 132.

28 For the general background see Turner, M.E., *Enclosures in Britain, 1750–1830*, London, 1984, especially pp. 16–35.

29 btlJohnson, op. cit., p. 130n.

30 Gray, loc. cit., p. 300.

31 ibid., p. 300.

32 ibid., p. 300.

33 Less than four shillings, four shillings to one pound, £ 1–5, £ 5–10, and over £ 10.

34 Davies, loc. cit., p. 105n.

35 Mingay, G.E., 'The Land Tax Assessments and the Small Landowner', *Ec.H.R.*, 2nd series, volume XVII, 1964, p. 381.

36 Turner, M.E., 'Parliamentary Enclosure and Landownership Change in Buckinghamshire', *Ec.H.R.*, 2nd series, volume XXVIII, 1975, p. 570.

37 Wilson, loc. cit., p. 71.

38 Outlined in among others Unwin, op. cit., pp. 9 onwards.

39 Mingay, loc. cit., p. 384. It is interesting to note that half a century earlier Gray had mentioned many of the same criticisms, Gray, loc. cit., pp. 299–301.

40 Mingay, loc. cit., p. 384.

41 Grigg, D.B., 'The Land Tax Returns', *Agricultural History Review*, volume 11, 1963, pp. 82–94; see also his 'A Source on Landownership: the Land Tax Returns', *The Amateur Historian*, volume 6, 1964, pp. 152–6, and *The Agricultural Revolution in South Lincolnshire*, Cambridge, 1966, especially pp. 82–94: Hunt, H.G., 'Landownership and Enclosure, 1750–1830', *Ec.H.R.*, 2nd series, volume XI, 1958–9, pp. 497–8; Thirsk, J., 'Agrarian History, 1540–1950', in volume 2 of the *Victoria County History of Leicestershire*, London, 1954, especially pp. 234–7.

42 Grigg, *The Agricultural Revolution*, pp. 87–8; idem., 'The Land Tax Returns', p. 94; see also Hunt, 'Landownership', pp. 497–505.

43 Martin, J.M., 'Landownership and the Land Tax Returns', *Ag.H.R.*, volume 14, 1966,

pp. 96–103, and generally in his thesis, *Warwickshire and the Parliamentary Enclosure Movement*, unpublished Ph.D., University of Birmingham, 1965.

44 Martin, 'Landownership', p. 98, and generally corroborated by me in *Some Social and Economic Considerations of Parliamentary Enclosure in Buckinghamshire, 1738–1865*, unpublished Ph.D., University of Sheffield, 1973.

45 Martin, 'Landownership', p. 100.

46 Neeson, J.M., *Common Right and Enclosure in Eighteenth Century Northamptonshire*, unpublished Ph.D., University of Warwick, 1977, p. 424.

47 This categorisation in terms of parish peer groups has become a tried and tested method of using the Land Tax, for an example see Turner, *Some Social and Economic Considerations*, pp. 130n, 157–62.

48 Wilson, loc. cit., pp. 66, 87–8.

49 Grigg, 'The Land Tax Returns', p. 86.

50 For an example see Mills, D.R., *Lord and Peasant in Nineteenth Century Britain*, London, 1980, p. 71.

51 It would be tedious to list all of the historians who proffer this advice, needless to say it is now commonplace in our literature.

52 Grigg, 1963, 1966; Martin, 1965, 1967, and 'The Small Landowner and Parliamentary Enclosure in Warwickshire', *Ec.H.R.*, 2nd series, volume XXXII, 1979, pp. 328–43; Yelling, J.A., *Common Field and Enclosure in England 1450–1850*, London, 1977, especially pp. 103–8, 113, 231; Turner, 1973, 1975, and *English Parliamentary Enclosure*, Folkestone, 1980, chapter 7; Neeson, op. cit.; Crowther, J.E., *Parliamentary Enclosure in Eastern Yorkshire, 1725–1860*, unpublished Ph.D., University of Hull, 1984.

53 Summarised in Turner, *Enclosures in Britain*, pp. 64–80.

54 Broad, J., 'Alternate Husbandry and Permanent Pasture in the Midlands, 1650–1800' *Ag. H.R.*, volume 28, 1980, pp. 82–3; Mills, op. cit., chapter 4.

55 Method first outlined in Turner, *Some Social and Economic Considerations*, pp. 143–50, 163–71, then published in 'Parliamentary Enclosure and Landownership Change'.

56 Davies, loc. cit., p. 91.

57 Chambers, 'Enclosure and the Small Landowner', p. 126.

58 Martin, *Warwickshire and the Parliamentary Enclosure Movement*, p. 120 and Appendix XX.

59 Walton, J.R., 'The Residential Mobility of Farmers and its Relationship to the Parliamentary Enclosure Movement in Oxfordshire', in Phillips, A.D.M., and Turton, B.J. (eds), *Environment, Man and Economic Change*, London, 1975, p. 243.

60 ibid., especially, p. 251.

61 Neeson, op. cit., especially, pp. 208–33.

62 Turner, 'Parliamentary Enclosure and Landownership Change', p. 568.

63 Neeson, op. cit., pp. 208–9.

64 Martin, 'The Small Landowner'.

65 Crowther, op. cit., pp. 464–76, especially p. 474 where we learn that on average from 33 parishes the rate of property turnover on and around enclosure was twenty eight per cent.

66 See also Noble, M., 'Land Tax Returns and Urban Development', *The Local Historian*, volume 15, 1982, pp. 86–92.

67 Wilson, G.J., 'The Land Tax Problem', *Ec.H.R.*, volume XXXV, 1982, p. 425. The other part of the country alluded to is Lancashire, for which see Wilson, loc. cit., pp. 81–2. Ashford, P.J., *The Structure of Land Ownership and Occupation in the Vale of Porlock (Somerset) 1760–1850*, unpublished B.Phil., The Open University, 1984.

68 Soltow, L., 'Wealth Distribution in England and Wales in 1798', *Ec.H.R.*, 2nd series, volume XXXIV, 1981, p. 60, my parenthesis because reading ahead to the section on

Land Tax Administration we discover the local distribution of the county quota was sometimes based on procedures which ante-dated 1692.

69 For a discussion of line entries and 'property bundles' see chapter 10 below, especially note 7.

70 For a discussion and critique of separating rural from urban and the unrealistic implication that rural families were in fact 'farm' families, see, Wilson, 'The Land Tax Problem', p. 425.

71 Soltow, 'Wealth Distribution', p. 69.

72 There are 121 volumes for 1798.

73 For which see Soltow, L., 'Long-Run Changes in British Income Inequality', *Ec.H.R.*, 2nd series, volume 21, 1968, pp. 17–29.

74 Ginter, D.E., 'A Wealth of Problems with the Land Tax', *Ec.H.R.*, 2nd series, volume XXXV, 1982, p. 418.

75 ibid., pp. 419–20.

76 ibid., p. 420; see also chapter 10 below, note 5.

77 ibid., p. 421.

78 Soltow, 'Wealth Distribution', p. 62.

79 Wilson, 'The Land Tax Problem', p. 423.

80 ibid., p. 423.

81 My emphasis, chapter 2 below, p. 40.

82 And see the important unpublished discussion in Neeson, op. cit., pp. 412–31.

83 Banks maintains that this discord in the dates of the two prime documents is not so important unless there was amalgamation or dispersion, as distinct to simply changing hands, thus changing the distribution of parish landownership. Arguably there was some kind of rationalisation in the post-1815 Agricultural Depression which was still present in the 1830s and which may account for some differences in the distribution of landownership between the land tax and the tithe.

84 Banks suggests re-appraising her table in this way herself, chapter 2, p. 44–5.

85 Unwin, op. cit., pp. 6–7.

86 The general proposition is set down in Turner, *English Parliamentary Enclosure*, chapter 7.

87 Though apart from the three chapters in this book we might usefully mention, Noble, loc. cit; idem., *Change in the Small Towns of the East Riding of Yorkshire c. 1750–1850*, Hull, 1979, and idem., *Growth and Development of Country Towns: the Case of Eastern Yorkshire c. 1700–1850*, unpublished Ph.D., University of Hull, 1982: Unwin, op. cit., pp. 13–14.

88 As noted in Chapter 10 below, note 7.

89 See Chapter 6, table 3.

90 See Noble, 'Land Tax Returns', p. 89.

91 For further reading on his technique of house repopulation see chapter 7 below, notes 1–4.

92 Wilson, 'The Land Tax and West Derby Hundred', pp. 68–70; see also Langton, J., *Geographical Change and Industrial Revolution: Coalmining in South West Lancashire, 1590–1799*, Cambridge, 1979, especially Appendix 4, Land Tax Assessment Returns as a source of Colliery Data.

93 And within counties the distribution of the county quota was uneven. In the West Riding the distribution among the various Wapentakes recognised the greater taxation capacity of the cloth producing towns, and the metal working and coal producing areas compared with the farming and lead mining communities, Unwin, op. cit., p. 6.

94 Beckett, chapter 9 below, p. 000, citing Sir John Sinclair. See also his note 52.

95 Beckett, J.V., and Smith, D.K., 'The Land Tax Returns as a Source for Studying the English Economy in the Eighteenth Century', *Bulletin of the Institute of Historical Research*, volume LIV, 1981, pp. 54–61, especially p. 56.

96 Wilson, R.G., *Gentlemen Merchants; the Merchant Community in Leeds 1700–1830*, Manchester, 1971, pp. 150–3.
97 Pressnell, L.S., *Country Banking in the Industrial Revolution*, Oxford, 1956, especially pp. 56–73.
98 Chapter 9 below, p. 163.
99 Chapter 10 below, p. 180.
100 But as Wilson points out, there were advantages for some townships in this situation. Those that were in a comparatively underdeveloped state in 1692 could be placed in more favourable circumstances as the eighteenth century proceded. For example, land reclamation which improved land values and increased the amount of agricultural land, thus spread the burden of taxation more thinly as long as township assessments remained fixed. Wilson, 'The Land Tax and West Derby Hundred', pp. 66–7; see also Unwin, op. cit., p. 19.
101 Indeed 'Revaluation seems in fact to be more clearly attributable to activity in the land market than to any other factor', chapter 10 below, p. 184; in West Yorkshire Unwin relates revaluation to the 1798 redemption Act because in many instances it occurred shortly after this provision, Unwin, op. cit., p. 10, and in general 9–12.
102 Chapter 11 below, p. 198; This is a variation on the Chambers labour supply thesis which also emphasises demographic changes as the key to lost rural opportunities of independence, and possible population migration. Chambers, J.D., 'Enclosure and Labour Supply in the Industrial Revolution', *Ec.H.R.*, 2nd series, volume 5, 1953, pp. 319–43.
103 Chambers, 'Enclosure and the Small Landowner', p. 122.
104 Chapter 12 below, p. 216–7.
105 Wordie, J.R., 'The Chronology of English Enclosure, 1500–1914', *Ec.H.R.*, 2nd. series, volume XXXVI, 1983, pp. 483–505.

PART II: THE RURAL LAND TAX : USES AND ABUSES

Chapter 2

Parish Landownership and the Land Tax Assessments in West Norfolk: a Comparison with the Tithe Surveys

SARAH BANKS

One of the main uses of the Land Tax Assessments has been as an indirect source of information on the numbers of owners and occupiers and the sizes of property holdings in English rural parishes during the period for which they are commonly extant, circa 1780–1832.[1] Since the Assessments were compiled to facilitate the collection of a tax rather than to produce a complete record of all owners and occupiers, lists of owners have to be inferred from lists of taxpayers and sizes of holdings inferred from amounts of tax paid. Although serious doubts have been raised, particularly by Mingay,[2] about the reliability of the Land Tax Assessments as a source for details of parish landholdings, these doubts have received little published attention since their rather summary dismissal by Martin in 1966.[3] This is probably because many recent studies using the Land Tax Assessments have avoided the most contentious issue, namely, the translation of pounds of tax assessed into acres held. Turner, for example, charted the changing fortunes of different categories of owner after parish enclosure by using the acreages given in enclosure awards and then tracing owners' names in the Land Tax Assessments of consecutive years.[4] Alternatively, the Land Tax Assessments have been used to calculate only very broad indicators of the distribution of parish landownership, such as the percentage of tax paid by owner-occupiers, density of owners per parish, or indices of concentration of ownership.[5]

This paper will consider two questions in relation to the use of the Land Tax Assessments in the study of parish landownership. First, are Mingay's doubts justified about translating sums of tax assessed into acres owned at a parish level? Second, what effects do the inaccuracies in the Assessments have in the calculation of the summary statistics of parish landownership distribution, such as concentration of ownership?

Mingay lists a number of problems and inaccuracies which might be likely to occur in the Land Tax Assessments, given the ways in which valuations were made and the categories of persons liable for payment.[6] For example, after 1798 tax could be redeemed by payment of a lump sum and small owners of properties of less than twenty shillings annual value were not chargeable. Thus it is possible that owners included before that date were subsequently omitted. Some owners apparently avoided paying tax altogether, and confusions exist in some of the early returns over the recording of occupiers as owners. Other problems are listed, but the most serious is the alleged inconsistency even within a single parish of the relationship between the individual assessments and the acreage of land upon which they were made. This inconsistency would arise because of the often arbitrary nature of the assessments, initial differences in use and values of land and the failure to reassess land as its use and value changed. One or two examples are included of problematic assessments, but the argument is essentially *a priori*. Martin, while apparently accepting the shortcomings mentioned by Mingay as theoretically possible, attempts to demonstrate empirically that the problems either do not occur, or are not sufficiently serious to invalidate the use of the Assessments to provide a complete and detailed list of owners, occupiers, and estimated acreages of land held in a sample of Warwickshire parishes. The most debated issue, which Mingay in replying to Martin still disagrees about,[7] is the possibility of accurately estimating acreages of individual properties, even given Martin's proviso that reliability could only be expected in parishes which were non-industrial and where the quality of land did not vary greatly.

This debate about the reliability of the Land Tax Assessments is particularly important as these documents constitute the most comprehensive survey of landholding in English parishes at any date in the late eighteenth and early nineteenth centuries. They are also the only source which can be used to trace change over time systematically for large numbers of parishes. Although it is possible to use the tithe surveys of circa 1840 to compare the landownership structure of different parishes at one date, these surveys exist for fewer parishes than the Land Tax Assessments and in many areas of the country coverage is very thin.[8] Some studies of changing ownership over time have avoided calculating the number of acres per unit of tax paid ('acreage equivalents'), but such studies have relied on reference to enclosure awards in order to discuss holding sizes. This obviously suits Turner's purpose which is to chart changes in ownership after parliamentary enclosure. However, enclosure awards do not exist for all parishes and they were made at different dates for different parishes. Therefore, any study of changes in landholding sizes for all the parishes in a particular area between fixed dates, say 1780 to 1830, has to use the Land Tax Assessments alone and to assume that one pound in tax assessed represents the same acreage on different holdings. Many of the early studies using the Land Tax Assessments made the assumption that an assessment of one pound for the Land Tax on a particular holding in a certain parish would represent roughly the same acreage of land as assessment of one pound on another holding in another parish. However, it is now generally accepted that differences in local administration and valuation of property meant that acreage equivalents could vary widely not only between counties, but within them as well. Therefore in order to standardise the Assessments to permit comparison of size of holdings between parishes it becomes necessary to calculate acreage equivalents separately for each parish.[9] If, as Mingay claims, it is not possible to do this accurately because of the variations within parishes between the amounts of tax assessed and the acreages of different landholdings, then this would cast serious doubt on the use of the Land Tax Assessments in studies of changing landholding sizes over time.

(i) *Comparison with the Tithe Surveys*

Although details of parish landholdings given in the Land Tax Assessments can be compared with other documents, for example, estate surveys or enclosure awards, such material can only provide random checks for a minority of parishes. In fact, the only documents which exist in large numbers and actually record details of owners, occupiers, and acreages at a date before 1850 are the tithe surveys. The surveys are relatively detailed and accurate and were drawn up for many parishes in England between 1838 and the mid 1840s following the Tithe Commutation Act.[10] In this paper a comparison will be made of the information derived from the Land Tax Assessments with that contained in the tithe surveys for eighty nine parishes in the poor law unions of Docking, Swaffham, and Freebridge Lynn in west Norfolk for which both tithe surveys and Land Tax Assessments are extant.[11] This is an area of predominantly agricultural parishes with little industry and no great variations in soil type.[12] Most of the tithe surveys date from around 1840, which is eight years after the last available complete set of land tax records. Obviously, therefore, in comparing the details of landholding recorded in the two sources, discrepancies could arise through changes in landownership and occupation during this period. However, this will not matter greatly unless the holdings were amalgamated or dispersed (as opposed to simply changing hands) thus altering the distribution of parish landholdings.

(ii) *Aggregative Statistics*

General measures of concentration and dispersion of ownership were calculated from both sources for each parish (see Table 1a). From the tithe surveys the percentage of land owned by the largest owner and by the four

Table 1

Comparison of Statistics of Parish Ownership Derived from the Tithe Surveys and the Land Tax Assessments

A Measures of Concentration and Dispersion per parish

	Mean		Median		Rho
	TS	LTA	TS	LTA	
% land owned by largest owner	72	63	79	67	0.89
% land owned by four largest owners	93	90	99	97	0.92
Number of acres per owner	354	430	148	200	0.89

B Size Categories

	Sum of all 89 parishes		Mean no. of owners per parish		Per cent owners per parish		Median no. of owners per p'h		Rho
	TS	LTA	TS	LTA	TS	LTA	TS	LTA	
Owners of over 1,000 acs	69	55	0.8	0.6	4	4	1	1	0.76
Owners of 500-999 acs	36	58	0.4	0.7	2	4	0	1	0.48
Owners of 100-499 acs	132	196	1.5	2.2	7	14	1	1	0.72
Owners of 10-99 acs	351	491	3.9	5.5	19	35	2	3	0.75
Owners of 1-9 acs	544	584	6.1	6.6	29	41	2	3	0.81
Owners of under 1 acre	747	24	8.3	0.3	40	2	2	0	0.25
All owners	1879	1408	21.0	15.9	101	100	10	9	0.95

Notes:

Number of parishes = 89 TS = Tithe Surveys LTA = Land Tax Assessments

Rho = Spearman's Rank Order Correlation Coefficients between tithe survey and corresponding land tax variables
Values greater than 0.21 are significant at the 95 per cent level
Those greater than 0.28 are significant at the 99 per cent level

largest owners in each parish was calculated for comparison with figures for the percentage of tax assessed on the largest and on the four largest owners recorded in the Land Tax Assessments. The number of acres per owner was derived from the tithe surveys by dividing the total parish acreage recorded in each parish survey by the total number of owners, while a comparable measure from the Land Tax Assessments was calculated by dividing the total number of owners recorded in each assessment by the parish acreage recorded in the 1831 census. Although these acreages were estimated rather roughly from parish maps, they are the only available measurements of parish acreages for the period circa 1830–40. For between this time and the first ordnance survey, many parish boundary changes had taken place.[13]

The owners listed in each parish tithe survey have been categorised into six groups according to how many acres they owned in that particular parish (see Table 1b). In order to group the owners recorded in the Land Tax in a similar way, acreage equivalents (that is, the number of acres represented by one pound in tax assessed) were calculated for each parish by dividing the total parish acreage recorded in the 1831 census returns[14] by the total amount of tax assessed in the parish Land Tax Assessment. The tax value at which the property of each individual owner in a parish was assessed was then converted into estimated acreages and categorised in the same way as the landholdings recorded in the tithe surveys.

It should be emphasised that the figures shown in Table 1 have been calculated at the parish level, where the basic unit is the amount of property owned by each individual owner. Therefore, when we talk in terms of the total number of owners in all eighty nine parishes (as in the first column of Table 1b), this is not equivalent to the total number of different owners in the eighty nine parishes as a whole, but is simply the sum of the total number of owners in each parish. Thus, these figures cannot be used to give a picture of landownership distribution over the whole area of land encompassed by the eighty nine parishes, as many owners held land in more than one parish and hence are included in the figures for a number of parishes.

Table 1a shows that the mean percentage of land owned by the largest and by the four largest owners per parish is higher according to the tithe surveys (seventy two per cent and ninety three per cent respectively) than according to the Land Tax Assessments (sixty three per cent and ninety per cent). The median values show a similar difference. The mean number of owners per parish is also greater according to the tithe surveys (twenty one compared with sixteen according to the Land Tax Assessments) and hence the mean number of acres per owner is less (354 compared with 430). However, in the latter case the median values are closer and much smaller, which reflects the fact that both sets of data are highly skewed.

So, the landownership statistics derived from the Land Tax Assessments present a picture of parish landownership distribution which is both less concentrated into the hands of few owners and less dispersed between many smaller owners than the corresponding picture derived from tithe survey variables. However, although it appears that in absolute terms the Land Tax figures do not match the tithe figures, they may be a good guide to the relative differences between parishes since these differences are similar to those revealed by the tithe surveys. The values of the correlation coefficients between the corresponding tithe survey and Land Tax variables are quite high (between eighty and eighty five per cent of the variation in one variable can be explained by variation in the other). Thus, the Land Tax Assessments appear fairly systematically to underestimate the concentration of ownership and the number of owners per parish. Therefore, it would appear that the Land Tax Assessments can be used with reasonable confidence to compare the relative concentration or dispersion of ownership between parishes at a certain date, as in the studies by Mills, Obelkevich, and Banks, for example.

However, when the distribution of ownership is broken down into more detailed size categories, as in Table 1b, the discrepancies between the tithe and land tax variables are greater and less obviously systematic. In absolute terms the differences are quite wide, as can be seen most clearly from the column headed 'sum', which shows the total number of owners in each category for all eighty nine parishes. There are fewer people in the over 1,000 acres category according to the Land Tax figures (fifty five) than recorded in the tithe surveys (sixty nine). Conversely, in the 500–999 acres group the figures derived from the Land Tax estimate the number of owners as fifty eight, while the tithe surveys record only thirty six. This suggests that the size of some of the holdings of over 1,000 acres might have been under-estimated using the Land Tax Assessments. In fact, the total number of owners estimated to fall within each of the categories is higher according to the calculations based on the Land Tax except in the largest (over 1,000 acres) and the smallest (less than one acre) categories. The range of the ownership distribution estimated from the Land Tax Assessments is less wide, with fewer extreme values than in the tithe documents. This is as would be expected, given what is known about the underestimation of the size of large holdings and the omission of small owners. Estimation of the number of owners of less than one acre from the Land Tax Assessments (twenty four compared with 747 recorded in the tithe surveys) will also be prone to error because those small owners who were included would often be cottage-owners, and the presence of a house would raise the value of the property and cause the acreages of these properties to be over-estimated. Therefore some of the people owning a cottage and less than an acre will have been put into the next size category, although it is likely that the majority were omitted from the Land Tax Assessments altogether. Because of these problems with small owners, in a study of agricultural landowners it would obviously be advisable to omit owners whom it was apparent from the documents owned a cottage and a few acres. However, the Land Tax Assessments do not always record a description of properties, and, of course, it is very often the small owner of about five acres and upwards in whom historians are interested.

It is likely, on the basis of Table 1b, that people owning less than one acre who were recorded in the Land Tax Assessments would generally be estimated as belonging to the category of one to nine acres, and that some of those really owning between one and nine acres (particularly if they also owned buildings) would be put into the next highest category, and so on until we reach the 1,000 acres plus category, when some holdings appear to have been underestimated as belonging to a smaller size category. However, the over- or under-estimation does not appear to conform to such a predictable pattern. The highest values of the correlation coefficients indicate that only between fifty and sixty per cent of the variation in one variable can be accounted for by the variation in the other variable. The correlations between the tithe and the Land Tax figures for categories 500–999 acres and less than one acre are very low, suggesting that even the relative rankings of parishes on these variables differ considerably between the tithe and the Land Tax data. This is not surprising, since many parishes had no, or very few, owners recorded in some of the size categories, therefore analysis at this aggregative level would not be expected to give much more insight into the variations in the data from the two sources.

However, there is no doubt that the conclusions we have drawn from this comparison of the tithe survey and the Land Tax data at an aggregative level are contrary to Martin's view that acreages calculated from the Land Tax Assessments are reasonably correct in parishes where the quality of land was relatively uniform and little industry existed. Since the Norfolk parishes used in the above analysis fulfil both these conditions, we would expect the numbers of owners in each of the size categories from the tithe and the Land Tax to be much more similar than they are.

(iii) *Comparison of individual properties*

The evidence in support of Martin's case was taken from five Warwickshire parishes where he compares the actual acreage of each land parcel recorded in the enclosure awards with acreages estimated from the amounts of tax assessed on the same property recorded in the Land Tax

Table 2

Comparison of the Acreages of the Same Properties in the Tithe Surveys and the Land Tax Assessments

Parish	Barwick		Great Bircham			Bircham Newton		
Acreages derived from:								
Tithe Surveys	768	507	3552	73	2	1075	48	5
LTAs/1831 Census areas	476	414	3079	441	10	921	217	11
LTAs/Tithe Survey areas	677	588	3114	446	10	893	211	11
Nos. of owners from:								
Tithe Surveys	2		3			8		
Land Tax Assessments	2		3			3		
% land owned by largest owner:								
From Tithe Surveys	60		98			96		
From Land Tax Assessments	54		87			80		

Parish	Castle Acre												
Acreage derived from:													
Tithe Survey	3013	21	9	2	2	1	2	1	1	1	1	1	<1*
LTA/1831 Census area	2984	21	53	11	5	11	5	11	5	5	5	5	5
LTA/Tithe Survey area	2967	21	52	11	5	11	5	11	5	5	5	5	5
Nos. of owners from:													
Tithe Survey	74												
Land Tax Assessment	29												
% land owned by largest owner:													
From Tithe Survey	97												
From Land Tax Assessment	93												

*14 properties of under one acre

Parish	Little Dunham				West Lexham			
Acreages derived from:								
Tithe Surveys	509	443	299	219	993	52	17	4
LTAs/1831 Census areas	460	430	267	191	737	195	26	130
LTAs/Tithe Survey areas	448	419	260	186	735	194	26	129
Nos. of owners from:								
Tithe Surveys	26				7			
Land Tax Assessments	22				9			
% land owned by largest owner:								
From Tithe Surveys	28				89			
From Land Tax Assessments	25				65			

Table contd...

Table 2 contd.

Parish	Great Massingham								
Acreage derived from:									
Tithe Survey	2556	1119	80	22	11	4	2	2	<1*
LTA/1831 Census area	1952	740	172	29	17	26	39	6	6
LTA/Tithe Survey area	1809	686	160	26	16	24	36	5	5
Nos. of owners from:									
Tithe Survey	24			*under one acre					
Land Tax Assessment	17								
% land owned by largest owner:									
From Tithe Survey	63								
From Land Tax Assesment	44								

Parish	Newton					
Acreage derived from:						
Tithe Survey	438	302	109	92	49	12
LTA/1831 Census area	391	314	136	78	65	43
LTA/Tithe Survey area	438	344	149	86	72	47
Nos. of owners from:						
Tithe Survey	8					
Land Tax Assessment	6					
% land owned by largest owner:						
From Tithe Survey	43					
From Land Tax Assessment	38					

Note: The acreages derived from the Land Tax Assessments are based, in the first case, on the estimate of the total parish area given in the 1831 Census, and, in the second case, on the surveyor's figure given in the Tithe Survey as being the total area of the parish.

Assessments.[15] Although he may have based his conclusions on more data than these, as they stand, the examples actually given prove nothing about the reliability of the Assessments in general. A much larger sample taken from a number of different parts of the country would have been more persuasive. The data analysed above are based on a much larger number of parishes, although from one area and at the aggregative level. Given that it is suspected that the Land Tax documents do not in all cases provide a complete list of owners, and that ownership may have changed between 1831 and circa 1840, the most convincing proof of the inadequacy of acreage estimates would be to compare individual land parcels which can be identified with a high degree of certainty as the same in the Land Tax and tithe records.

Table 2 gives information for eight parishes, simply to demonstrate examples of some of the discrepancies which may occur. The acreages of the properties as given in the tithe surveys are listed in the first column, followed by two estimates of the acreages of the same properties calculated from the Land Tax Assessments. The first estimate is based on acreage equivalents calculated by dividing the 1831 census figures for parish acreage by the total tax assessed. In deriving the second estimate, the total acreage recorded as owned in the tithe survey (that is, excluding roads, rivers, wastes, and common lands) has been used instead of the acreage recorded in the census. The former should be a closer approximation to the amount of land privately owned and hence included in the tax documents. The two sets of estimates are not, in fact, markedly different, so it could not be hypothesised that the use of the census acreage figures is causing errors in the estimates. In the right hand columns figures showing the general features of the distribution of land in each parish are included to show how many owners have been omitted from the analysis, and to demonstrate the extent to which the measures of landownership concentration differ between the eight parishes.

These figures do not definitively prove a case, any more than Martin's examples prove the opposite. They do suggest, however, that while acreage estimates derived from the Land Tax Assessments may be relatively accurate in some parishes, they are not in others. It may be possible to suggest why this is so. The estimated acreages shown in Table 2 are on the whole more accurate in parishes where the land is more equally distributed amongst its owners, and above all where there is no single dominant owner. Barwick, Little Dunham and Newton are examples. Not surprisingly, the two Warwickshire parishes for which Martin lists details in full are of this type. In the other Norfolk parishes, with the exception of Castle Acre, the acreages of the predominant owners are markedly under-estimated, which necessarily entails that some of the smaller holdings will be over-estimated. Error seems to be greatest in parishes where there are few owners, such as Great Bircham and Bircham Newton. Careful study of the description of the properties in the tithe surveys (and in the Land Tax records, if given) can often help explain why some of the acreages are over-estimated. In Newton, for example, the forty nine acres estimated at sixty five acres includes a mill, which would add more to the value of the holding. However, although reasons can often be suggested for the discrepancies when studying the Land Tax information in conjunction with other documents, this is not so easy given the Land Tax Assessments alone, especially if descriptions of each property are not given (which they are not generally in the Norfolk Assessments).

It could be that some of the differences between the estimated acreages derived from the Land Tax Assessments and the acreages recorded in the tithe surveys arise because owners are excluded from the Assessments in certain parishes, and therefore calculating the number of acres equivalent to one pound in tax using the whole parish acreage is misleading. However, if some owners are omitted, whether arbitrarily or systematically (systematically in the sense that a certain type of owner would always be omitted or under-represented), then although the estimated acreages of those remaining will be wrong, they should all be over-estimated to the same degree. This does not seem to be the case, as Table 2 shows. On the whole, large owners are not omitted from the Land Tax documents, even when they are exonerated from payment. Occasionally medium-sized owners of fifty to two hundred acres appear to be missed out, although it is possible that they might have been bought out by another owner before the date of the tithe surveys. Sometimes glebe land recorded in the tithe surveys is not entered in the Land Tax lists, but this usually amounts to no more than fifty acres. The main group of people which tends to be under-recorded is that of small owners, especially those owning little more than one acre, or simply a cottage and garden. This is not unexpected, since we know that properties of less than twenty shillings annual value did not have to be included in the Assessment. However, cottage owners are not totally excluded from the Tax Assessments. Some are included and some are not – probably for complicated reasons depending on the history of their plots of land, or what happened at the time of enclosure in particular parishes. For example, in the Castle Acre Land Tax Assessment there are eighteen people listed as paying four shillings tax, the majority of whom can be identified in the tithe survey as owning only cottages and gardens. In the tithe survey itself, however, there is a total of sixty three owners of cottages and gardens. Nevertheless, the omission of small owners who would own much less than ten acres of parish land between them would not seriously affect the calculation of acreage estimates and hence the distribution of other owners amongst the various size categories.

Since we know that large owners tended to pay proportionately less tax in relation to the acreage they owned, and that the very small owners paid more, might it not be possible to adjust the estimated acreages using a sliding scale according to the amount of tax paid by each individual? In fact, it is difficult to employ such a correction factor. For the extent to which, say, a large owner's holding will be under-estimated using a parish acreage equivalent will depend not simply on how much tax he pays, but on how many other owners there are in a parish. For example, if a parish is known to consist of 3,000 owned acres and has only one owner paying ninety five pounds tax, then using an acreage equivalent of 3,000 divided by ninety five, we will infer quite correctly that he owns 3,000 acres. However, in a parish known to be of 3,500 acres, if one owner is assessed at ninety five pounds for 3,000 acres, while a number of owners together are assessed at thirty pounds for 500 acres, then using an acreage equivalent of 3,500 divided by £125, the large owner's holding will be under-estimated (2,660 acres) and the land owned by the rest over-estimated (840 acres). An error of 340 acres amongst 3,000 is not very large (eleven per cent) and would not usually result in the large owner being put in a lower size category. However, an error of 340 acres amongst 500 is more serious (sixty eight per cent) and would probably result in a number of owners being put in the wrong size category. The kind of situation outlined above might cause problems for analyses of changes in the detailed distribution of ownership over time, whether it is thought that valuations of property might have changed over the years or not. For if a number of small holdings were amalgamated to form one large one, the large owner might then secure a reduction in the amount of tax he paid, hence although the acreages of the remaining owners in the parish might still be the same, the acreage estimates derived from the Land Tax Assessments would be higher than previously. Alternatively, if the Tax Assessments of the amalgamated small holdings were retained as they stood, this particular large owner might then pay roughly the same rate of tax per acre as other remaining small owners. So, it cannot be straightforwardly assumed that the estimated acreage of owners of a large proportion of land in a parish is always an under-estimation.

Conclusion

Martin's optimism regarding the accuracy of the Land Tax Assessments has not been vindicated in the case of the west Norfolk parishes analysed here. One explanation might be that the Norfolk Assessments are less reliable than those in other parts of the country, or at least compared with the Warwickshire examples given by Martin, perhaps because of the vagaries of local administration or because it was an area of very large landowners. Martin does not give figures for concentration of ownership in the parishes used in his study, but it is likely that there were fewer parishes in Warwickshire owned largely by one or a few people than in Norfolk. In terms of the average number of owners per parish, however, the figure for Martin's 110 Warwickshire parishes derived from the 1825 Land Tax is 13.7,[16] which is very similar to the figure of 15.8 for the eighty nine Norfolk parishes in 1831. Even if Martin's Warwickshire examples are regarded as more representative of England as a whole (although there is no reason to assume this), the fact that in west Norfolk the Land Tax Assessments are less reliable suggests that considerable care should be taken in analysing the data on ownership found in the Assessments in other parts of the country.

In conclusion it appears that the picture of the distribution of landholding derived from the Land Tax Assessments can be used with reasonable confidence in the comparison of relative differences in concentration and dispersion of ownership between parishes, although the absolute figures will be lower than those derived from the tithe surveys. However, if details of the absolute number of owners, occupiers and amounts of land held are required, then much more caution must be exercised. The distribution of parish landownership into size categories using the Land Tax Assessments and a parish acreage equivalent for eighty nine parishes in west Norfolk differs quite markedly from the picture given by the tithe surveys. It may be possible to see why some of the errors have occurred, particularly if each individual holding in each parish is scrutinised closely, but there does not seem to be an easy way of correcting the Land Tax figures. Parishes where the Tax or land was distributed very unequally amongst its owners seem more subject to error than places where greater equality prevailed. We may conclude, therefore, that the accuracy of the landownership distribution calculated from the Land Tax Assessments in west Norfolk depends not only upon the absence of industry and variation of soil types within parishes as Martin claims, but differences in landownership structure.

Footnotes

1 For example, Johnson, A.H., *The Disappearance of the Small Landowner*, Oxford, 1909, pp. 128–154; Davies, E., 'The Small Landowner 1780–1832 in the Light of the Land Tax Assessments', *Economic History Review*, first series, volume 1, 1927, p. 87–113; Chambers, J.D., 'Enclosure and the Small Landowner', *EcHR*, first series, volume 10, 1940, pp. 118–127; Hunt H.G., 'Landownership and Enclosure, 1750–1830', *Ec.H.R.*, second series, volume 11, 1959, pp. 495–505; Martin, J.M., 'The Parliamentary Enclosure Movement and Rural Society in Warwickshire', *Agricultural History Review*, volume 15, 1967, pp. 19–39; Martin, J.M., 'The Small Landowner and Parliamentary Enclosure in Warwickshire', *EcHR*, second series, volume 32, 1979, pp. 328–343.

2 Mingay, G.E., 'The Land Tax Assessments and the Small Landowner', *Ec.H.R.*, second series, volume 17, 1964, pp. 381–388.

3 Martin, J.M., 'Landownership and the Land Tax Returns', *AHR*, volume 14, 1966, pp. 93–103.

4 Turner, M.E., 'Parliamentary Enclosure and Landownership Change in Buckinghamshire', *Ec.H.R.*, second series, volume 28, 1975, pp. 565–581.

5 Grigg, D.B., 'The Land Tax Returns', *AHR*, volume 11, 1963, pp. 83–94, Mills, D.R., *Lord and Peasant in Nineteenth-century Britain*, London, 1980, pp. 91–97; Obelkevich, J., *Religion and Rural Society: South Lindsey, 1825–1875*, Oxford, 1976, pp. 7–13; Banks, S.J., *Open and Close Parishes in Nineteenth-century England*, unpublished Ph.D. thesis, University of Reading, 1982, p. 195ff.

6 Mingay, op. cit., p. 31; idem., *Enclosure and the Small Landowner in the Age of the Industrial Revolution*, London, 1968, passim.

7 Mingay, G.E., Letter to the Editor, *AHR*, volume 15, 1967, p. 18.

8 Kain, R.J.P., 'Tithe Surveys and Landownership', *Journal of Historical Geography*, volume 1, 1975, pp. 39–48.

9 Grigg, op. cit., pp. 84–5.

10 Evans, E.J., *Tithes and the Tithe Commutation Act, 1836*, London, 1978.

11 Norfolk and Norwich Record Office, Land Tax Assessments 1831: Public Record Office, Tithe Surveys, I.R. 29/23.
12 Banks, S.J., op. cit., p. 181.
13 *Guide to the Census Reports: Great Britain 1801–1966*, London, 1977, p. 262.
14 Census, Abstract of Answers and Returns, *British Parliamentary Papers*, volumes 36–38, 1833.
15 Martin, op. cit., 1966, pp. 100–103.
16 Martin, op. cit., 1967, p. 33.

Chapter 3

Parish Landownership and the Land Tax Assessments in Twelve Buckinghamshire Parishes: a Comparison with Enclosure Awards[1]

MICHAEL TURNER

Introduction

The role of this chapter is to review once again the usefulness of the Land Tax Assessments as an indication of relative landownership sizes and landownership size distributions in a rural society. The 1960s debate which was concerned with the viability of converting the money measurements of the Land Tax into an 'acre equivalent' unfortunately became entrenched in a discussion of estimating the *precise* size of an individual's land. For example, J.M. Martin estimated from the Land Tax of five Warwickshire parishes the acreage of sixty three individual estates and compared those estimates with actual estate sizes from contemporary surveys. For thirty three of them he described the differences in the actual and estimated sizes as negligible. In a further eighteen the difference was less than twenty per cent in each case, and in ten it was between twenty and thirty three per cent.

> 'Only in estimating the size of some small holdings was the error more than twenty per cent; this is not surprising, of course, since on small estates a greater proportion of the tax would represent the landowner's dwelling-house.'[2]

Furthermore, in spite of these errors of estimation on the individual estates, when the total acreage of the sixty three landowners was taken together the total error of estimation was very small. From enclosure awards the estates amounted to 6,738 acres compared with 6,934 acres estimated and summated from the Land Tax, an error of plus 196 acres or three per cent. As an indication that errors were greatest for the smaller estates Martin found that for forty four of them, each of fewer than 100 acres the actual total acreage was 1,902 compared with an estimated

2,007, an error of plus 105 acres or less than six per cent. For nineteen estates of over 100 acres each the acreages were 4,836 as surveyed from the enclosure awards compared with 4,927 as estimated from the Land Tax, an error of plus 91 acres or less than two per cent.[3]

That seemed at the time an emphatic demonstration, admittedly on a small scale, of the reliability of the technique of 'acre equivalent' conversion from the money based Land Tax. But there were and still are some reservations. Two important ones spring to mind: first, not only did Martin's method subsume a great number of estates for which the errors of estimation were very large; but second, those errors were randomly distributed such that the final aggregate error was small by virtue of the mutual cancelling of excessively under- and excessively over-estimated estate sizes. To give a flavour of the problem, in the parish of Harbury Martin discovered neglibible differences between the estimated and actual surveyed acreages of fourteen estates out of a total of twenty six, but in the remaining twelve the errors were minus 21, 12, 27, 21, 26, 36, and 22 per cent and plus 14, 15, 33, 19, and 17 per cent.[4] This does not inspire confidence in using techniques of acre equivalent conversions. But using percentages in this way can be highly misleading. To estimate the size of a four acre estate as only two acres is ultimately less important, and, in terms of broad landownership and social distribution, less distorting of reality than to estimate the size of a 400 acre estate as only 200 acres, yet the error in both cases is the same at 100 per cent. However, possibly a more important issue is, having estimated estate sizes by converting the money Land Tax into acreages is it possible to describe accurately the social distribution or social composition of a parish or township, or group of parishes or townships, not simply by the mutual cancelling of over- and under-estimated estates but by confidently allocating estates into those which were large, medium, or small, depending on definitions of those terms but regardless of individual errors of estimation. This is in effect what Sarah Banks does in chapter two above when she compares size distributions derived from the Land Tax with actual distributions taken from tithe surveys. As I have suggested in my introductory chapter, the broad differences when the very smallest owners are omitted are not very great and would not lead the historian into seriously misrepresenting the actual social/landed distribution of a collection of parishes. Martin gave a hint of this approach when he said that,

> 'Of the 44 small landowners in possession of under 100 acres, only three marginal landowners would have been classified in the wrong category, that is placed with landowners in possession of 1–200 acres.'[5]

Richard Grover in his 1981 Land Tax conference paper also suggested this possible confident use of the Land Tax,

> 'the relationship between tax and acreage is sufficiently strong so as to permit confidence in a size distribution of holdings computed by applying a parish-based tax per acre ratio to the tax assessments, though not in the computation of any individual holding.'[6]

As yet neither Martin nor Grover give enough cases for the issue to be resolved, and Banks, though she gives enough cases perhaps does not investigate enough group frequency variation in those cases.

Group Frequency Landed Distributions

From enclosure awards Martin extracted the actual sizes of estates to check against the acreage estimates of the same estates derived from the Land Tax. Unfortunately enclosure awards are not a source which can be used in this way in every case. When enclosures occurred not all of the land in a township or parish was enclosed at the same time, and some land may have been enclosed at an earlier date. The enclosure commissioners and their surveyors were not bound to survey the whole parish, unless directed to do so by the enclosure act, but thankfully sometimes they did. The following analysis is based on twelve of the Buckinghamshire parishes for which the enclosure awards give a complete parish survey measured in statute acres. The acreages of individual landowners itemised in these enclosure awards have been compared with the estimated acreages derived from the Land Tax Assessments for the same landowners in the same parishes for closely associated years.[7] As John Broad indicates in his chapter below, not always will there be a close correlation in names between the two sources. The date of an enclosure in relation to the month of collection of the Land Tax is important, though more significant is the fact that it took time for the tax assessors to catch up with the buying, selling, and exchange of land. J.R. Walton found that they did this fairly shortly after such transactions took place.[8] From the twelve Buckinghamshire parishes in this analysis 304 landowners have been traced in both the enclosure awards and the Land Tax of the same or the following year, including landowners of those estates where it has been possible to trace the buying, selling, and exchange of land. By the familiar method of converting the money Land Tax into an acre equivalent these landowners have been categorised into landownership groups, nine in number ranging from landowners with more than 500 acres to those with less than one acre. The landownership distribution so produced is illustrated in figure 1.

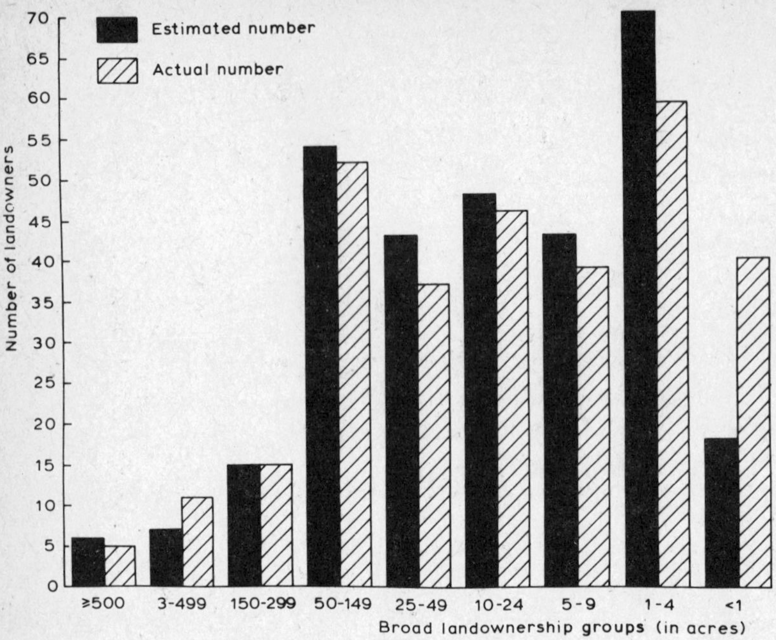

Figure 1. The Distribution of Landownership in Twelve Buckinghamshire Parishes, 1796–1812, Comparing Estimated Numbers from the Land Tax with Actual Numbers from Enclosure Awards.

The visual correlation of the distribution of the estimated and actual numbers between the groups is very impressive. One would go further and suggest that if asked to describe the landownership distribution from either source, almost identical descriptions would emerge. These are not particularly broad acreage groups but are really quite detailed. At its worst, those ninety nine owners with fewer than five acres derived from the enclosure awards composed fifty nine with one to four acres each and as many as forty with less than one acre each, compared with eighty eight owners with fewer than five acres estimated from the Land Tax composed of seventy with one to four acres each and only eighteen very small ones with less than one acre each. This is the familiar tale exposed by Gray in the pioneering days of Land Tax studies,[9] and more recently by Martin and Banks, among others. From the Land Tax it is very difficult to identify the very smallest landowners. We usually maintain that this is because of the disproportionate contribution of assessment on buildings in the Land Tax payments of these small landowners. Table 1 reproduces figure 1 to show

Table 1

Distribution of Landownership in Twelve Buckinghamshire Parishes, 1796-1812, Comparing Estimated Numbers from the Land Tax with Actual Numbers from Enclosure Awards

Strategy 1					Strategy 2				
Acreage	Landowners				Acreage	Landowners			
Groups	Estimated		Actual		Groups	Estimated		Actual	
	No	%	No	%		No	%	No	%
Over 500	6	2.0	5	1.6	Over 300	13	4.3	16	5.3
300-499	7	2.3	11	3.6	200-299	8	2.6	3	1.0
150-299	15	4.9	15	4.9	100-199	26	8.6	30	9.9
50-149	54	17.8	52	17.1	50-99	35	11.5	34	11.2
25-49	43	14.1	37	12.2	25-49	43	14.1	37	12.2
10-24	48	15.8	46	15.1	10-24	48	15.8	46	15.1
5-9	43	14.1	39	12.8	5-9	43	14.1	39	12.8
1-4	70	23.0	59	19.4	Under 5	88	28.9	99	32.6
Under 1	18	5.9	40	13.2					
Total	304	99.9	304	99.9		304	99.9	304	100.1

Source: Buckinghamshire County Record Office, adapted from Enclosure Awards and Land Tax Assessments for the parishes itemised in figure 2

the distribution of landownership under two different strategies. On the one hand this indicates the absence of bias in the choice of landownership groups and on the other it solves the difficulty of identifying the very smallest landowners by subsuming them in one group owning fewer than five acres.

It could reasonably be suggested that as with my criticism of Martin, the table and the figure subsume the mutual cancellation of over- and under-estimated estate sizes and therefore any broad description of land or social distribution might be the consequent randomness of this over- and under-estimation. Once again this is not a conclusion which would inspire confidence in the continued use of the Land Tax in this way. From table 1, strategy 2, of the 304 landowners 232 of them appear in the same landownership group whether by estimation from the Land Tax or by direct allocation from the enclosure awards. Of the remaining seventy two landowners only three are located in a group derived from the Land Tax which is more than one group removed from their true location from the enclosure awards, and one of these landowners was three groups removed. Of the remaining sixty nine landowners forty five of them drop into a lower landownership group when comparing the estimated distribution with the true distribution, that is they were over-estimated, and twenty four climb into a higher group, that is they were under-estimated. This shows that estimates calculated from the Land Tax tend to inflate the sizes of larger numbers of landowners, than they deflate the sizes of smaller numbers of landowners; much the same conclusion that has been formed by other users of the Land Tax.

The next stage in the analysis shows that even where landowners were estimated to appear in one group but actually should be placed in a higher or lower group, predominantly, these were very small landowners. In rounded terms, eighty per cent of all errors in allocating landowners to landownership groups in table 1 strategy 2 occurred at or below the ten acre boundary level, and sixty per cent at or below the five acre boundary level. But does it matter whether in absolute specific terms a landowner was estimated to own four acres but actually owned six acres, or whether he was estimated to own six acres but actually owned four acres? He is, by any stretch of analysis and imagination, no more nor less than a very small landowner. Such examples abound and in broad terms they occur mainly among the very smallest landowners, and mainly, though not exclusively, highlight the problems of the disproportionate influence of buildings in the Land Tax Assessments of these small estates. On the other hand, examples of *gross* distortions of an individual's position on the agricultural ladder are rare, thus in terms of frequency distributions, on the basis of parish acre equivalents, the suggestion is that the Land Tax can be used with confidence.

Rank Order Landownership Distribution

It may matter, however, that there are errors of estimation using techniques of acre equivalents, not because it weakens attempts to describe general social distributions, but because it will alter the personal positions of individuals on the agricultural ladder, as distinct from their group positions. Figure 2 demonstrates the problem. The first part of each of the twelve parish diagrams is the estimated rank order of landownership as computed from the Land Tax. The second part shows the actual rank order of those landowners as measured from the enclosure awards. If a landowner occupies the same rank order in both the estimated and actual rankings then he will be represented by a straight line. If he does not occupy the same relative position then he will climb up or down the ladder by however many places are appropriate. To show the location of the problematic areas of ranking the 100, 50, 10, 5, and 1 acre boundary levels have been included as well. As was indicated earlier, the main problems of estimating the sizes of individual estates occurs in the smaller acreage groups, especially on or around the ten acre boundary level. By most measures of social landownership distribution these people will be classified as very small. The two exceptions to this general rule are Little Kimble parish (number 9), where the problematic area is on or around the 100 acre boundary level, and Marsworth (number 10), where no clear message emerges when rank orders are compared. But even in this confused example it is on or under the ten acre boundary level where landownership distribution is most difficult to predict in terms of rank order.

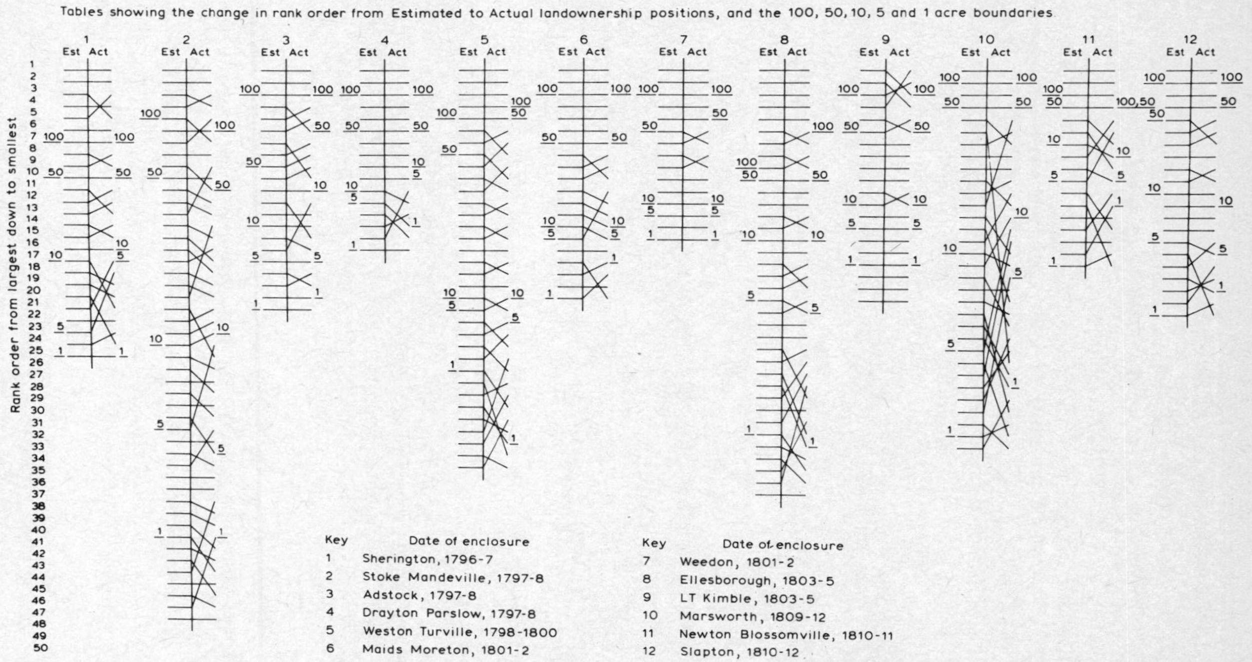

Figure 2. Landownership in 12 Buckinghamshire Parishes, 1796–1812, comparing Estimated rank order from the Land Tax (computed acreage equivalents), with Actual rank order from Enclosure Awards (measured statute acres).

Of the 304 landowners in this analysis 115 of them appear in the same rank order in the estimated and actual rankings in their respective parishes; ninety five of them change order by plus or minus one rank order place. Thus seventy per cent of all landowners appear in the correct order or within one place of their correct order. Thirty five landowners were displaced by two rank order places, twenty by three places, eighteen by four places, and twenty one by more than four places. The worst examples occur in Marsworth parish (number 10) where one landowner appears in the estimated rank order as sixth largest tax payer, but in actual fact was twenty fifth largest landowner out of thirty two. Only three other landowners were displaced by as many as ten places and they also all occur in Marsworth. In fact nine of the twenty one landowners who were displaced by more than four places occur in Marsworth. This bad example of Marsworth holds up a mirror to the great accuracy of displaying rank order landownership from the Land Tax in the other parishes.

Finally, of the twenty one landowners who were displaced by more than four places in this rank order exercise, twelve of them were in possession of fewer than five acres, five were between five and ten acres in size, and only four were greater than ten acres in size. In the majority of these cases of large displacement in rank order therefore we run the risk of asking the Land Tax and techniques of acre equivalents to measure accurately, perhaps even to the nearest acre, rood, or even perch. This is an unrealistic measure of accuracy but a measure which in the past if it has not been accomplished has lead to considerable criticism of acre equivalent techniques in our historiography of the subject. A similar exercise on three Lancashire parishes by G.J. Wilson revealed similar conclusions; the accurate prediction of rank order for larger landowners and increasing difficulty in those predictions the smaller the landowner, but only rarely with a displacement in rank order of greater than one place.[10]

Conclusion

It is possible to give these kinds of exercise more precise quantitative expressions, but because the margins of error in estimating landownership sizes for individuals can be very large I think it wiser to avoid giving what may turn out to be spurious accuracy. In terms of frequency distributions however, and in discussions of the social differentiation of rural places, the Land Tax is an invaluable source. Wilson summarises it neatly,

> 'While a rank order of land tax assessments would correspond closely with a rank order of holdings by acreage, deductions made about the actual size of the holding, based on the land tax assessments alone, could be misleading.'[11]

They could be misleading, but by judicious handling of the data and by asking only those questions which it is capable of answering, the Land Tax can be used with confidence for analysing landownership distribution in rural society.

NOTES

1 My thanks to Derek Waite of the drawing office in the Department of Geography at Hull University for preparing the diagrams in this chapter and to the photographic department of the University Library for preparing prints for publication. Unlike others in this book, this essay has been prepared with the benefit of seeing all other contributions. This is the editor's prerogative but I would like to thank Sarah Banks whose chapter stimulated some of my own ideas.

2 Martin, J.M., 'Landownership and the Land Tax Returns', *Agricultural History Review*, volume 14, 1966, p. 100.

3 ibid., pp. 100–1.

4 ibid., pp. 102–3.

5 ibid., p. 101.

6 R. Grover, 'Procedures for Exploiting the Land Tax Assessments', Land Tax Conference Paper, September 1981, p. 19.

7 Buckinghamshire enclosure awards found in Buckinghamshire County Record Office either as enrolments in Quarter Sessions Records or as photoduplicates taken from enrolments in the Public Record Office. Land Tax Assessments found as duplicates in Buckinghamshire County Record Office. My thanks to the Twenty Seven Foundation for a grant towards the expense of purchasing photocopies of these duplicates and to the staff of the Buckinghamshire Record Office for preparing them.

8 Walton, J.R., 'The Residential Mobility of Farmers and its Relationship to the Parliamentary Enclosure Movement in Oxfordshire', in Phillips, A.D.M., and Turton, B.J., (eds), *Environment, Man and Economic Change*, London, 1975, p. 243.

9 Gray, H.L., 'Yeoman Farming in Oxfordshire from the Sixteenth Century to the Nineteenth', *Quarterly Journal of Economics*, volume XXIV, 1910, p. 300.

10 By my observation and calculation from Wilson, G.J., 'The Land Tax and West Derby Hundred 1780–1831', *Transactions of the Historical Society of Lancashire and Cheshire*, volume 129, 1980, pp. 89–91.

11 ibid., p. 78.

Chapter 4

The Land Tax and the Study of Village Communities

JOHN BROAD

Land Tax Assessments can be used in a number of different ways to examine the structure of landownership in individual parishes in the later eighteenth and early nineteenth centuries. Michael Turner's pioneering work looked at changes in landlords and tenants over successive years and his and other 'turnover studies' have shown how parliamentary enclosure was a time when much land was bought and sold in the village, and the structure and personel altered as well as the physical layout of the land. It now also appears possible to use the large numbers of pre-1780 Assessments in some counties to do comparative studies over much longer periods, and to analyse the changing distribution of eighteenth- and early nineteenth-century landownership at the parish level.[1]

There are greater doubts about translating Land Tax payments into acreages in any precise manner. Donald Ginter's work shows that the relationship between tax payments and acreages varied considerably from parish to parish and that the variation did not necessarily reflect local differences in land values.[2] However, even if we cannot make useful comparisons of acreage equivalents between parishes, it is possible to examine the relationship within parishes, and this is most productive in slowly changing rural settlements. In urban and industrial areas, where housing, factories, and other industrial premises were assessed for tax, the relationship is considerably distorted. Areas which went through rapid change of any kind, for instance, large-scale drainage or reclamation work or any major change in agricultural use and value, are also likely to give misleading results. John Beckett has shown that the Land Tax was often assessed on the same basis for long periods during the eighteenth century, and may reflect values that go back as far as the Civil War. There are also properties, particularly charitable bequests of land to the village community, that remained exempt from Land Tax as a condition of gift.[3]

Despite such distortions Land Tax Assessments probably reflect the character of land-distribution and tenant farming in individual parishes, at least in slow-changing rural areas. However, they are an isolated set of documents, remarkable mainly for their long time-span and wide geographical coverage. To test their validity in a wider context, I undertook the task of combining Land Tax data and values with other nominal data that could expand our perception of the structure of society in that period. Three parishes from north Buckinghamshire were selected for a trial because the economy was rural and little affected by industrial change in the later eighteenth century. Buckinghamshire is also remarkable in having a large militia-type listing called the Posse Comitatus for 1798.[4] This recorded the names of all males between the ages of 16 and 60 who were not already in the militia. Some 25,000 names are given, and for almost all of them the occupation is also recorded. Although there are problems with this source – the percentage of the 1801 population recorded in it varied quite widely – it provides a unique nominal data set that can be compared with the Land Tax of the period and can give some indication of the range of village inhabitants that it picks up.

To compare two data sets of this kind provides interesting results, but to widen the scope of the enquiry I sought out three parishes that enclosed within a year of the Posse. This was not easy, as several parishes with the right date enclosed only a part of their land area – such as Adstock and Steeple Claydon – while for others the layout of the enclosure award did not make it a simple task to tabulate all the land redistributed. Choosing parishes that were in the throes of enclosure has its drawbacks. Precisely because landownership tended to change rapidly around the time of enclosure the three sources are likely to be aiming at moving targets, and may not catch them at the same point. Nevertheless the addition of a third series of documents for comparison was judged to outweigh the disadvantages and also makes it possible to compare Land Tax Assessments and enclosure acreages and measure the statistical relationship.[5]

Comparing three sets of documents with hundreds of names, many of which have duplicate entries, both in the Land Tax and enclosure awards, is a tedious task which requires great patience and in which it is possible to make considerable errors. To make the process much easier I wrote a computer program for the BBC micro-computer, model B, which could sort and combine data and made it possible to analyse the total information on any one individual very easily. Data was presented under five headings: the name, type of record (or subdivision within record), enclosure acreage, Land Tax sum paid, and occupational designation in the Posse. All the information from the three sources was typed in verbatim, so there were many multiple entries from the Land Tax and enclosure awards. The Land Tax data was most complex, because the fullest picture could only be presented by differentiating tenant holdings from ownership, and owner-occupied land from absentee ownership. This was done by providing separate type headings for all three.

Typing in the data in itself produced problems, particularly with the Land Tax, where the classic problem of how entries such as 'himself', 'ditto', and 'the same' should be treated emerged. With careful scrutiny of the context many of the ambiguities were sorted out but a few inevitably remained. Once data from the three series had been typed in, with tenant holdings from the Land Tax entered quite separately from owners, the computer was used to sort them all alphabetically by name, a process which took only a few seconds for three hundred entries. At this stage I printed out all the entries alphabetically. From this it is possible to standardise the styles of address used in the three separate sources. Mrs Lucas and Sarah Lucas, one paying Land Tax only, and the other awarded land at enclosure, were clearly the same person, as were John Baker and Mr Baker, where no other Bakers are named. All entries like this were given the fullest sensible designation e.g. Mrs Sarah Lucas. It is also important to ensure that there are no hidden spaces typed in at the end of words because at the next stage of the process, the computer will not recognise that two identically spelt names, one with an extra space at the end of it, refer to the same person.

The next operation handled by the computer program was the most crucial. It processed the revised alphabetical data, and combined all the entries attached to identical names. The new list of names that emerges includes, where appropriate, information on the amount of land awarded to each person at enclosure, the amount of Land Tax paid as an owner, any occupational designation that exists, and information as to whether the person is an owner occupier, or a tenant, and how much Land Tax is paid on any such holding. The uses of this are obvious. They make it possible to compare the three sources and their coverage at a glance. The computer also calculates the numbers of separate names occurring on each of the three source lists, as well as the numbers of names which can be found in various categories on any two or three lists. Finally the computer program includes a section that correlates Land Tax payments and enclosure awards for the parish as a whole.

The three parishes chosen for the survey were Grandborough, Wingrave, and Sherington. Grandborough, near Winslow is a parish of 1,580 acres that had a population of 230 in 1801 and lay in clayey soil in the vale of Aylesbury. Wingrave lay further to the south-east near Leighton Buzzard, on sandier soils more suited to arable agriculture, and its population of 602 in 1801 lived in a parish some 2,488 acres in extent. Sherington's history has been well chronicled by A.C. Chibnall. It was a more densely populated village with 671 inhabitants making a living in a parish of only 1,805 acres in 1801. Sherington also lies on clayey soil, but in the north-east of the county, near Newport Pagnell.[6]

The results of the computer analysis are presented in table 1:

Table 1

Three Buckinghamshire Parishes, c.1798

Parish	Grandborough	Wingrave	Sherington
A. General Specifications			
Enclosure Award date	1797	1799	1797
Parish acreage	1580	2488	1805
Award acreage	1482	2249	1742.5
Population in 1801	230	602	671
Total Land Tax paid	£95.92	£252.1	£174.86
Acres per £1 tax paid	15.45	8.92	9.97
B. Names			
Total No. of different names	98	204	217
In Enclosure Award	43	57	60
In Land Tax Assessments	34	57	75
In Posse Comitatus	53	127	152
Names of owners common to Awards and Assessments	30	35	45
Pearson Correlation for enclosure acreage/tax paid	0.993	0.953	0.989
Spearman Rank Order Correlation	0.567	0.796	0.95
Owners occurring in Award but not Land Tax Assessment	13	22	15
Owners occurring in Land Tax Assessment but not Award	8	30	30

Note: These numbers take into account, for instance, people of the same name who cannot be distinguished from each other by the computer program used, eg, Posse entries where both name and occupation are identical, perhaps father and son in the same trade.

Sources: as in notes 4 and 5

The three parishes were enclosed almost in their entireties, and the difference between the parish acreage, and the amount awarded to named owners can be accounted for by the roads and verges which were excluded from calculations, and perhaps by some central village land that lay outside the field system.

A number of features are apparent from the computer analysis. Most marked, and interesting, though not altogether surprising in view of Turner's work, is the extent to which the names of Land Tax and enclosure owners do not coincide even though the dates of enclosure are no more than one year from the 1798 Land Tax. The process works both ways: in two villages there are more people listed in the enclosure award but not paying Land Tax, than the other way round, while in the third the opposite position prevailed. The proportion of owners appearing in both Land Tax Assessments and enclosure awards is greatest in Grandborough, the smallest village. The biggest discrepancy is in Wingrave, which was enclosed in 1799, after the Posse and Land Tax Assessments perhaps because the greatest activity in the land market preceded enclosure, as Turner found.

The Pearson correlation shows a high degree of consistency between Land Tax payments and enclosure acreages for those owners found in both sources. This appears true in all three parishes, but the finding is in practice not very significant. The correlation coefficient is designed to measure like with like, but in these villages, the range of enclosure acreages and Land Tax payments is enormous, and the mean of both figures conceals an huge range of values (standard deviations range from 886 to 10,487). All the test confirms is that large Land Tax payments went hand-in-hand with large acreages, as might be expected. To use the test properly you would need to be able to take a small range of acreage sizes and Land Tax payments, but the size of the sample for any single village is far too small. Since we already know that it is unsound to suggest acreage equivalence for Land Tax data even for adjoining villages, no proper test can be made. The Spearman rank order test was also run by the computer. It ranked the names of those owners with both enclosure acreages and Land Tax payments in ascending order for each source, and then correlated the rankings for each name according to a standard formula. This test suffers in part from the same problem, but by reducing the range of differences to rankings rather than absolute figures gives a better but a less comforting picture. The result in Grandborough in particular shows much less correspondence.[7]

So far the analysis has concentrated on the relationship between Land Tax and enclosure figures, and relatively little has been said about the third source, the Posse. This source brings out clearly just how small a part of the village community were listed in the Land Tax Assessments and enclosure awards. In all three villages, the number of names noted in the Posse lists was considerably larger than those on the enclosure or Land Tax lists. In Sherington 35 names from the Posse can be cross-referenced to owners or tenants in the village, but some 115 are otherwise unidentified. A very similar situation prevailed in the other villages. The Posse took into account only males between 16 and 60 (incidentally concealing the extent of the major local industry, lacemaking, which in north Buckinghamshire was largely a female occupation) and thus demonstrates how limited a section of village society is found in Land Tax and enclosure documents.

The Posse information also sometimes obscures rather than clarifies problems in Land Tax and enclosure awards. One striking feature that the alphabetical listing of names reveals is just how many duplicate names are to be found in a village at the same time, and many of these are not adequately differentiated. Where occupations were different the Posse needed to do nothing, while where the names were father and son, senior and junior were commonly used. Even within the Posse there are problems. In Grandborough there were five duplicated names where the occupation was also the same. How these can be matched to their counterparts in enclosure and Land Tax documents presents a very considerable quandary and illustrates just how great a risk those who confidently link names on the basis of Land Tax records alone are taking.

A good example of this problem is the Mortimer family in Wingrave. There were at least five adult male Mortimers in the village at the end of the eighteenth century, and apart from one who was listed as a servant they appear to be carrying on potentially prosperous trades as victuallers, butchers, and shopkeepers. The problem of identification centres around the William Mortimers. There were at least two of these, Senior and Junior, identified in the Posse as a butcher and victualler respectively, and also in the Land Tax. They were both owner-occupiers and tenants and among the middle-ranking villagers. How though, do we match them with the other three entries.

1) William Mortimer, with no further designation who paid over £4 in Land Tax as an owner, but did not occupy it himself.
2) William Mortimer (Bell) presumably a publican who received just over a quarter of an acre in the enclosure award.
3) William Mortimer (Rose and Crown) who received almost an acre and a quarter at enclosure?

Now it is possible that there were only two William Mortimers, both running pubs, but one calling himself a butcher. Certainly one of the pubs must be identified with the victualler – but which one? Alternatively the undesignated William Mortimer might be a publican but was too old, or important, to be listed in the Posse. Our quandary is this: there may be only two William Mortimers, but we certainly cannot be sure which was which; or there could be reasonably up to four different individuals, or just conceivably five.

The linkages made possible by adding the Posse entries also have other applications. In the first place, they throw some light on the nature of the Posse listings, and who was and was not included. Surveying the northern Buckinghamshire hundreds as a whole, and comparing the 1801 census estimates (admittedly not the most perfect of sources) with the numbers of men listed in the Posse for each parish, it emerged that the ratio between Posse totals and population in each parish varied to a much greater degree than would be expected if all males between 16 and 60 who were not serving in the militia were included. The mean ratio was 1:4.43, and the standard deviation 1.47 from a sample of 91 north Buckinghamshire parishes. This indicates that just under a quarter of the population were included, a figure that could rise to above one third, or, in the case of the parish of Buckingham fall to only about one tenth of the population.

Finally, one of the most interesting applications of the database is to analyse the peculiarities of particular groups of people. Such a collection of information could be the starting point for much wider analysis of village communities at this time using other more disparate sources. An excellent case in point is that much analysed group, the owner-occupier, often referred to without too much discrimination as the small landowner. Table 2 below sets out rather more detail about various categories of landowners in 1798 obtained from the computer files:

Table 2

Subgroups of Landowners and Tenants, 1798

Parish	Grandborough	Wingrave	Sherington
Numbers of:			
Owner-Occupiers	16	26	28
Owner-Occupiers only	13	8	14
Owner-occupiers and Landlords	0	5	6
Owner-occupiers, Landlords and Tenants	0	1	2
Owner and Tenant	1	10	7
Owner-Occupiers with Posse occupation,	3	10	17
of which, farming occupations	2	3	7
trade and craft occupations	1	7	10

Notes. These columns do not add up, since the categories overlap.
'Farming occupations' include gentleman, farmer, labourer, gardener.
'Craft and trade' occupations include poulterer and butcher, which are very clearly agriculturally derived, as well as more obviously non-agricultural occupations, but they do not preclude the possibility that the people involved also farmed their land.

Sources: as in notes 4 and 5.

What is interesting about the group of people who were owner-occupiers is how miscellaneous they were. Far from being the last remnants of some ancient peasant caste, they include a variety of different types. One or two were large landowners who apparently kept a small home farm, or residence, for which they paid Land Tax as owner-occupiers. Some were men who farmed quite large farms, but most of it was held as tenanted land. Others were both owner-occupiers and tenants, but at the same time were letting out land, or more usually cottages, as landlords. Finally, in this picture of a highly complex structure of landholding in these late eighteenth century Buckinghamshire villages, there were those who were landlords, letting out land or housing, and not occupying it themselves, but at the same time they were tenants for other land within the same parish. All these variations existed within one parish, and ignore any holdings that owners or occupiers may have held in other communities. Yet we know from documents such as eighteenth-century pollbooks that there were many men who owned land in one community, and lived and farmed in another. Many years ago, Chibnall noted the way that outsiders bought investment property in Sherington and sublet it to villagers while living elsewhere, often in London or local towns. The patterns that emerge from these three Buckinghamshire villages is that there were many other types of landholders in the countryside.[8]

The occupational information from the Posse also brings out the variety of types of owner-occupiers in the villages. In Sherington these included a tailor, victualler, poulterer, gardener, carpenter, grocer, and matmaker, as well as gentlemen, clergy, and farmers. Most of these small tradesmen do not appear as tenants and landlords as well. One feature of the Grandborough Posse listing is that hardly any of the larger owners appear at all – only two farmers and one publican who owned land were included – and occupational designations were normally confined to those who were tenants, or apparently had no important stake in the land at all. At Wingrave the craftsman owner-occupiers included a carpenter, two shopkeepers, baker, brewer, victualler, butcher, but there were also two labourers who owned their land. That archetype of eighteenth century rural studies, the man who tried to farm twenty or thirty acres as an owner-occupier, is more or less non-existent.

Men designated as labourers, and in many of the other common rural occupations, appear more commonly as tenants than owner-occupiers in all three villages, as might be expected. It is also apparent that large numbers of village craftsmen do not appear at all within the landholding classes as defined by the Land Tax and enclosure awards. Some of those named were undoubtedly the sons of families who do appear, but sufficient numbers of new names without any other designation remain unlinked to enclosure and Land Tax records to reinforce the suspicion that although the Land Tax will always remain an important source of information about eighteenth century village landholding society, it only scratches at the surface of that large underbody of tradesmen, craftsmen, and labourers who made up the core of the rural community. They were often sub-tenants, or living in shared accommodation or newly erected dwellings that avoided the tax, in an era of rapid population change over the whole of England. The Land Tax covers none of these, and for many of the rural artisans who retained property as owners, it was at least as likely that it lay in some other community, as that they retained some remnant of an ancestral villein holding in the village of their birth and upbringing.[9]

NOTES

1 See especially Turner, M.E., 'Parliamentary Enclosure and Landownership change in Buckinghamshire', *Economic History Review*, 2nd series, volume 28, 1975, pp. 565–81; and Neeson, J.E., *Common Right and Enclosure in Eighteenth-century Northamptonshire*, unpublished Ph.D. thesis, University of Warwick, 1977, chapter 4.

2 Ginter, D., 'A Wealth of Problems with the Land Tax' *EcHR*, 2nd series, volume 35, 1982, pp. 416–21 and conversations with Dr. Ginter at the Agricultural History Conference 1984.

3 For a specific example of exempted land see Buckinghamshire County Record Office, PR51/12/1, East Claydon overseers accounts, where a condition of William Abell's charity was that the land endowed should be free of tax.

4 The Land Tax Assessments are at Bucks. C.R.O. reference Q/RPL. Copies of the Posse Comitatus exist at the Buckinghamshire Record Office, and British Library, Stowe Manuscripts, 802–3. An edition of the Posse is in press for the Buckinghamshire Record Society, volume 22.

5 The enclosure awards at Bucks. C.R.O. are filed in series. For Sherington the information came from Public Record Office MPL 38. The general context for Buckinghamshire enclosures is set out in Turner, M.E., *Some Social and Economic Considerations of Parliamentary Enclosure in Buckinghamshire 1738–1865*, unpublished Ph.D. thesis, University of Sheffield, 1973.

6 Chibnall, A.C., *Sherington: Fiefs and Fields of a Buckinghamshire Village*, Cambridge, 1965.

7 For similar work attempting to link Land Tax to tithe records see Banks, S. above.

8 Chibnall, op. cit. pp. 237–43.

9 For a summary of the arguments see Turner, M.E., *Enclosures in Britain 1750–1830*, London, 1984, chapter 5.

Chapter 5

Enclosure, Topography, and Landownership in Eastern Yorkshire

JANICE E. CROWTHER

The value of the Land Tax Assessments as a source of information on landownership during the parliamentary enclosure period has been widely recognised by historians. There is a continuing debate on their accuracy, and today we accept that they must be used with caution, and that they are generally inappropriate for assessing in detail the holdings of individuals. Nevertheless they constitute the only general source on landownership in the later eighteenth and early nineteenth centuries, and they have much valuable information to tell us about the broader aspects of landownership distribution. In this study they are used for one region – eastern Yorkshire – in the 'traditional' way of many Land Tax studies of the past half century or more. There are 219 townships in the region, and they have been divided into three groups, according to the date of their enclosure. The incidence of owners in these three groups is examined, and the position of owner-occupiers, both in terms of their numbers, and of the proportion of land they owned, is evaluated.

(i) *Eastern Yorkshire – Enclosure History*[1]

The Land Tax Assessments are preserved in county collections, and for this reason have tended to be used on a county basis, although when the information that they contain is aggregated in this way the result often conceals more than it reveals. Most counties have varied topographies, and landownership distribution often, if not always, reflected physical geography. A study of parliamentary enclosure in eastern Yorkshire soon demonstrates that in this region, as in many more, topography, enclosure history, and landownership structure were probably closely linked. In order to bring out these features the region is divided into seven districts, five upland and two lowland.

In figure 1, district 1, the Jurassic hills district, is situated in the north-western corner of the region. At the opening of the parliamentary

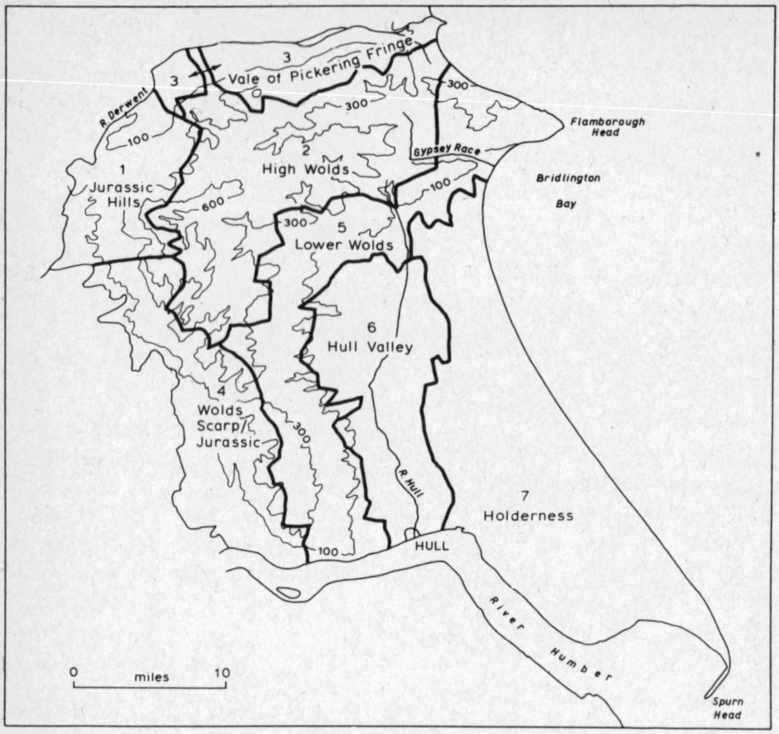

Figure 1. The Seven Districts of Eastern Yorkshire

enclosure period, c. 1725, this district was already predominantly enclosed: less than twenty per cent of the total acreage was still open (table 1). Physically it differs markedly from the high Wolds district nearby; the landscape of the Jurassic hills district was, and still is, well wooded, with numerous streams and valleys. District 2, the high Wolds, comprises those townships situated in the northern part of the Wolds. At the beginning of the parliamentary enclosure period over sixty per cent of the acreage of this district was still open, the chalk hills were almost bare of trees, and the settlements were surrounded by vast fields interspersed with sheep walks and rabbit warrens. District 3, the Vale of Pickering fringe, comprises those townships which run down the steep scarp face of the Wolds on their northern side into the valley of the rivers Derwent and Hertford. The low ground was of very little value agriculturally in the eighteenth century, being frequently flooded. Over fifty per cent of this district was enclosed by act, much of it in association with the drainage of the low ground. District 4, the Wold scarp/Jurassic ridge district, runs down the western escarpment of the Wolds. Most of the townships in this district have a share of wold land, as well as of land under the scarp, and on the low lying ground of the Vale of York. Over sixty five per cent of the acreage of this district was still open in 1725. The fifth district, the lower Wolds, is situated on the eastern side of the Wolds, where the land slopes gently down to the valley of the River Hull. District 5 also had a high proportion of land – sixty five per cent – still unenclosed in 1725. District 6, the Hull valley, comprises the townships lying on either side of the River Hull. This district was of low value agriculturally, especially in the vicinity of the river, until the large scale drainage schemes of the later eighteenth century partially alleviated the flooding which usually occurred for much of the year. About thirty per cent of district 6 was still unenclosed in 1725; much of the enclosure which took place after that date was concerned with common pastures only, since the open fields, which were situated on higher ground, had generally been enclosed in the seventeenth century or earlier. District 7, Holderness, is a clayland area, with scattered belts of gravel and sand. Although low lying, it is not as flat as the Hull valley. The Holderness landscape may be described as hummocky, and in parts it rises to fifty feet or more above sea level. About forty per cent of this district was still open in 1725.

Parliamentary enclosure took place in eastern Yorkshire in two distinct waves of activity. The first began fully in the early 1760s and petered out in the late 1770s, whilst the second began in the mid 1790s, coinciding broadly with the French Revolutionary and Napoleonic Wars (figure 2). The earliest complete set of Land Tax Assessments for eastern Yorkshire is for the year 1787. This is approximately halfway through the trough between the two waves of enclosure activity, so that an investigation of

Table 1

Acreage Enclosed after 1725 in the Seven Districts of Eastern Yorkshire

Districts	Total acreage in district	Enclosed after 1725 Acres	Enclosed after 1725 Percentage
1 Jurassic Hills	38,020	6,372	16.8
2 High Wolds	113,181	74,083	65.5
3 Vale of Pickering Fringe	37,705	20,271	53.8
4 Wold Scarp/Jurassic Ridge	66,421	43,585	65.6
5 Lower Wolds	109,419	72,980	66.7
6 Hull Valley	78,051	25,608	32.8
7 Holderness	148,378	55,872	37.7
Eastern Yorkshire	591,175	298,771	50.5

Source: Humberside County Record Office, Enclosure Awards

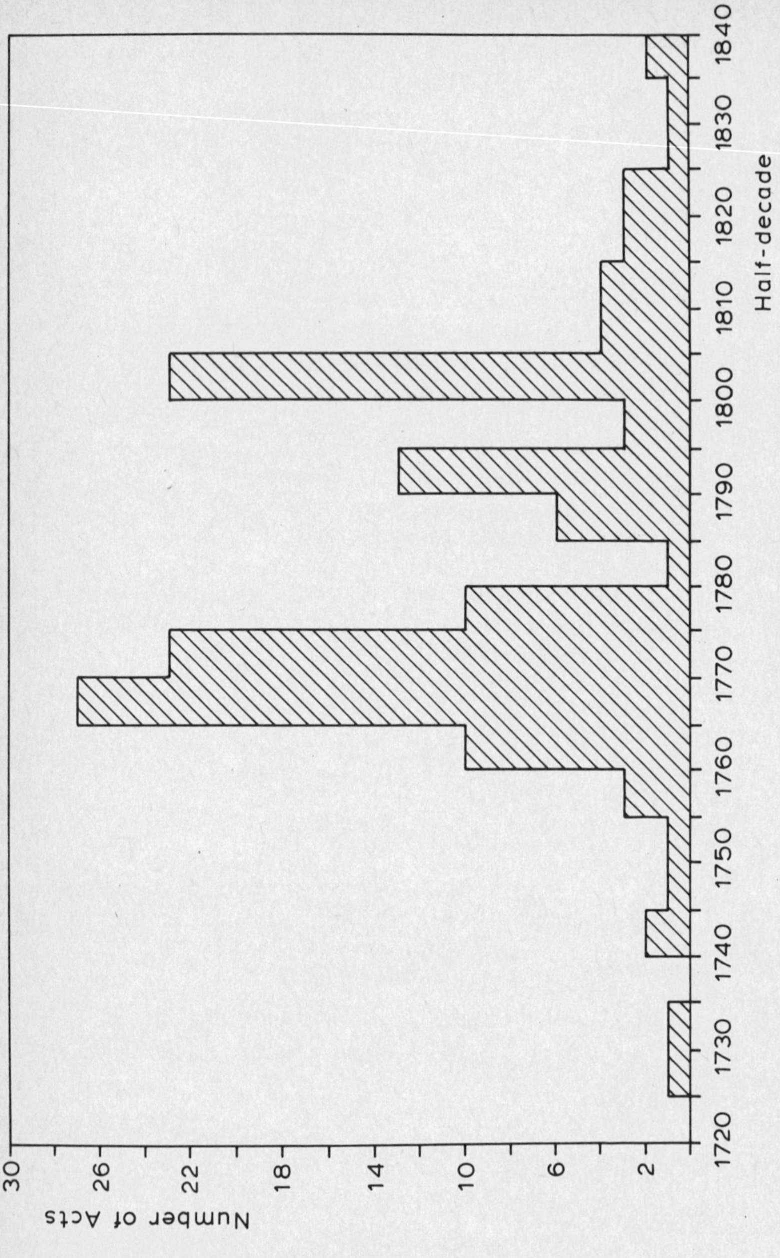

Figure 2. Eastern Yorkshire Enclosure Act by Half Decade.

the landownership distribution in that year in old enclosed (that is enclosed before 1725), recently enclosed (between 1725 and 1779), and open field townships should bring out any associations between enclosure history and landholding. Since the townships are also divided into physical regions such a study should reveal topographical differences, if any.

(ii) *The Land Tax – Ownership and Enclosure, c. 1787*

Table 2 shows the average number of owners per township paying Land Tax in 1787 in each district, divided into townships which were old enclosed, recently enclosed, and still at least partly open. The information for the lowland and upland districts has been conflated to bring out more general patterns. As revealed in other areas where the Assessments have been used in this way[2] the information for eastern Yorkshire shows that there were fewer owners in old enclosed townships than in those enclosed during the parliamentary enclosure period. The table also shows that physical factors as well as enclosure date had a bearing on landownership distribution. In old enclosed upland townships there were only 4.6 owners per township, whereas in the lowlands the comparable figure was 7.0.

Table 2

Average Number of Owners per Township Paying Land Tax in 1787 in Eastern Yorkshire

Districts	Townships old enclosed		Townships enclosed 1725-79		Townships open in 1787	
	No.	Aver.no.owners per township	No.	Aver.no.owners per township	No.	Aver.no.owners per township
1 Jur. Hills	12	7.2	3	11.7	4	10.0
2 High Wolds	7	3.3	13	13.2	12	15.5
3 Vale Fringe	3	1.3	6	14.2	6	10.3
4 Wold/Ridge	2	3.5	18	30.1	4	17.8
5 Lower Wolds	11	3.9	11	21.4	18	19.3
6 Hull Valley	7	4.3	8	22.4	3	31.3
7 Holderness	28	7.7	27	26.0	16	17.8
Upland Districts 1-5	35	4.6	51	20.9	44	15.9
Lowland Districts 6-7	35	7.0	35	25.2	19	21.6
Region	70	5.8	86	22.7	63	17.3

Source: Humberside County Record Office, Land Tax Assessments, QDE 1 1787

When the information is shown separately for the seven districts a considerable variation is revealed, from as low as 1.3 owners on average for the Vale of Pickering fringe townships, to as high as 7.7 for Holderness.

Many of the old enclosed townships were situated at a higher elevation, or in a less favourable physical location, than were those which retained their open fields until the parliamentary enclosure period. They were often the sites of depopulated settlements, and usually the land in such townships in the uplands had been converted to sheep walks and rabbit warrens. Typical of this category of township was Wharram Percy, enclosed probably in the early sixteenth century, and with only four Land Tax payers in 1787.[3] In other cases the concentration of property and early enclosure is explained because the townships were the sites of former religious communities: in Watton in the Hull valley only two people paid tax in 1787, the township was the site of a Gilbertine priory, and the enclosure had probably taken place in the seventeenth century;[4] in Meaux in the same district three people paid tax in 1787, the township was the site of a Cistercian abbey, and the enclosure date, though not known, was certainly well before the eighteenth century.[5] The proximity of the mansion and principal estate of a long established gentry family explains the early enclosure and property distribution in some old enclosed townships: for example, at Burton Constable, the property of the Constable family since medieval times, the land had been enclosed from an early date.[6] A number of eastern Yorkshire families had been resident for many generations in a particular district, and over several centuries they had systematically bought suitable property in the vicinity of their mansions. Many of them had benefited from the redistribution of monastic estates during the Dissolution, and intermarriage with other gentry families had often increased their estates still further. As the principal, often the only, owners of land in the township, they were able to carry out an enclosure when it suited their personal circumstances. Many 'estate' villages of eastern Yorkshire were thus early enclosed, although the actual date of enclosure is often unknown.

Examination of individual Assessments shows that in the lowlands early enclosure was not always associated with the concentration of property. In a few Holderness townships which were enclosed well before the parliamentary enclosure period the land was still in the hands of a quite numerous body of owners: Seaton, enclosed in 1657 and with twenty three owners in 1787;[7] Owstwick, enclosed c. 1649 and with seventeen owners in 1787;[8] and Fitling, enclosed in 1640 and with nineteen owners in 1787,[9] show this feature most prominently. Enclosure was evidently achieved in such townships with general agreement. A prime motive for enclosure in these cases may have been the desire to convert some land from arable to pasture.[10]

Conversely, the concentration of property into a few hands did not always lead to early enclosure. There are a number of townships where one family owned either the whole, or almost the whole, of the land in 1787, and had done so for several centuries, and yet the enclosure did not take place until the parliamentary enclosure period. Most such townships were situated in the uplands, though there is one case of single ownership and late enclosure in the lowlands; when Lisset in Holderness was enclosed in 1771–2 only the lord of the manor and the church were involved.[11] An act of Parliament was probably used because the tithes were commuted.

Despite these exceptional cases the information in table 2 demonstrates that there was an association between early enclosure and the consolidation of property. The table also shows some interesting patterns in townships which were enclosed during the parliamentary enclosure period. In 1787, of the 149 parliamentary enclosed townships in the study, 63 of them (42.3 per cent of all townships) still remained open. The majority of these, 44 (69.8 per cent), were situated in the upland districts. When the recently enclosed townships are compared to those still in open fields some divergences are apparent. Comparing upland and lowland districts we see that there were fewer owners per township in open townships than there were in recently enclosed ones. Turning to the figures for the seven districts, except in two this pattern is again present. Only in district 2, the high Wolds, and in district 6, the Hull valley, is the pattern reversed. However, in district 6 the average of 31.3 owners for open townships is based upon only three townships: Leven, with fifty one people paying tax; North Frodingham, with seventy three; and Beswick, with only one.[12] The low number of cases suggests that too much importance should not be attached to the figure in this instance. In the case of the high Wolds district the difference between the two figures is negligible.

One possible reason why generally more owners paid tax in recently enclosed townships than in open field ones relates to the effects of enclosure upon those people who owned cottages with common rights but no other land. After enclosure some of them became landowners for the first time as a result of the small allotments they received in lieu of their common rights. They may thereafter have qualified as taxpayers, whereas in open field townships such people were not always included in the tax. However, inclusion in the Assessments did not inevitably follow enclosure; the tax was levied at a local level, and close examination of individual Assessments at the time of enclosure shows that in many cases the new owners of very small allotments were not taxed.

In order to check the accuracy of the Assessments as a guide to the number of owners we can turn to another source, the enclosure awards. Table 3 shows the average number of allottees per township for townships enclosed during the first and second waves of enclosure in the seven districts of eastern Yorkshire. The information in tables 2 and 3 is not directly comparable because enclosure awards understate the number of owners in a township since they do not necessarily include people with old enclosed land only, and the Assessments understate owners since they may exclude cottagers. Moreover the two sources relate to different dates. Nevertheless both tables show the same pattern; in almost every district there were more owners in townships enclosed in the first wave of enclosure activity than in those enclosed during the second.

Table 3

Average Number of Owners per Township at Enclosure in Eastern Yorkshire

	TOWNSHIPS ENCLOSED 1725–79			TOWNSHIPS ENCLOSED AFTER 1790		
Districts	Number of townships	Aver. no. owners per township		Number of townships	Aver. no. owners per township	
		Award	1787 LTA*		Award	1787 LTA*
1 Jur. Hills	3	11.7	11.7	4	5.4	10.0
2 High Wolds	13	14.2	13.2	12	16.3	15.5
3 Vale Fringe	6	8.3	14.2	6	10.0	10.3
4 Wold/Ridge	18	30.0	30.1	4	17.5	17.8
5 Lower Wolds	11	23.5	21.4	18	18.2	19.3
6 Hull Valley	8	27.0	22.4	3	36.0	31.3
7 Holderness	27	24.7	26.0	16	14.2	17.8

*From Table 2

Source: Humberside County Record Office, Enclosure Awards

A recent study of landownership and enclosure in Buckinghamshire may be compared with the present study. Turner found that in that county 'parishes . . . enclosed before 1780 had fewer owners than those enclosed after 1780', and he suggested that the trends in landownership were linked with the timing of enclosure, and that the higher numbers of owners in later enclosed townships could be seen as 'a direct reason for delaying enclosure'.[13] The evidence for eastern Yorkshire shows an opposite trend and demands a different hypothesis. It suggests that in townships with numerous owners the restrictions imposed by the open field system were felt more heavily by the beginning of the parliamentary enclosure period than in those townships where there were relatively few landowners. There was therefore more impetus to enclose early in the parliamentary enclosure period in townships where the land was divided amongst many owners. Enclosure by act was expensive, and landowners needed to be convinced that the benefits were considerable before they embarked upon it. Yet the new institutional method of enclosure seems to have been seized upon with great enthusiasm by many of the landowners of eastern Yorkshire,[14] and information from both the enclosure awards and the Land Tax Assessments suggests that the presence of many owners was not usually a bar to enclosure.

Perhaps it is significant that in the district with most owners, district 4, the Wold scarp/Jurassic ridge district, almost all the enclosures were carried out between 1730 and 1779. South Cave was one of the few townships in this district where enclosure was delayed until after 1779, but here we know that many attempts were made to obtain an act, beginning at least as early as 1766.[15] This was a township with many proprietors – a total of sixty four people were allotted land in the enclosure award[16] – and the disposition of the land before enclosure is well illustrated in a pre-enclosure plan and survey which was made in 1759.[17] One example of the scattering of strips in the open fields will suffice. One man, a Mr Appleton, owned a total of 171 acres in 101 separate holdings. Most of his arable strips were less than two acres in extent, and since South Cave was a very extensive township – the open fields covered over three miles from east to west – Appleton's tenant or tenants had a considerable distance to travel from one area to another. Throughout the period of negotiating the South Cave Enclosure Act there seems to have been general agreement on the part of the owners that an enclosure was required. It was only the opposition of the tithe owners which delayed the matter until 1785.[18] Throughout the 1760s and 1770s, at the same time as negotiations were in hand for an enclosure, new crops such as turnips and potatoes were introduced into the open fields.[19] The fragmentation of holdings which the 1759 plan demonstrates must have made it difficult for progressive farmers to improve the cultivation of their land as much as they would have wished, and therefore it seems understandable if they, or their landlords, favoured enclosure in the 1760s and 1770s. In townships with only a few owners it would have been relatively easy, by informal agreement, to rearrange the balance of arable to pasture, change rotations, and introduce new crops.[20] Moreover, in such townships the land was less fragmented.[21]

Many examples could be given of eastern Yorkshire townships with very few proprietors, where enclosure was delayed until well into the second wave of activity: an act to enclose open field land at Scrayingham in the Jurassic hills district was passed in 1825, and the land was allotted to only two people;[22] the enclosure of Foxholes in the high Wolds took place in 1836–40, and the land was allotted to eight owners;[23] two townships in the vale of Pickering fringe – Ganton and Binnington – were enclosed in 1803–4 and only one owner was involved in each case.[24] Such cases support the argument that pressure to enclose was strongest in townships with numerous owners.

In a study of yeoman farming in Oxfordshire Gray found that there were a number of townships in that county where only a few people owned the land, and yet the enclosure was long delayed. He suggested that:

> 'enclosure was sometimes delayed, not so much because there were so many interests to harmonise as because landlords were indifferent. With their holdings probably not badly scattered, owners were not troubled by inconveniences to their tenants (which perhaps the latter did not feel) and did not care to incur the expense of parliamentary act and award.'[25]

Clearly many factors influenced the decision to enclose, but scattering of holdings, which may have been effective for a variety of reasons before the eighteenth century, seems to have held back progress by the parliamentary enclosure period.[26]

(iii) *The Land Tax – Owner-Occupancy and Enclosure, c. 1787.*

The Assessments include the names of occupiers as well as those of owners, and they have been used by many researchers to trace the fortunes of the owner-occupiers, who have long evoked considerable interest. There are variations in the way that owner-occupiers are recorded in the Assessments. Most frequently in Eastern Yorkshire the word 'self' is used in the occupier column, but 'occupier' is sometimes used, and some returns repeat the name of the owner. The use of 'ditto' can sometimes cause uncertainty as to whether it refers to the owner or to the occupier above. Familiarity with the records, scrutiny of the usual form of words, and reference to previous years' returns can usually solve this problem.

The Assessments can be used in a number of ways to show the position of owner-occupiers and to suggest relationships between enclosure history and spatial distribution. The owner-occupiers may be expressed in average numbers per township, as percentages of all owners, or the tax that they paid may be expressed as a percentage of the total tax paid in the township or in the district, giving an indication of their landowning strength. Table 4 shows the average number of owner-occupiers per township in the seven districts of eastern Yorkshire in townships which were old enclosed, recently enclosed, and still open. It also shows the information aggregated for all upland districts and lowland districts. Taking these figures first we see that in old enclosed townships in the uplands there were only 0.7 owner-occupiers per township in 1787, which means that only 13 per cent of owners were also the occupiers of their land. In the lowlands there were 1.7 owner-occupiers per township, which was about one quarter of the total owners. For recently enclosed townships in the uplands the average number of owner-occupiers per township was 9.9, almost half of all

Table 4

Average Number of Owner-Occupiers per Township Paying Land Tax in 1787 in Eastern Yorkshire

OLD ENCLOSED TOWNSHIPS

Districts	1	2	3	4	5	6	7	1-5	6-7	All
No. of town'ps	12	7	3	2	11	7	28	35	35	70
Owner-occupiers:										
Ave. no. per t'p	0.9	1.0	NA	0.5	0.5	1.4	1.8	0.7	1.7	1.2
As % all owners	12.5	30.3	NA	14.3	12.8	32.6	23.4	13.2	24.3	21.0

TOWNSHIPS ENCLOSED 1725-1779

Districts	1	2	3	4	5	6	7	1-5	6-7	All
No. of town'ps	3	13	6	18	11	8	27	51	35	86
Owner-occupiers:										
Ave. no. per t'p	5.3	5.7	5.3	15.3	9.7	8.2	12.0	9.9	10.8	10.0
As % all owners	45.3	43.2	37.2	50.8	45.3	36.6	46.1	47.4	42.9	44.3

TOWNSHIPS OPEN IN 1787

Districts	1	2	3	4	5	6	7	1-5	6-7	All
No. of town'ps	4	12	6	4	18	3	16	44	19	63
Owner-occupiers										
Ave. no. per t'p	4.0	5.1	4.3	6.3	8.1	22.0	5.9	6.2	8.5	6.9
As % all owners	40.0	32.9	41.7	35.4	42.0	70.3	33.1	40.0	39.4	39.8

Key to districts:
1 Jurassic Hills
2 High Wolds
3 Vale of Pickering Fringe
4 Wold Scarp/Jurassic Ridge
5 Lower Wolds
6 Hull Valley
7 Holderness
1-5 Uplands
6-7 Lowlands
All Whole region

Source: Humberside County Record Office, Land Tax Assessments, QDE 1 1787

owners, whilst in the lowlands the comparable figure was 10.8 owner-occupiers per township, about forty per cent of all owners. For both upland and lowland townships still remaining open almost forty per cent of all owners were also the occupiers of their land.

It is apparent from the table that in all districts owner-occupiers were very weak numerically in old enclosed townships. In other regions of England this was also the case. Davies found that in 1780–6 owner-occupiers 'could hardly be said to exist' in 605 of 737 old enclosed Midland parishes.[27] Martin found that in Warwickshire in 1780 the majority of old enclosed parishes had no owner-occupiers,[28] and Chambers found a very similar picture in Lindsey.[29] In eastern Yorkshire not only were there few owner-occupiers in old enclosed townships, but in parts of the uplands there were very few occupiers. Many of these townships had been converted to pasture at an early date, and in a number of cases a single farm covered the whole township. Cowlam in the high Wolds was typical. In 1787 it was owned by one man, who let it out in its entirety to one farmer.[30] There were similar townships in the lower Wolds: the Duke of Devonshire let his estate at Bracken to one tenant; two owners of the land at Eastburn let their land to one man, so that this township, although owned by two people, was cultivated as a single farm.[31]

In all but one of the seven districts owner-occupiers were weaker, both numerically and as a proportion of all owners, in townships still open in 1787 than they were in those which had been recently enclosed. When this finding is compared with information from other counties some interesting divergences as well as similarities become apparent. Davies found that in the Midlands, in 1780–6:

> 'occupying owners . . . were more widely distributed and numerous in parishes already enclosed by Act than in those yet wholly or partly open'[32]

and Martin found that in Warwickshire in 1780 owner-occupiers were strongest in parishes enclosed in the period 1730–79.[33] However, in Lindsey Chambers found that in 1790 this group was stronger in open field parishes than in those newly enclosed,[34] whilst in Buckinghamshire Turner found a similar pattern for 1785.[35]

When owner-occupiers are expressed as a percentage of all owners they appear to be quite strong in eastern Yorkshire; generally by 1787 they constituted about forty per cent of owners in townships enclosed by act in the six decades before 1780, and also about forty per cent of owners in townships still open in 1787 (table 4). In Buckinghamshire owner-occupiers formed approximately thirty six per cent of all owners;[36] in eastern Yorkshire they were clearly somewhat stronger.

The relationship between the incidence of owner-occupancy and the timing of enclosure, if there is one, is not easy to discern. Certainly in eastern Yorkshire there is no evidence that a strong class of owner-occupiers had delayed enclosure in those townships which still remained open in 1787.[37] Conversely there is no reason to suppose that the townships enclosed between 1725 and 1779 were enclosed during that period because they had a higher number of owner-occupiers. Detailed investigation of the enclosure process in the region demonstrates quite clearly that the promoters of enclosure were the gentry owners,[38] and they were almost always landlords rather than owner-occupiers. Furthermore the numbers of owner-occupiers tell us little about their landowning strength. When the weight of opinion for and against an enclosure was being assessed it was the land owned rather than the individuals concerned that was used as the criterion.

Accordingly an alternative, and rather more revealing way of showing the importance of owner-occupiers is to look not at their numbers but at the proportion of the total tax they paid, and hence indirectly, the proportion of land they held. The Assessments are well suited to such a purpose, although we need to be cautious when interpreting the figures, because the amount of tax paid is unlikely to be an exact reflection of the land owned or occupied. Broad generalisations from the aggregated figures may safely be made however, and table 5 shows the information on the proportion of tax paid by owner-occupiers for the seven districts of eastern Yorkshire.

Table 5

Percentage of Total Land Tax Paid by Owner-Occupiers in 1787 in Eastern Yorkshire

Districts	Townships old enclosed		Townships enclosed 1725–79		Townships open in 1787	
	No.	% tax paid by owner-occup'rs	No.	% tax paid by owner-occup'rs	No.	% tax paid by owner-occup'rs
1 Jur. Hills	12	5.9	3	5.8	4	7.5
2 High Wolds	7	2.1	13	10.7	12	17.8
3 Vale Fringe	3	NA	6	9.1	6	14.3
4 Wold/Ridge	2	49.8	18	21.1	4	18.9
5 Lower Wolds	11	4.7	11	16.5	18	17.6
6 Hull Valley	7	25.2	8	9.8	3	17.8
7 Holderness	28	8.3	27	17.9	16	14.0
Upland Districts 1–5	35	8.4	51	15.1	44	15.7
Lowland Districts 6–7	35	13.0	35	15.5	19	14.7
Region	70	11.5	86	15.3	63	15.3

Source: Humberside County Record Office, Land Tax Assessments, QDE 1 1787

Looking first at the conflated figures for the uplands and lowlands we see that in both regions owner-occupiers were stronger in terms of tax paid in townships enclosed after 1725 than they were in old enclosed townships. The figures for townships enclosed by act, whether before or after the 1780s, are remarkably imilar; about 15 per cent of the land in parliamentary enclosed townships was apparently owner-occupied in 1787. It would seem that although numerically this class was quite strong in townships enclosed by act – comprising forty to fifty per cent of all owners – yet territorially they were weak.

Turning to the information on owner-occupancy in the seven districts we see that there is considerable regional variation. We must take care not to read too much into certain results: the figure for old enclosed townships in district 4, the Wold scarp/Jurassic ridge district, is based upon only two townships, and in one, Kilnwick Percy, the lord of the manor had most of the land in hand in 1787;[39] in district 6, the Hull valley, the inclusion of Watton, where the two principal owners farmed their own land,[40] inflates the proportion of owner-occupied land considerably.

In certain uplands owner-occupiers seemingly were very weak. In the three townships enclosed between 1725 and 1779 in district 1 only 5.8 per cent of the land was owner-occupied, despite the fact that such owners constituted almost half the total number of owners (table 4). In district 2 in the townships enclosed between 1725 and 1779 owner-occupiers were also weak, as they were in district 3. Examination of the landownership structure at enclosure in these upland townships shows that much of the land was in the hands of people with estates of over 500 acres,[41] and the Assessments indicate that almost without exception such landowners were landlords. Even Sir Christopher Sykes, who took a very close interest in his property, let most of it to tenant farmers.[42] With the contemporary custom that an enclosure act could pass with the consent of the owners of three-quarters to four-fifths of the property,[43] even had every owner-occupier in these districts opposed enclosure without other support they could not have prevented the passage of an act.

The district with the highest proportion of land in the hands of owner-occupiers in 1787 was district 4, the Wold scarp/Jurassic ridge. Here as much as one-fifth of the land was owner-occupied in townships enclosed between 1725 and 1779, and almost as much in townships still in open fields. This is also the district with the highest number of owners in 1787 (table 2), as well as that which experienced most of its parliamentary enclosure in the first wave of activity.

In most districts owner-occupiers held a slightly higher proportion of the land in 1787 in open-field townships than they did in those recently enclosed. However there is little in table 5 to suggest that the strength or weakness of this class had a bearing upon the timing of enclosure; the proportion of the land they held was such that, with the sole exception of district 4, in no district could the owner-occupiers on their own have prevented an act from going through Parliament. Researchers looking at other areas have found slightly different patterns and reached different conclusions. In Buckinghamshire for example, analysis of the Assessments for 1785 showed that owner-occupiers were stronger in townships which were to remain open until after 1800 than in those enclosed before that date, and Turner suggested that in such parishes a higher degree of owner-occupancy may have delayed enclosure.[44]

All studies of the Assessments and owner-occupancy so far undertaken show that this group held a relatively low proportion of the land by the end of the eighteenth century. In some areas the proportion seems to have been particularly low. The studies of ownership and occupancy made by Davies and by Gray suggested a level of only ten per cent in the Midland counties. Davies looked at the Assessments for 1,395 parishes in Derbyshire, Leicestershire, Lindsey, Northamptonshire, Nottinghamshire, and Warwickshire, and concluded that owner-occupiers in 1780:

> 'contributed only 10.4 per cent of the land tax, so that nearly 90 per cent of the land was in the occupation of tenant farmers.'[45]

Gray stated that in Oxfordshire:

> 'only nine per cent of the county's rural estate was in the hands of the independent farmer in 1785.'[46]

Since these two studies were published early in this century other people have examined the level of owner-occupancy, and have produced results consistently higher than either Davies or Gray. Hunt found that in 105 Leicestershire parishes owner-occupiers paid nineteen per cent of the tax in 1780.[47] Turner showed that in 1785 in Buckinghamshire this group paid between fifteen and twenty one per cent in townships enclosed by act, and six per cent in old enclosed townships.[48] In eastern Yorkshire table 5 shows that the level of tax paid by owner-occupiers was generally well above ten per cent, except in old enclosed townships, and the average for parliamentary enclosed townships was fifteen per cent. It would appear that owner-occupiers were distributed somewhat unevenly throughout the country. This class of 'yeoman' farmer had certainly not disappeared, but except in a few places their share of the land was not large, even though numerically they were still quite strong.

(iv) *Owner-Occupancy and Topography, c. 1787*

The relationship of enclosure chronology to ownership structure has been

Table 6

Landownership and Occupancy in 1787 in Eastern Yorkshire

District	1	2	3	4	5	6	7
Total no. of townships	19	32	15	24	40	18	71
Average number of owners per township	8.5	11.8	10.1	25.5	15.6	18.6	16.9
Average no. of owner-occupiers per township	2.3	4.4	4.0	12.6	6.5	7.8	6.6
Owner-oocupiers as a percentage of all owners	26.7	37.3	39.7	49.4	41.3	42.2	38.9
Percentage of tax paid by owner-occupiers	6.2	10.9	8.9	23.4	13.8	16.9	13.8

Key to districts and Source: see Table 5 above

dealt with by many researchers, but few have looked closely at the influence of topography. As tables 2–5 have demonstrated, when the townships of eastern Yorkshire are grouped into physical regions they show differing patterns of landholding. In table 6 the information on landownership and occupancy in each of the seven districts irrespective of enclosure history is shown. The table highlights the very marked differences between the districts, the greatest contrast being between districts 1 and 4. In Lincolnshire too the distribution and landowning strength of owners and owner-occupiers reflected topography. Using the Assessments Grigg found that in the fenlands of South Lincolnshire at the turn of the eighteenth century owner-occupiers were numerous, whilst on the limestone heath and in the boulder clay central region they were 'almost entirely absent'. In parishes on the scarp foot of the Wolds, in the west, and on the Lias clay they were numerous but rather more irregularly distributed than they were in the east.[49] In her study of landownership in Lindsey using the Land Tax Assessments, Fuller found that at the beginning of the nineteenth century owner-occupiers were most numerous along the coast in the marshes, where they paid between twenty and fifty per cent of the tax. In the mid-clay vale and in the southern Wolds they were less strong, whilst in the northern and central Wolds there were large tracts with almost no owner-occupiers.[50]

We have no earlier records on landownership to compare with the Land Tax Assessments, so any attempt to account for variations in landholding, in eastern Yorkshire or elsewhere, must be speculative. Possibly in regions like district 1, the Jurassic hills, where owner-occupiers were very weak in 1787, they had once been quite strong and for reasons linked to the nature of the soil they had declined. Certainly by the end of the eighteenth century pasture farming prevailed in this district.[51] In areas more favourable to mixed farming, such as on the western side of the Wolds in district 4, small-scale farmers seem to have flourished. They were fortunate in having a variety of land types available within their townships. They had a 'relative abundance of meadowland', pasture on the low lying Vale of York, arable land under the scarp, and sheep pastures on the Wolds.[52] They were thus able to carry on a broadly based mixed farming, and it may have been this which enabled the small owner-occupier to change farming patterns relatively easily and to survive, whereas in more homogeneous districts he sold his property and either left the area or became a tenant farmer. Alternatively there may never have been high numbers of owner-occupiers in certain areas; in some parts of the high Wolds for example the nature of the soil and the elevation of the land made it unsuitable for small scale farming, and it seems unlikely that the structure of landownership and occupancy differed much in the seventeenth century from the pattern shown in the 1787 Assessments.

It is difficult, perhaps impossible, to separate the influence of topography from that of enclosure history when attempting to explain differing patterns of landownership. Grigg concluded that although in South Lincolnshire there was an undoubted relationship between the date of enclosure and the presence of owner-occupiers, this was not the only factor relevant to the distribution of this group. He suggested that a distribution in space as well as in time was important in discussing the changing importance of the owner-occupier.[53] The information extracted from the Land Tax Assessments for eastern Yorkshire corroborates this view.

Conclusion

In this study attention has been focussed upon the numbers of owners and owner-occupiers, and the relative strength of owner-occupiers in eastern Yorkshire, using the Assessments for one year only, although this source is admirably suited for use in a study of landownership change, using any dates between c. 1780 and c. 1832.[54] The year 1787 was chosen because it stands at a mid-point between the two waves of parliamentary enclosure activity. By dividing the 219 townships of the region into seven districts, according to their topography, and by subdividing within each district by enclosure date, it has been possible to reveal some of the different patterns of ownership and occupancy.

There seemed to be a relationship between enclosure history and the number of people owning land; owners were most numerous in townships which had been recently (between 1725 and 1779), enclosed by act, they were slightly less numerous in those still in open field, whilst in old enclosed townships they were generally very few. Apparently parliamentary enclosure occurred earlier in townships where the land was most sub-divided, and it may be that this was because in such townships proprietors (or their tenants) experienced more inconvenience from the scattering of their holdings than did those in townships where owners were less numerous. Moreover, as an alternative to enclosure, agreements to change cropping and cultivation were easier to arrive at in townships with relatively few owners. It may be significant that there were a number of townships, still open in 1787, where such agreements pre-dated enclosure by some years, and in these townships owners were not numerous.

The study reveals that owner-occupiers were weak both numerically and territorially in 1787 in old enclosed townships, a finding which mirrors the pattern found by researchers in other parts of England. In townships enclosed by act owner-occupiers were more numerous, and they held a higher proportion of the land than in those enclosed before 1725. When the owner-occupancy in townships enclosed between 1725 and 1779 is compared to that in those still open in 1787 the differences between the two groups is small; it is difficult to detect any significant relationship between the date of enclosure by act and the level of owner-occupancy. Certainly the study demonstrates that owner-occupiers were, without support from absentee owners, too weak successfully to oppose an enclosure act. Only in one district, the Wold scarp/Jurassic ridge district, did their landowning strength exceed twenty per cent.

Enclosure history and topography are closely linked to one another, and it is difficult to assess which had more bearing upon the structure of ownership and occupancy. Table 6 showing the patterns of landholding in the seven districts irrespective of enclosure history reveals considerable divergences from one district to another. A variety of factors must have contributed to these differences, the most important being the degree of old enclosure in the district, the type of farming systems, the elevation, and the soil. Perhaps owner-occupiers had once been strong in all districts, and had only survived in strength in some areas where a system of mixed farming prevailed. Alternatively this group may never have been strong in districts like the high Wolds, where poor soils and a high elevation meant that farms had to be large to be profitable, which relegated small family farms to relative oblivion.

The information from this joint study of enclosure and the Land Tax Assessments for eastern Yorkshire suggests that in any region with a varied landscape it is necessary to look at the spatial distribution of owners and occupiers as well as their distribution in townships with different enclosure histories. There are many influences on ownership structure, but by using the Assessments it is possible to begin separating them from one another.

NOTES

1 Eastern Yorkshire is not synonymous with the East Riding. Eastern Yorkshire omits those parts of the Vale of York which are in the East Riding because to include the Vale of York would necessarily involve parts of the North and West Ridings. The Land Assessments on which this study is based can be found in the Humberside Record Office, Beverley (hereafter HCRO), QDE 1. My thanks to Mr K.D. Holt and his staff for their helpful assisstance.

2 Martin, J.M., *Warwickshire and the Parliamentary Enclosure Movement*, University of Birmingham, unpublished Ph.D. thesis, 1965, p. 64; Turner, M.E., *English Parliamentary Enclosure: its Historical Geography and Economic History*, Folkestone, 1980, p. 163. See also Hunt, H.G., 'Landownership and Enclosure, 1750–1830', *Economic History Review*, 2nd series, volume 11, 1958–9, pp. 501–3.

3 Allison, K.J., *The East Riding of Yorkshire Landscape*, London, 1976, p. 104; HCRO, QDE 1 1787.

4 HCRO, DDRI/33/7; HCRO, QDE 1 1787.

5 Allison, op. cit., p. 94; HCRO, QDE 1 1787.

6 Harris, A., *The Rural Landscape of the East Riding of Yorkshire*, Oxford, 1961, Figure 14, p. 45.

7 HCRO, PE/144; QDE 1 1787.

8 HCRO, DDCC/69/1; QDE 1 1787.

9 HCRO, DDCC/39/3–4; HCRO, QDE 1 1787.

10 Harris, op. cit., p. 44.

11 HCRO, AN/391/27.

12 HCRO, QDE 1 1787.

13 Turner, op. cit., p. 164.

14 Crowther, J.E., *Parliamentary Enclosure in Eastern Yorkshire, 1725–1860*, University of Hull, unpublished Ph.D. thesis, 1984, Appendix III, pp. 573–85.

15 Hull University Library (hereafter HUL), DDBA/4–5. My thanks to Mr. N. Higson for his helpful assistance.

16 HCRO, BG/139/12.

17 HUL, DDBA/4/31–2.

18 HUL, DDBA/4–5.

19 *Victoria History of the County of York: East Riding*, volume 4, London, 1979, p. 49.

20 This was indeed the case in a number of eastern Yorkshire townships: at Helperthorpe in 1773 the farmers agreed to sow turnips and clover in the open fields, HUL, DDSY/70/125; at nearby Weaverthorpe and East and West Lutton turnips and clover were also grown in the open fields well before enclosure, Harris, A., *Pre-enclosure Agricultural Systems in the East Riding of Yorkshire*, University of London, unpublished M.A. thesis, 1951, pp. 19–20. In all these townships there were few landowners.

21 The Land Tax Assessments show that in most upland townships with few owners the farms were generally very large.

22 6 Geo. IV, c.68; HCRO, DQ/233/9.

23 6&7 Wm. IV, c.115; HCRO, Enrolment Book H, p. 11.

24 43 Geo. III, c. 89; HCRO, CA/320/43.

25 Gray, H.L., 'Yeoman Farming in Oxfordshire from the Sixteenth Century to the Nineteenth', *Quarterly Journal of Economics*, volume 24, 1910, p. 322.

26 For a discussion of the inefficiency of the open fields by the beginning of the parliamentary enclosure period see Turner, M.E., *Enclosures in Britain, 1750–1830*, London, 1984, pp. 37–9.

27 Davies, E., 'The Small Landowner, 1780–1832, in the Light of the Land Tax Assessments', *EcHR*, 1st series, volume 1, 1927, p. 105.

28 Martin, J.M., 'The Parliamentary Enclosure Movement and Rural Society in Warwickshire', *Agricultural History Review*, volume 15, 1967, p. 34.
29 Chambers, J.D., 'Enclosure and the Small Landowner', *EcHR*, 1st series, volume 10, number 2, 1939–40, p. 123.
30 HCRO, QDE 1 1787.
31 ibid.
32 Davies, loc. cit., p. 103.
33 Martin, 'The Parliamentary Enclosure Movement', p. 32.
34 Chambers, loc. cit., p. 123.
35 Turner, *English Parliamentary Enclosure*, pp. 163–4.
36 ibid., p. 163.
37 As they may have done in Buckinghamshire, Turner, ibid., p. 164.
38 Crowther, op. cit., Chapter 5, passim.
39 HCRO, QDE 1 1787.
40 ibid.
41 Crowther, op. cit., Table 7.1, p. 347.
42 HCRO, QDE 1 1787.
43 Homer, H., *An Essay on the Nature and Method of Ascertaining the Specific Shares of Proprietors upon the Inclosure of the Common Fields*, Oxford, 1766, p. 36.
44 Turner, *English Parliamentary Enclosure*, p. 165.
45 Davies, loc. cit., p. 110.
46 Gray, loc. cit., p. 301.
47 Hunt, loc. cit., p. 283.
48 Turner, *English Parliamentary Enclosure*, p. 164.
49 Grigg, D.B., 'The Land Tax Returns', *AgHR*, volume 11, 1963, p. 89.
50 Fuller, H.A., *Landownership in Lindsey, circa 1800–1860*, University of Hull, unpublished M.A. thesis, 1974, p. 45.
51 Harris, *The Rural Landscape*, p. 58.
52 Sheppard, J.A., 'Field Systems of Yorkshire', Chapter 4 of Baker, A.R.H. and Butlin, R.A., (eds.), *Studies of Field Systems in the British Isles*, Cambridge, 1973, p. 161.
53 Grigg, loc. cit., p. 94.
54 For Eastern Yorkshire see Crowther, op. cit., pp. 437–443.

PART III: THE URBAN AND INDUSTRIAL LAND TAX

Chapter 6

The Land Tax Assessments in the Study of the Physical Development of Country Towns

MARGARET NOBLE

The traditional use of the Land Tax Assessments has rested on their application to the study of landownership and agrarian change in rural areas, leading to considerable debate as to whether the tax paid could be justifiably interpreted as proportional to the assessed acreage.[1] More recently debate has centred on the usefulness of the Assessments for measuring wealth and income distribution in England and Wales.[2] One major problem in using them for either purpose is that it was not a tax on land alone, but also an assessment of property such as dwelling houses, cottages, warehouses, and industrial premises, often failing to distinguish between such units and land itself.[3] The recognition of the importance of entries relating to built property in the Assessments suggests therefore that the tax might prove an important source for investigating change in semi-urban and urban parishes. To date, however, the traditional application of the Land Tax to the analysis of rural and agrarian change has continued and in only one or two cases have the returns been employed in the analysis of landownership and property change in urban areas.[4] The lack of use of the Land Tax in urban areas is perhaps not surprising for the numerous problems that face utilisers of the tax in rural areas are compounded in urban areas, due largely to the large number of entries involved.[5] It is suggested, however, that the Assessments, if used in conjunction with other contemporary sources, may provide valuable insights into the nature of land and property ownership changes in towns, particularly country towns or market towns situated in semi-rural parishes. This chapter demonstrates the applicability and usefulness of the Assessments in investigating physical change in urban communities through an analysis of eight East Yorkshire country towns in the period 1782 to 1832 in conjunction with available enclosure and tithe awards, poor rate assessments, and printed census returns.

(i) *The Study Towns*

East Yorkshire is a large rural area, not dominated by industrialisation but, nevertheless, containing a diversity of economic activity. The settlement structure of the area in the eighteenth and nineteenth centuries was of fairly homogeneous character comprising farms, villages, and market towns with only two large urban centres, York and Hull, disturbing this pattern; and the region, unlike its industrial counterparts, experienced no phase of town creation during this time. Within the inherited urban system, however, significant demographic and economic changes occurred. Between 1780 and 1820 the population of the region's country towns generally increased threefold, with in-migration a significant force in this growth.[6] It was also a period in which significant economic development took place within these communities. Expansion in two main economic sectors of retailing and manufacturing activity made several of them into important service centres within the region. The growth of the region's country towns was reflected in structural changes within the urban area.. These changes are most strongly represented by the erection of several hundred new dwelling units and the establishment of new commercial and industrial premises within the urban area. The principal forces in the pattern and process of internal restructuring were the demolition and rebuilding of existing properties, infilling of vacant land, and the subdivision of plots. To the long-established pattern of two or three main streets were added numerous lanes, alleys, courts, and yards, whilst infilling behind the main street frontages was particularly marked in all towns. In none of the country towns of the region was physical structure so compact as to preclude new building within the existing built area, but in the most dynamic growth centres of the region there was an obvious need for areal expansion.

While contemporary maps can be utilised to demonstrate the pattern of this expansion, the nature and operation of the process is less obvious. It is suggested, however, that the Assessments are a valuable tool in investigating the operation of the building process within these communities, particularly where Assessments were made for individual town wards as opposed to the community as a whole, which might include rural areas. The important questions that have to be asked are, how accurate are the Assessments and what problems arise in their application to the study of physical change in country towns?

(ii) *The Assessments and the Study Towns*

Property descriptions were first included in the Assessments in the period after 1825 (see figure 2 in chapter 1 above) and provide valuable insights into the amount and nature of built property that was taxed. Table 1 indicates the proportion of all Assessment entries relating to built property for the eight East Yorkshire country towns. Entries referred not only to dwelling houses and land but also to commercial and industrial premises such as inns, shops, tanyards, breweries, mills, and warehouses. On average almost two-thirds of entries related to built property of some kind; the standard deviation of 16.5 indicates some deviations among the towns but only Beckside ward in Beverley and the town of Great Driffield registered significantly low values of more than one standard deviation below the mean. Using the Assessments in conjunction with available enclosure and tithe plans it is evident that entries relating to land only generally referred to larger units of agricultural land within the parish, for within towns there were few large tracts of land with no attached property.[7] Clearly, therefore, the Assessments must include a considerable proportion of the built environment within each of these urban parishes, but how much and how representative are they?

Table 1

Property Descriptions Recorded in the LTAs for East Yorkshire Towns

Town	BBW*	BNBW*	Hedon	Pockn	Patrn	Howdn	G.Dfd	M.Wtn	S.Cave
Date	1792	1802	1832	1832	1832	1832	1832	1832	1832
No of entries	86	51	82	301	98	187	123	257	116
% of entries									
House	26.7	56.9	-	41.9	36.7	44.9	41.5	23.7	-
House/garden/land	4.6	9.8	89.0	8.3	38.8	26.7	-	31.5	64.4
Commercial premises	4.6	3.9	-	7.0	.0	2.1	-	-	-
Industrial premises	1.2	7.8	1.2	2.6	-	1.1	0.8	0.4	-
All built property**	37.5	78.4	90.2	59.8	77.6	74.9	42.3	55.6	64.4
Land	58.1	21.6	9.8	39.9	20.4	22.4	57.7	44.0	36.6
Other/unknown	3.5	-	-	0.3	2.0	2.7	-	0.4	-

* BBW = Beverley Beckside Ward; BNBW = Beverley North Bar Within

** Mean of percentages of all built property = 64.5; S. D. = 16.5

Source: Humberside County Record Office LTA/QDE

The Assessments made for the country towns of Beverley, Driffield, Pocklington, Hedon, Howden, Market Weighton, Patrington, and South Cave were analysed at a variety of levels and for various dates in the period 1782 to 1832. For seven of the towns (viz, Great Driffield, Pocklington, Market Weighton, Hedon, Howden, South Cave, and Patrington) the returns were sampled at ten year intervals from 1782 to 1832 giving six study dates. For three of these towns, each of which enjoyed a different pattern of growth during the late eighteenth and early nineteenth century, namely Driffield, Pocklington, and Hedon, the Assessments were also analysed for intervening five year periods providing a total of eleven study dates. Assessments for Beverley Borough were the only ones among the towns to be made at ward level, but unfortunately these are only available for the period 1792 to 1802 and thus analysis had to be confined to three dates in this period viz. 1792, 1796, and 1802.[8]

The overall comprehensiveness of the Assessments presented no problems among the study towns because even that property which was exonerated from payment still continued to be included in the document in the period after 1798. The main difficulties arise first due to the removal, following the 1798 act, of all properties with an annual rental value of less than twenty shillings from liability to assessment, and second to the re-assessment that could result from redemption procedures.[9] For each of the study towns for which a consistent run of data is available there

Table 2

Land Tax Quotas Payable and Estimated Tax Per Acre for East Yorkshire Towns

Town	1782 Quota £ s d	1782 Estd.** Tax per ac Shillings	1832 Quota £ s d	1832 Estd.** Tax per ac Shillings	Percentage Difference
Gt Driffield	135 8 0*	0.55	115 0 8	0.47	-15.0
Hedon	47 4 0	2.90	42 0 0	2.40	-11.1
Pocklington	127 4 0	0.99	108 11 0	0.84	-14.6
Mkt Weighton	126 7 0	0.43	116 7 0	0.40	-8.0
Howden	179 5 4	1.22	160 4 0	1.09	-10.7
Patrington	145 16 0	0.78	127 16 0	0.68	-12.4
South Cave	130 3 11*	0.60	129 17 11	0.60	-0.7
Beverley	648 10 11*	5.39	Not available		
Mean		1.61		0.95	10.9
Standard Deviation		1.61		0.70	4.5

* The 1792 LTA has been substituted for the 1782 LTA in these three cases
** The acreages used are those from the 1891 Census Report

Source: Humberside County Record Office, LTA/QDE

was a reduction in the quota payable of about ten to twelve per cent over the period 1782 to 1832 (Table 2). The explanation for this reduction may arise from the removal of the poorest properties from liability to assessment but it is also evident that certain towns were revalued at the turn of the century. Ginter has recently cited the case of the town of Patrington in South Holderness where a new valuation of rents resulted from redemption, altering the statutory rent to tax ratio of 5:1 to a new mean ratio of 25.3:1.[10] The effect of reduction in quotas payable and of re-assessment on the taxation structure of townships is not altogether clear, for individual properties could be subject to changing assessment due to the sale or acquisition of land, which in a period of accelerated urbanisation was undoubtedly a very common process. However, evidence from the study towns suggests that alterations in the amounts of tax payable were relatively small in magnitude and do not tend to alter the constitution of the different tax paying groups, except occasionally amongst the very lowest valued properties.

Periodic fluctuation in the methods adopted by assessors in compiling the returns poses problems in the use of the Assessments. Prior to the alphabetical listing of landowners around the turn of the eighteenth century it was common practice to list separately each individual taxable unit, and this was indicated by the frequent appearance of proprietors names in the Assessments. Later, however, individual taxable units owned by one proprietor were often grouped and listed in the Assessments as a single gross taxable sum. Thus the number of taxable units listed in any settlement may appear to fall in total, obscuring the underlying trend for the period of an increase. Comparison of the number of taxable properties listed in the Assessments with the number of buildings listed for each parish in the printed census returns of 1801 to 1831 demonstrates clearly that the number of properties in each of the towns rose, but that this increase was not fully reflected in the Assessments. On average, the number of entries in the Land Tax was only half the number recorded in the Census returns. (Table 3).

The reasons for under-enumeration in the Assessments may be due to changes in compilation methods already mentioned, but there is a suggestion that new buildings often escaped Land Tax.[11] In the light of this it is suggested that the Assessments cannot be used to measure any detailed quantitative changes in the structure of land and property ownership, but may be most usefully employed as aggregate representative samples indicating relative increase or decrease in respect of a number of variables.

Further evidence of the difficulty of using the Assessments for precise quantitative measurement is provided by comparing the property ownership structure as indicated by the Land Tax with available enclosure and tithe data. Estimation of the possible size of holdings in urban parishes

Table 3

Numbers of Properties in East Yorkshire Towns, 1782-1832

	1782		1792	1802			1812		1822			1832		
Town	LT	PR	LT	LT	PR	C	LT	C	LT	PR	C	LT	PR	C
Gt Driffield	NA		118	118	-	320	130	399	139	459	488	123	-	541
Howden	224	221	216	182	228	313	185	314	180	-	395	187	374	448
Hedon	62	-	79	81	-	136	81	163	83	-	179	82	-	195
Patrington	5	-	58	87	-	161	87	190	87	-	253	88	-	288
South Cave	NA		95	92	-	-	101	-	93	-	-	116	-	-
Pocklington	121	-	140	198	-	367	290	381	236	-	431	301	-	451
Mkt Weighton	139	-	126	141	-	175	148	324	150	-	317	257	-	371
Beverley	NA		553	643	-	-	NA		NA			NA		

LT = Land Tax Assessments, which progressively improved as an index of properties
PR = Poor Rate Assessments
C = Censuses of 1801, 1811, 1821, and 1831 respectively

Sources: Humberside County Record Office, LTA/QDE, PR847. Census Reports.

from the Land Tax is fraught with difficulties as the contentious acreage equivalent loses much of its validity when the majority of entries relate to built property. Nevertheless, an attempt was made to estimate size of holdings from the Assessments in order that their representativeness could be tested. For both enclosure and tithe awards land and property owners were divided into seven groups; those owning less than five acres, five to ten acres, ten to fifty acres, fifty to one hundred acres, 100 to 500 acres, 500 to 1,000 acres, and those owning more than 1,000. Land and property owners listed in the Land Tax were also allocated to these groups according to the amount of tax paid. Amounts of tax paid per acre varied considerably among the townships from 0.55 shillings in Great Driffield to 2.9 shillings in Hedon and 5.39 shillings in the county town of Beverley (Table 2). As Table 4 demonstrates, there was a measure of correlation between the land ownership structure as evidenced by enclosure and tithe awards and the Land Tax Assessments, particularly among the larger proprietors, but it is evident that attempts to quantify the size of holdings in urban parishes using the Assessments must be regarded with severe caution. Examples of individual holdings may serve to clarify this point further.

Jane Le Marche, the second largest landowner in Great Driffield, owned almost 630 acres at the time of tithe apportionment, yet in 1832 she paid only £2 16 shillings tax, while Thomas Clark of the same town owned only five acres but paid 5 shillings and 9d Land Tax, double the estimated tax per acre for the township. In the town of Hedon there was perhaps greater correlation for James Iveson, gentleman, who owned twenty three acres

Table 4

Land and Property Owners Listed in Enclosure Awards, Land Tax Assessments, and Tithe Awards

Ownership Groups in acres		Under 5	5-10	10-50	50-100	100-500	500-1000	Over 1000	Total Owners
				Great Driffield					
Enclosure 1742	N	42	18	11	3	10	-	1	85
	%	47.7	21.2	12.5	3.4	11.4	-	1.1	
LTA 1792	N	21	24	26	4	4	2	1	82
	%	28.6	29.3	31.7	4.9	4.9	2.4	1.2	
LTA 1802	N	36	24	36	8	5	2	1	112
	%	32.1	21.4	32.1	7.1	4.5	1.8	0.9	
LTA 1832	N	33	28	17	9	10	-	1	108
	%	30.5	25.9	25.0	8.3	9.3	-	0.9	
Tithe A. 1845	N	190	18	24	3	5	2	1	252
	%	75.4	7.1	9.5	1.2	2.0	0.8	0.4	
				Patrington					
Enclosure 1768	N	117	9	15	10	3	2	-	156
	%	75.0	5.8	9.6	6.4	1.9	1.3	-	
LTA 1782	N	4	17	19	8	6	1	-	55
	%	7.3	30.9	34.5	14.5	10.9	1.8	-	
LTA 1802	N	24	15	27	7	8	-	1	82
	%	29.3	18.3	32.9	8.5	9.7	-	1.2	
LTA 1832	N	28	14	26	3	7	-	1	79
	%	35.4	17.7	32.9	3.8	8.9	-	1.3	
				Market Weighton					
Enclosure 1776	N	40	7	33	10	5	1	1	97
	%	41.2	7.2	34.0	10.3	5.1	1.0	1.0	
LTA 1782	N	-	27	47	14	6	1	1	96
	%	-	28.1	48.9	14.6	6.2	1.0	1.0	
LTA 1802	N	-	18	79	13	6	1	1	118
	%	-	15.2	66.9	11.0	5.1	0.8	0.8	
LTA 1832	N	16	20	70	12	7	1	1	127
	%	12.6	15.7	55.2	9.4	5.5	0.8	0.8	
Tithe A. 1846	N	108	8	2	-	-	-	-	118
Town land only	%	91.5	6.8	1.7	-	-	-	-	
				Hedon					
LTA 1782	N	49	7	6	-	-	-	-	62
	%	79.0	11.3	19.7	-	-	-	-	
LTA 1802	N	65	4	5	-	-	-	-	74
	%	87.8	5.4	6.7	-	-	-	-	
LTA 1832	N	48	4	10	-	-	-	-	62
	%	77.4	6.5	16.1	-	-	-	-	
Tithe A. 1849	N	82	5	4	1	-	-	-	92
	%	89.0	5.4	4.3	1.1				

Sources: Humberside County Record Office, DDBD 45/6, DDCK 32/23, DDPY 14/2 IA, LTA/QDE, PR 993 TA, PR 1067, RDB A5, RDB AK/98/8, RDB B/153/42. Borthwick Institue of Historical Research, TA 378 S.

and paid £2 16 shillings tax, but in Market Weighton John Smith, who owned a little over three acres paid 5 shillings in tax. Town property was clearly taxed at a much higher rate per acre than outlying parish land and it is this that largely invalidates the use of acreage equivalents in semi-rural parishes.

The problems of comparing the Assessments with these other sources are further compounded by the fact that only in a few cases do the enclosure and tithe data provide a complete coverage of the township in question. Market Weighton enclosure award covered only 77 per cent of all parish land and the tithe award for the same town dealt with only 134 acres of town land, representing just 2.2 per cent of all parish land, and the tithe award for Howden covered just 64 per cent of the township.[12]

Despite all the aforementioned difficulties the Assessments must remain one of the most important sources for investigating the process of urban development in country towns in this critical transitional period around the turn of the eighteenth century. For small country towns, which experienced much less dynamic growth than many of their industrial counterparts, comprehensive sources of a comparable nature that might be found for larger towns and cities are generally lacking and for much investigation it is necessary to have recourse to 'traditionally rural' sources and apply them to an urban situation.

(iii) *Urban Development c. 1780–1830*

(a) Property Development.

One of the easiest ways in which the growth of a community can be investigated is through an analysis of the changing number of properties. Evidence can be found in three principal sources, the Land Tax Assessments, poor rate assessments, and the printed census returns. There are problems associated with using the first to estimate the degree of development in individual towns for they are seldom consistent in their recording of properties under the ownership of a single individual. In the case of Great Driffield, for example, the Assessments indicate no highly significant increase in the number of taxable units, yet this town grew faster than any of its regional counterparts resulting in considerable physical expansion of the urban area. Richard Langley, Lord of the Manor of Great Driffield, held land and property taxed at more than £30; in the early Assessments his individual properties are listed, but in later years they were grouped as one single gross taxable sum and although one might hazard a guess as to the total number of units, there is no clear indication as to whether a policy of fragmentation or consolidation had occurred. For each of the study towns there was an increase in the number of taxable units recorded in the Assessments and in the number of properties listed in

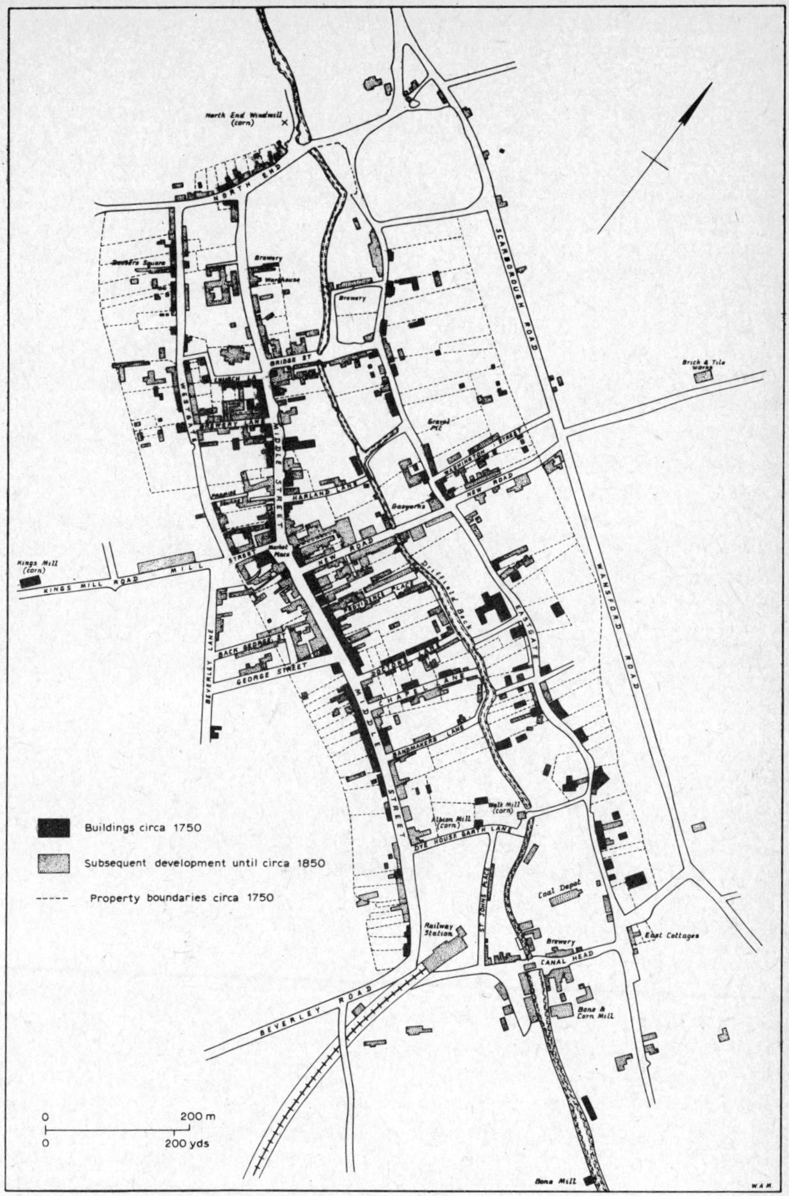

Figure 1: The Expansion of the Built Area of Great Driffield, c. 1750–1850.

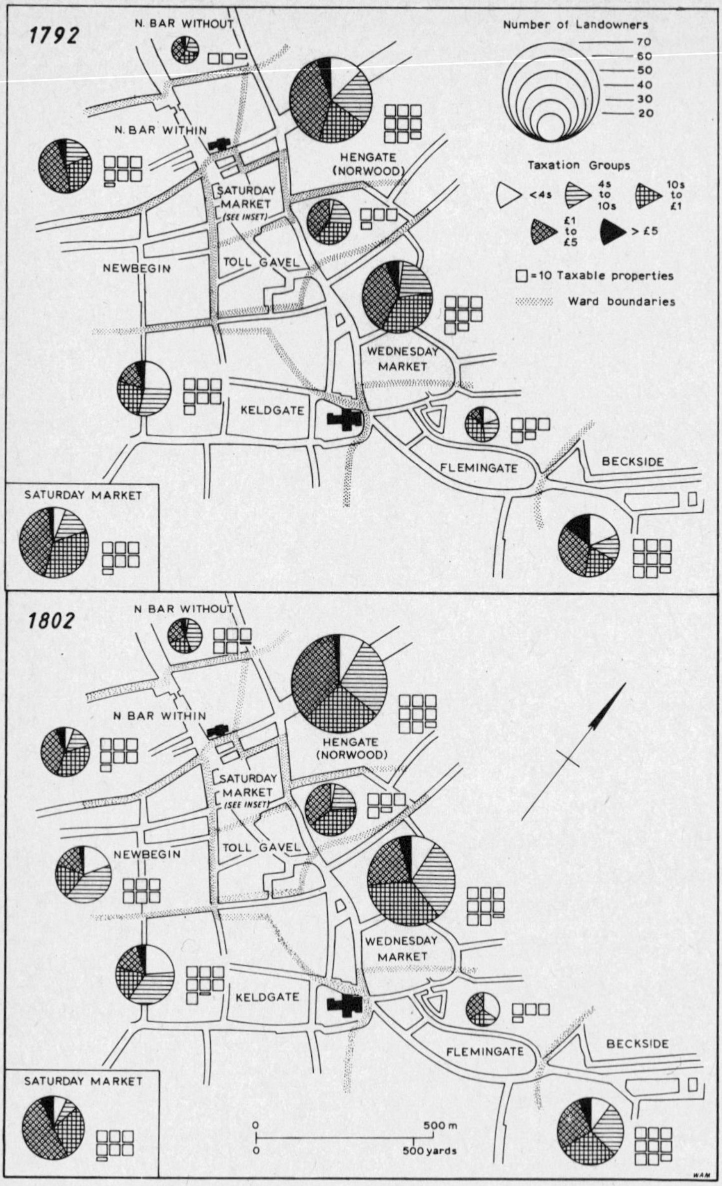

Figure 2: Taxable Properties and Property Ownership in Beverley, 1792 and 1802.

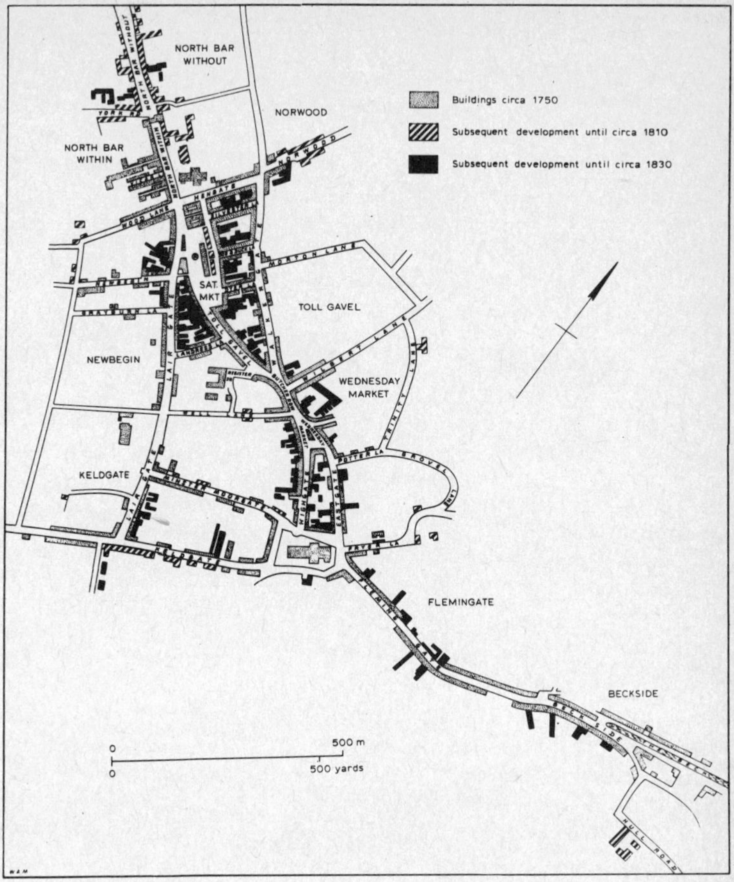

Figure 3: The Expansion of the Built Area in Beverley, c. 1750–1830.

the census during the period 1780 to 1830, evidence of a process of property development (Table 3). The increase in the number of taxable units averaged 46 per cent, but the high standard deviation of 47.1 indicates considerable inter-urban variation. For the period 1801–31 the census returns suggest that the real increase in the number of properties was three times this amount. Inter-urban variation in the degree of property development in these country towns was clearly related to differential rates of demographic growth and economic and social expansion.

During the century after 1750 the country towns of the region each underwent one of four types of growth experiences, dynamic growth, expansion, stability, and decline.[13] Dynamic towns experienced the highest rates of demographic growth, considerably expanded their functional status within the region and emerged as social and nodal centres of regional significance. Expanding centres enjoyed similar but more tempered growth to that of dynamic centres; they too experienced fairly high rates of demographic growth and witnessed significant expansion in their service activities, but most of this growth was absolute and they failed to alter their relative standing within the settlement system of the region. Relative loss in both demographic and functional standing within the region characterised stable centres. Although they experienced some growth in both population and functions their poor geographical location and ill-developed trade and commerce rendered them unable to transcend their position as middle to lower order centres in the regional urban hierarchy. Declining centres were towns that at the start of the eighteenth century could already be considered on the margins of urban status, for, their markets and fairs apart, they possessed few attributes that set them apart from rural society which they were designed to serve. Limited demographic growth and functional expansion in the ensuing century and a half ensured further erosion of their already weak standing within the region.

Pocklington, Market Weighton, and Beverley were each expanding towns and, as table 3 demonstrates, they each experienced a marked increase in the number of recorded taxable units, by 131.5 per cent in Pocklington over the period 1782 to 1832 and by 85 per cent in Market Weighton, while in Beverley they rose by 116 per cent in the decade 1792 to 1802. By contrast Hedon and Howden, both predominantly stable towns, experienced a much less marked increase in their number of taxable properties, perhaps reflecting the low level of demand for new housing by a more slowly expanding population. A similar situation characterised the declining town of South Cave. The dynamic town of Great Driffield clearly experienced significant growth at this time (Figure 1), but the Assessments for this town fail adequately to represent the rate of physical growth.

Both Land Tax Assessments and poor rate assessments made for individual town wards indicate more precisely the detailed patterns of property change within country towns. Within Beverley the Land Tax Assessments indicate that two wards, Tollgavel and North Bar Without, experienced significant property development in the period 1792 to 1802 (Table 5, Figures 2 and 3). The former was developing as a secondary retail node to the already congested central core of Saturday Market, and the latter as an upper class residential area.[14] Surprisingly Beckside Ward,

Table 5

Taxable Properties in Beverley Wards, 1792-1802

Date	1792 No	1796 No	1792-1796 per cent increase	1802 No	1796-1802 per cent increase	1792-1802 per cent increase
Newbegin	NA	51	-	59	15.7	-
Hengate	86	82	-4.6	85	-3.6	-1.1
North Bar Within	63	71	12.9	64	-11.3	1.6
Flemingate	47	33	-34.0	35	6.1	-14.9
North Bar Without	25	28	12.0	51	82.1	104.0
Wednesday Market	77	81	5.2	83	2.5	7.8
Saturday Market	65	64	1.5	63	1.6	-3.0
Tollgavel	36	36	0.0	45	25.0	25.0
Keldgate	68	68	0.0	72	6.0	6.0
Beckside	86	NA		86	-	0.0
Mean			-1.0		13.8	13.9
Standard Deviation			13.7		26.0	33.4

Source: Humberside County Record Office, LTA/QDE

which centred on the town's navigable link to the River Hull and the Humber, registered very little change, although Beverley Beck was bringing considerable trade and industry to this part of the town.[15] In Howden, over the period 1780 to 1830, poor rate assessments indicate an increase of almost 170 per cent in the available dwelling stock, the period after 1800 witnessing the greatest degree of change (Table 6). From this time a large number of new properties were erected in the town with two areas, St. John's Street and Applegate, and Pinfold Street and Corn Market Hill, adding considerably to their percentage share of all housing.[16] The growth of these areas was related to the establishment of two extensive tanyards which provided the focus for the town's leather industry with more than 40 per cent of leather workers residing in these areas.[17]

(b) Landownership Change.

How was land made available for development? The analysis of the changing structure of property ownership may provide an answer. The difficulties encountered in the preceding analysis of property development due to the frequent aggregation of taxable units under one head leading to an underestimation of the rate of growth of buildings, particularly in the period after 1800, were absent in this part of the analysis. Here concern is with individuals or property owners and not properties, and in no case are property owners grouped together under a single line entry in the Assessments, except in cases of joint ownership.

For most towns in the 1790s there was a marked increase in the number

Table 6

Housing Development in Howden, 1781-1831

Street	Houses in 1781 No	%	Houses in 1801 No	%	Houses in 1831 No	%
Market Place	39	17.6	48	21.0	58	15.5
Church Yard	13	5.9	13	5.7	16	4.3
St John's St. and Applegate	20	9.0	18	7.9	45	12.0
Pinfold Street and Corn Market Hill	6	2.8	6	2.6	47	12.6
Bridegate	64	28.9	64	28.0	75	20.0
Hailgate	66	29.9	70	30.7	109	29.1
Flatgate	13	5.9	9	3.9	24	6.4
Total	221	100.0	228	99.8	374	99.9

Source: Humberside County Record Office, PR 847

of property owners, the town of Patrington, for example, registering a 64 per cent increase. Conversely in the first two decades of the nineteenth century there was stability and/or decline reflecting the end of the war-time boom on the property market. Moving into the second quarter of the nineteenth century the number of property owners within towns again appeared to be increasing, a trend substantiated by the more detailed five year analysis for the towns of Great Driffield, Hedon, and Pocklington, and the evidence from the tithe apportionments of the 1830s and 1840s. Land Tax Assessment data for five year periods shows that the years 1797–1802 and 1822–27 were especially marked for increase and tithe data (Table 7) suggests that increases in the total number of property owners may have been of even greater magnitude than the Assessments reveal. In the case of both Howden and Market Weighton the tithe award covers only 64 per cent and 2.2 per cent of parish land respectively, the latter being concerned entirely with town land, while for Hedon and Great Driffield, where the tithe award dealt with the whole township, the number of listed proprietors is significantly higher than that found in the Assessments.

Within country towns there is thus evidence to suggest that the years surrounding the turn of the eighteenth century may have been of particular significance for their development. In Beverley in all but two of the wards, namely Saturday Market and North Bar Within, there was an increase in the total number of property owners in the period 1792 to 1802; in three of the wards, North Bar Without, Wednesday Market and Toll Gavel, these increases were between 20 and 25 per cent (Table 8, Figure 2). Analysis of the land and property ownership turnover rate (i.e. a measure of the rate at which new proprietors entered the ownership

Table 7

Property Owners in East Yorkshire Towns, 1782-1832

	Hedon	Howden	Mkt.Wtn.	S.Cave	Gt.Dfd.	Pocklgn.	Patrgtn.
Enclosure							
Date	-	-	1776	1787	1742	1757	1768
No. owners	-	-	97	69	86	88	156*
1782 LTA							
No. owners	62	144	96	-	-	121	55
1792 LTA							
No. owners	78	145	91	81	82	127	50
% change	+25.8	+8.7	-5.2	-	-	+4.9	-9.0
1802 LTA							
No. owners	74	159	118	91	112	157	82
% change	-5.1	+9.6	+29.7	+12.3	+36.8	+23.6	+64.0
1812 LTA							
No. owners	71	151	110	92	113	153	74
% change	-4.0	-5.0	-6.8	+1.1	+0.9	-2.5	-9.7
1822 LTA							
No. owners	66	141	107	85	107	156	79
% change	-7.0	-6.6	-2.7	-7.6	-5.3	+2.0	+6.8
1832 LTA							
No. owners	62	152	127	91	108	143	79
% change	+6.1	+7.8	+18.9	+7.1	+0.9	-8.3	0.0
1782-1832							
% increase	0.0	5.6	32.2	12.3	31.7	18.2	43.6
Tithe Award							
Date	1849	1844	1846	-	1848	-	-
No. owners	92	111	118	-	252	-	-

	1782-1792	1792-1802	1802-1812	1812-1822	1822-1832	1782-1832
Mean change	+2.5	+24.4	-3.7	-2.9	+4.6	+20.5
Standard deviation	10.4	20.6	3.6	6.0	7.8	14.7

*The Patrington Enclosure Award includes owners of old enclosure

Source: See Table 4

Table 8

Number of Property Owners in Beverley Wards, 1792-1802

Date	1792 No	1796 No	1792-1796 pe cent change	1802 No	1796-1802 per cent change	1792-1802 per cent change
Newbegin	NA	35	-	41	+17.1	-
Hengate	60	67	+11.7	70	+4.5	+16.7
North Bar Within	38	35	-7.9	34	-2.8	-10.5
Flemingate	25	23	-8.0	26	+13.0	+4.0
North Bar Without	20	20	0.0	25	+25.0	+25.0
Wednesday Market	52	54	+3.8	64	+18.5	+23.1
Saturday Market	50	47	-6.0	45	-4.2	-10.0
Tollgavel	31	34	+8.8	37	+8.8	+19.3
Keldgate	39	39	0.0	42	+7.7	+7.7
Beckside	42	NA	-	48	-	+14.3
Mean Change			+0.3		+9.7	+9.9
Standard Deviation			7.0		9.1	12.5

Source: Humberside County Record Office, LTA/QDE

Table 9

Turnover* of Land and Property in East Yorkshire Towns, 1782-1832

Town	Percentage Turnover 1782-1792	1792-1802	1801-1812	1812-1822	1822-1832
Great Driffield	NA	58.9	51.3	33.6	27.7
Howden	42.7	34.6	35.0	25.5	44.7
Pocklington	41.7	53.5	41.8	32.1	51.7
Market Weighton	46.1	44.9	29.1	27.6	47.2
Patrington	50.0	69.5	40.5	22.8	44.3
Hedon	59.0	39.2	21.1	33.3	41.9
South Cave	NA	35.2	30.4	37.1	45.3
Mean	47.9	50.0	35.6	30.3	43.3
Standard Deviation	6.3	12.2	9.2	4.7	6.9

*Turnover taken to mean the number of new owners entering the property ownership structure in a given period

Source: Humberside County Record Office, LTA/QDE

structure) provides further evidence of development within these towns (Table 9).

Between c. 1780 and 1830 decennial land/property turnover generally averaged between 30 per cent and 50 per cent although there was measurable inter-urban variation in this process. In Howden ownership turnover never exceeded 45 per cent compared with extreme peaks of 70 per cent in Patrington (1792–1802) and 60 per cent in Hedon (1782–1792). The overall trend was for the highest rate of change to come between c. 1780 and c. 1800, in particular during the 1790s, followed by a decline and later a secondary peak in the 1820s (Table 9). The structure of property ownership was seldom static and it is suggested that the intrusion of new property owners may have been an important factor in stimulating the transactions of the land market, and in ensuring that new land was made available for urban expansion. Analysing landownership change for five year periods indicates an even more fluid situation; turnover was particularly high between 1787–1792, 1797–1802, and 1822–1827. The town of Beverley demonstrates in greater detail how this fluidity in the land and property market was related to growth areas within the town. In Beverley turnover rates were lowest in Saturday Market and North Bar Within, two wards which by the turn of the eighteenth century were already well-developed commercial and residential cores within the town. Ownership change was most significant in Toll Gavel and North Bar Without where considerable commercial and residential development was taking place at this time.[18]

It is, however, the changing aggregate taxation structure of ownership that provides greatest insight into the way in which land was provided for urban development. For this analysis property owners were classified into seven taxation groups; viz, those whose property was taxed at under 4 shillings, 4–10 shillings, 10 shillings to £1, £1 to £5, £5 to £10, £10 to £20, and over £20, and three broad categories of property ownership were identified. Small property owners were classified as those paying under £1 tax and generally holding town land. Intermediate property owners were those with buildings and land taxed between £1 and £5, and commonly owned larger tracts of parish land or valuable properties within the urban area. The large landowners, whose holdings were taxed at £5 or more and who were noticeably unrepresented as a group in the town of Beverley, represented on average less than 4 per cent of all taxpayers and owned extensive areas of parish land.

Over the period c. 1780 to c. 1830 the number of very small property owners, i.e. those paying less than 4 shillings tax steadily increased while those paying between 10 shillings and £1 declined in number. A positive correlation is found between the total number of landowners and the number who paid less than 4 shillings tax, significant at over 99 per cent in four of the study towns[19] (Table 10). These figures suggest that space for urban development was provided not by the release of larger units of land held by wealthy proprietors, but through the release of smaller units generally owned by those paying between 4 shillings and £1 tax. Change in property ownership thus seemed to involve smaller plots of land. The

Table 10

Mean Percentages of Property Owners in each Taxation Class, in East Yorkshire Towns, 1782-1832*

Taxation Classes in £s	Mean percentages of all property owners occurring in each taxation class					
	1782	1792	1802	1812	1822	1832
Under £0.25	12.7	23.3	34.4	33.6	33.8	35.0
£0.25 - £0.5	48.4	38.7	35.4	34.7	34.1	33.3
£0.5 - £1	16.6	17.8	14.0	13.9	13.0	13.0
£1 - £5	17.7	16.1	13.3	14.5	16.3	15.6
£5 - £10	2.7	2.0	1.5	1.4	1.5	1.3
£10 - £20	0.8	0.9	0.5	0.9	0.5	1.0
Over £20	1.1	1.2	0.9	1.0	0.8	0.8

*Calculated from data relating to all study towns except Beverley

Source: Adapted from Land Tax Assessments 1782-1832, HCRO LTA/QDE

land of the lesser proprietors was sold and divided to form new building plots while that of their larger counterparts remained virtually intact. The latter, paying over £5 Land Tax, generally owned little town land and their property was largely confined to more extensive tracts of agricultural land outside the built up area. The evidence of property boundaries from contemporary maps, like enclosure and tithe maps, substantiates the observation that it was largely smaller plots of land that were released and subdivided for urban development. The predominant pattern, whereby entrepreneurs purchased large tracts of town land and erected numerous uniform dwelling types, that characterised many larger urban centres was not common in East Yorkshire.[20] Development in country towns was principally a piecemeal process in which few large building schemes were undertaken by wealthy tradesmen and industrialists although tradesmen such as Robert Thomas in Pocklington and John Sissons in Market Weighton occasionally built and leased small groups of houses.[21] Although one can suggest broadly similar patterns of development in country towns over the period c. 1780 to c. 1830 there were important distinctions in the pattern and process of physical expansion comparing so called dynamic with expanding, stable, and declining towns.

(c) Morphological Change.

In the 'classified' dynamic town of Great Driffield population growth and the accompanying functional development necessitated physical expansion of the built area and a considerable degree of restructuring. In the period 1750 to 1850 both intra-mural and extra-mural development occurred in Great Driffield. Within the loosely defined early eighteenth century built area bounded by Westgate, the Beck and Dye House Garth Lane, new streets were laid and infilling took place as former smallholdings and garden plots were sub-divided and built on (Figure 1). Extra-mural development occured in two main areas, to the east of the Beck and to the south of the town around the canal basin.[22] While in most country towns land for development was provided by lesser landowners who released small units of land within the town, in dynamic towns there is evidence to suggest that larger landowners also came to play a part in acquiring and developing land. While the proportion of taxpayers paying between 10 shillings and £1 declined from 14.6 per cent to 7.4 per cent in the period 1792–1832, and the proportion of those taxed at less than 4 shillings increased from 29 per cent to 41 per cent, the intermediate group of property owners increased their share of property. The proportion of taxpayers paying between £1 and £5 rose from 13 per cent to 17 per cent of all property owners.

In expanding country towns the general tendency in physical growth over the period 1750 to 1850 was inward. The predominant development process was one of infill with outward expansion occurring on only a limited scale. Many of these centres had organically developed into towns from large market villages and, in contrast to borough or corporate towns, possessed little formal layout. The absence of any real core in towns such as Market Weighton and Pocklington, and the loose nature of the urban fabric had morphological implications for it meant that structural change took place largely within the established frame of the built area. While there was some physical extension in these towns towards small plots of land on the urban fringe, most development occurred in the central area where garden plots behind the main street frontages were sub-divided to create numerous small terraces and yards that became characteristic of the morphology of these towns. Here intermediate landowners seem to have played very little part in the development process. In Market Weighton the most marked change in the taxation structure of property ownership occurred among the lowest taxed groups. Property owners who paid between 4 shillings and 10 shillings declined from 57 per cent to 34 per cent of all taxpayers over the study period while those paying less than 4 shillings increased from 5 per cent to almost 27 per cent of all taxpayers. In Pocklington, where at the enclosure of 1757, smaller landowners already constituted a significant proportion of all proprietors,[23] in the period after 1782 there was a further strengthening of their numbers. Between 1782 and 1832 the proportion of land and property owners taxed between 10 shillings and £1 declined from 16.5 per cent to 11 per cent while the proportion paying between 4 shillings and 10 shillings increased from 32 per cent to 41 per cent.

The Assessment data for the borough town of Beverley enables further investigation of internal restructuring of country towns at this time. It should be noted, however, that as the county town of the East Riding Beverley perhaps experienced proportionately greater development than its expanding counterparts. Analysing all town wards it is evident that similar processes were operating as in the other expanding towns of the region. Over the period 1792 to 1802 the number of small property owners, those paying less than 4 shillings tax, increased from 10.4 per cent to 12.5 per cent of all owners and those paying 4 shillings to 10 shillings from 21.5 per cent to 26.0 per cent. Conversely those taxed at more than £1 fell from 38 per cent to 33 per cent (Table 11). Wards in which the most significant changes occurred were North Bar Without, Wednesday Market, and Newbegin, in each of which the number of larger landowners declined and the number of lesser proprietors increased (Figure 3). The taxation structure of the individual wards shows internal differentiation within the town. North Bar Within and North Bar Without, Wednesday Market, Saturday Market, and Toll Gavel all had relatively few smaller proprietors and properties taxed at a low level. The two 'Bars' were areas of high class residence with many large dwellings, principally town residences of country gentry; the other three wards formed the principal retail axis in Beverley and therefore contained relatively few cottage dwellings. Keldgate, Flemingate and Newbegin had a majority of smaller proprietors indicating their development as predominantly working class residential areas, while Hengate Ward, or Norwood as it became known after 1800, fell somewhere in between with a mixture of dwelling types and proprietors.[24]

The limited demographic and economic development of stable towns exerted little pressure on urban form and consequently by the middle of the nineteenth century these country towns retained a good deal of their earlier plan. As in the expanding towns of the region the direction of physical growth was predominantly inward and there was little extension of the early eighteenth century urban area. Although along the main street frontages in these towns there was considerable infilling, the creation of small alleys and lanes behind these frontages and the replacement of garden plots with courts and yards were far less characteristic processes in stable centres. Land was provided for development in a manner similar to that operating in expanding towns. Few larger land and property owners were involved in the building process and it was lesser proprietors who came to dominate ownership. In Howden the proportion of taxpayers paying less than 10 shillings increased from 60 per cent to 70

Table 11

Taxation Distribution in Beverley, 1792–1802

Taxation Classes in £s	Percentages of all property owners occurring in each taxation class		
	1792	1796	1802
Under £0.25	10.4	10.5	11.8
£0.25 - £0.5	20.7	19.8	26.2
£0.5 - £1	28.6	30.8	28.0
£1 - £5	35.0	35.6	30.3
£5 - £10	4.8	2.8	3.0
£10 - £20	0.6	0.6	0.5
Over £20	-	-	0.2

Source: Humberside County Record Office, LTA/QDE

per cent over the course of the study period while the proportion paying between 10 shillings and £1 declined from 17 per cent to 10 per cent, and in Patrington the figures were 47 per cent to 61 per cent and 18 per cent to 16 per cent respectively. The outward extension of the urban area and the creation of successive fringe belts was thus not characteristic of stable towns, most development was related to inward-lying or intra-mural areas. Poor rate assessment data for Howden indicates something of the socio-spatial patterns that emerged in these towns.

During the last quarter of the eighteenth century more than two-thirds of the houses in Howden had a yearly rental value of under £5, almost one quarter a value of £6 to £20, and only one-tenth a rental value in excess of £20.[25] At this time the long main streets of the town were associated with an intermix of housing types, although the loosely compacted structure did give rise to certain groupings. Most of the poorer housing was located in Bridegate and Hailgate and the highest quality housing in Flatgate. Over the period 1780 to 1830 most of the new urban population was housed in dwellings of inferior stock. During this time the number of houses valued at between £1 and £5 increased from 108 to 224, while the number of houses with an annual rental of £20 or more only increased by seventeen from twenty-three to forty. Location quotients can be usefully employed to indicate something of the internal restructuring that occured (Table 12). Whereas structural development in towns experiencing more rapid regional growth led to the creation of residentially distinct areas and to

Table 12

Location Quotients* of Rental Values in Howden, 1781-1831

	Annual Rentals								
	Under £1			£1 - £5			£5 - £10		
Streets	1781	1801	1831	1781	1801	1831	1781	1801	1831
Market Place	0.3	-	0.4	0.7	0.9	0.7	2.0	1.1	2.2
Church Yard	-	-	0.7	1.1	1.4	0.9	1.2	1.6	0.5
St. John's Street and Applegate	1.4	2.9	0.9	0.9	0.7	1.2	0.4	1.5	0.6
Pinfold Street and Corn Market Hill	2.5	-	0.7	0.7	1.4	1.2	-	-	0.7
Bridegate	0.8	0.4	1.8	1.1	0.8	0.7	1.5	1.5	1.2
Hailgate	1.6	2.1	1.1	1.1	1.3	1.1	0.4	0.4	0.5
Flatgate	1.2	-	-	0.3	1.5	1.3	-	0.6	0.7
Total no. dwellings	43	17	35	105	108	224	28	43	44
Rental Groups as Percentages of all Housing	19.4	7.5	9.4	47.5	47.4	59.9	12.7	18.8	11.8

	£10 - £20			£20 - £50			£50 - £100		
Streets	1781	1801	1831	1781	1801	1831	1781	1801	1831
Market Place	2.0	2.2	1.8	1.0	-	1.7	0.9	1.0	1.4
Church Yard	2.3	-	2.1	1.0	-	-	-	-	2.0
St. John's Street and Applegate	1.5	-	0.5	0.6	0.8	0.5	1.8	2.8	0.7
Pinfold Street and Corn Market Hill	-	1.1	0.5	2.1	-	1.0	-	4.2	0.7
Bridegate	0.4	0.7	1.1	1.0	2.5	1.0	-	0.8	1.5
Hailgate	0.4	0.9	0.9	0.4	0.8	1.1	0.5	0.4	0.4
Flatgate	1.6	0.7	0.4	3.0	-	-	8.4	2.8	1.4
Total no. dwellings	22	35	33	17	16	15	6	9	23
Rental Groups as Percentages of all Housing	10.0	15.4	8.8	7.6	7.0	4.0	2.8	3.9	6.1

*Location quotients are measures of spatial concentration, showing the extent to which an area departs from some norm. A quotient of under 1.0 indicates under-representation, a quotient of over 1.0 over-representation. The higher the quotient, the greater the degree of concentration of a rental group in an area.

considerable improvement in the urban fabric,[26] in stable centres the patterns and processes of morphological change were far less distinct. Indeed there is evidence that limited eighteenth and nineteenth century development in these towns tended to obscure earlier patterns of spatial differentiation, particularly in the corporate and historically important of their number.[27] In Howden the status of Flatgate was clearly eroded over the course of the study period as Bridegate and the Market Place increased their share of high value properties and, with the exception of the location of most of the town's poorer dwellings in St. John's Street, Applegate, and Pinfold Street, the structure of the town demonstrated an even greater degree of intermix by the second quarter of the nineteenth century.

In the declining town of South Cave low level growth in the period 1750 to 1850 necessitated only limited development of the physical structure. Property development occurred in a circumscribed way and the increase in both property owners and taxable properties was of much lower magnitude than in her regional counterparts. As a predominantly agricultural town the strength of the larger landowning groups remained undiminished and indeed there was an increase from 8 per cent to 12 per cent in the proportion paying between 10 shillings and £1 tax. Growth concerned only the lowest tax paying groups with those paying between 4 shillings and 10 shillings declining from 36 per cent to 22 per cent over the course of the study period while those paying less than 4 shillings increased from 32 per cent to 45 per cent.

Conclusion

For investigating the pattern and process of internal change in country towns the Land Tax Assessments, if used in conjunction with other available data sources of the same period, may prove to be an important but hitherto underused source. Although considerable problems face the user of the Assessments largely due to the inconsistent nature of the recording of information, the records provide one of the major ways in which insights can be obtained into the nature of development and the provision of new building space in country towns. It is evident that small towns were highly individualistic in character and this is reflected in the inter-urban variation in growth experience. This paper has largely approached the study of change in an aggregate way but clearly opportunities present themselves for investigating individual properties so that a more detailed pattern of change can be established. Tracing the fortunes of certain properties in retrospective fashion from the date at which property descriptions were first recorded in the Assessments, analysing variables such as tenure and unit size, might enable a more comprehensive picture of property ownership change and property partition to emerge. More detailed use of the Assessments, however, is likely to pose considerable problems, first due to the general recognition of the imprecise nature of information recorded and second to the difficulties of establishing firm links between individual line entries in the Assessments and town properties, particularly when enclosure or tithe apportionment took place at some time before or after the period 1780 to 1832. In the same way further analysis at the aggregate level such as an investigation of the changing structure of property taxation which would make the data more directly comparable with available poor rate assessment, presents severe constraints to the researcher due to the difficulty of ascertaining whether individual line entries refer to one or several properties. Perhaps at best we must conclude that the role of the Land Tax Assessments must remain that of an aggregate sample indicating the general nature of development and change in both urban and rural communities, but incapable of being used for precise quantitative measurement.

NOTES

1 For example, Mingay, G.E., 'The Land Tax Assessments and the Small Landowner', *Economic History Review*, 2nd Series, volume 17, 1964, pp. 381–88; Martin, J.M., 'Landownership and the Land Tax Returns', *Agricultural History Review*, volume 14, 1966, pp. 96–103.
2 Soltow, Lee, 'Wealth Distribution in England and Wales in 1798', *EcHR*, 2nd series, volume 34, 1981, pp. 60–70; Ginter, D.E., 'A Wealth of Problems with the Land Tax', *EcHR*, 2nd series, volume 35, 1982, pp. 416–21; Wilson, G.J., 'The Land Tax Problem', *EcHR*, 2nd series, volume 35, 1982, pp. 422–26.
3 Mingay, loc. cit.; Hunt, H.G., 'Landownership and Enclosure 1750–1850', *EcHR*, 2nd series, volume 11, 1958–59, pp. 497–505.
4 For example, Noble, M., 'The Land Tax Returns and Urban Development', *The Local Historian*, volume 15, number 2, 1982, pp. 86–91; Unwin, R.W., *Search Guide to the English Land Tax*, West Yorkshire County Record Office, 1982, pp. 13–14.
5 These could be as many as 300 for a town of only 800 persons.
6 Noble, M., *Change in the Small Towns of the East Riding of Yorkshire c. 1750–1850*, (Hedon Local History Series number 5) Hull, 1979; Noble, M., *Growth and Development of Country Towns: the Case of Eastern Yorkshire c. 1700–1850*, unpublished Ph.D. thesis, University of Hull, 1982.
7 All enclosure and tithe awards for the study towns are located either at the Humberside County Record Office, Beverley (HCRO), or at the Borthwick Institute of Historical Research, York (BIHR).
8 All the Land Tax Assessments cited in this chapter are deposited in HCRO, LTA, QDE.
9 Unwin, op. cit., pp. 3, 8.
10 Ginter, loc. cit., p. 421.

11 Unwin, op. cit., p. 3.
12 HCRO, DDBD 45/6; BIHR, TA 378 S, cD 10 AL.
13 Noble, M., 'Growth and Development', chapter 4.
14 Detailed accounts of the development of Beverley are found in Hall, I. and E. *Historic Beverley*, York, 1973; MacMahon, K.A., *Beverley*, Dalesman, Clapham, 1973.
15 Noble, M., 'Inland Navigations and Country Towns: the case of East Yorkshire c. 1700–1850', in Sigsworth, E.M., *ed.*, *Ports and Resorts in the Regions*, Hull, 1981, pp. 79–100; Duckham, B.F., *The Inland Waterways of East Yorkshire 1700–1900*, East Yorkshire Local History Society, number 29, York 1973.
16 HCRO, PR 847.
17 Noble, M., 'Growth and Development', p. 448.
18 Hall, op. cit., pp. 59–69 : MacMahon, pp. 48–67.
19 Coefficients were Great Driffield 0.95, Pocklington 0.90, Patrington 0.98, Market Weighton 0.90, each with an associated probability greater than 0.01; Howden 0.78 with an associated probability greater than 0.05; South Cave 0.4, Hedon 0.07 each with an associated probability of less than 0.05; all cases with six degrees of freedom. For five year periods the coefficients were Pocklington 0.92, Great Driffield 0.85 with an associated probability greater than 0.01; Hedon 0.65 with an associated probability greater than 0.05; all with ten degrees of freedom.
20 For example, Chalklin, C.W., *The Provincial Towns of Georgian England*, London, 1974; Chapman, S.D., *The History of Working Class Housing*, Newton Abbott, 1971.
21 HCRO, DDPY 19/4, DDEV 7/13.
22 The area east of the Beck centering on Eastgate, Washington Street, and New Road developed due to the dispersal of formerly centrally located agricultural activity as pressure for space within the central area grew, and also the desire of high status households to distance themselves physically from the remainder of the population.
23 At enclosure in 1757 the average acreage held by each owner was 20.7, no owners held more than 500 acres and the majority of land was held in units of less than 100 acres, with two-thirds of all landowners holding less than 10 acres.
24 Hengate ward (or Norwood as it later became known) contained the town's assembly rooms, hospital, numerous houses, and closes.
25 HCRO, PR 847.
26 In Great Driffield, for example, between 1800 and 1840 only about one dozen houses in the central core of the town are thought to have remained unaltered, HCRO, DDX 17/15. In Beverley refurbishing of houses took place to a considerable extent, Hall, op. cit.
27 Noble, M., 'Growth and Development', pp. 464–65.

Chapter 7

House Repopulation from the Land Tax Assessments in a Derbyshire Market Town, 1780–1825

ADRIAN HENSTOCK

For many English provincial towns the late eighteenth and early nineteenth centuries were a period of transformation. The expansion of commerce, the improvements in transport, and the increased productivity of both industry and agriculture immediately before and during the so-called 'industrial revolution' were all reflected in the increased prosperity of the towns. Coupled with a rising population, these factors resulted in much expansion and rebuilding in the towns which transformed both their physical appearance and economic status.

Detailed local studies of individual country towns at this period can shed light on the mechanics of this transformation. A research method we can use as the basis of such a study is 'house repopulation'. This is the process of 'repopulating' the houses of a local community with the people who inhabited them at any given date.[1] For a large number of communities this is possible for the early Victorian period, and in certain fortunate but exceptional cases for the sixteenth century or even earlier.[2] The viability of such projects depends on the existence of two classes of historical record of near-contemporary date – a map distinguishing each property in reasonable detail, and a detailed list of inhabitants. Normally a close correlation in date between the two sources is vital to the success of house repopulation, but the object of this paper is to demonstrate how it is possible for certain communities to work retrospectively back from the 1840s to the 1780s and to repopulate the houses with both owners and occupiers for each year from 1780 to 1832. This can be achieved by using the widely-available tithe maps of the 1840s as a cartographic base and working systematically through the Land Tax Assessments.[3]

House repopulation alone can be a mere antiquarian exercise, but it is invaluable in providing significant information on a variety of social and economic aspects of a community's history and enabling this to be displayed in statistical or cartographic form. It can reveal detail about the physical development of towns in terms of infilling, rebuilding, and suburban expansion, as well as more subtle information about the structure and operation of local society. By linking people with properties, an insight can be gained into their social and economic status in the community.

This paper describes the house repopulation project undertaken by an adult education research group as part of a wider study of the history of the Derbyshire town of Ashbourne between 1725 and 1825.[4] Ashbourne in 1800 was a market town of some 2,500 people situated in a largely agricultural region on the borders of the Peak District and the Midland Plain. Its role was largely that of a marketing and servicing centre but at this period it witnessed the growth of small industries and nearby cotton-spinning mills. Its position on the main coaching road from London to Manchester combined with its proximity to the Derbyshire spa-towns caused it to develop as a minor resort for fashionable tourists and residents, and a large number of Georgian town houses survive to this day.

(i) *The Ashbourne Land Tax Assessments*

The Assessments for Ashbourne Township are preserved in the Derbyshire Record Office for each year from 1780 to 1832, with the exceptions of 1781, 1794, and 1814 which are missing. In addition to the standard property tax, they include at varying periods tax chargeable on three non-property elements:

(a) commercial stock-in-trade of the better-off tradesmen, between 1780 and 1785 only. Some twenty-five trades-men each contributed tax varying between 6d and 2s 5d on their stock in addition to their property tax.

(b) profits of the market – cattle and corn tolls and stallage – throughout the period. These were farmed out by the lord of the manor to a private lessee.

(c) profits of office of the two or three excise officers resident in the town between 1780 and 1811, assessed at £10 each. There were normally three but only two in the years 1789, 1791, and 1795–1805.

All the properties in Ashbourne Township are represented on the Assessments, with the exception of the church, chapels, grammar and charity schools, and almshouses, and total between 280 and 312 separate taxable units. Unlike the neighbouring town of Bakewell, no substantial blocks of property in Ashbourne were owned by any one great landowner, and so none of the properties are subsumed under one major entry. Following the Act of 1798 enabling owners to compound their land tax for a lump sum, the Assessments are divided from 1802 onwards into two columns for those 'exonerated' and 'not exonerated'. Again, unlike the Assessments for some communities, the 'exonerated' names continue to be recorded up to 1832, including all changes of owners and occupiers.

The tax quota for Ashbourne Township was £63 2s 6d, which appears at the head of each annual assessment up to 1811, but in practice the actual sum assessed varied considerably over the whole period. Between 1780 and 1785 it fluctuated between £98 8s 6⅓d and £98 15s 6⅓d. Following the disappearance of the tax on commercial stock it fell between 1786 and 1798 to sums varying from £86 14s 11d to £96 17s 7d. The majority of these considerable excesses can be accounted for by the addition of the tax from each excise officer. In 1799 all the properties in the township were re-assessed and their liability proportionally reduced so as to produce the required quota of £63 2s 6d. This was totally independent of the provisions for 'exoneration' and was achieved by *including* the £20 from the two excise officers; the restoration of a third excise officer in 1806 afforded the assessors the opportunity of a further proportional reduction in the tax throughout the township. In 1812, however, when the excise officers disappear entirely from the Assessments and the revenue dropped dramatically to £33 2s 6d, no compensating upward reassessment was made! This figure was accepted as the quota until the end of the period in 1832.

Other minor anomalies occur. In three cases a taxable property unit disappears mysteriously from the Assessments. One of these was the Talbot inn, the principal seventeenth-century hostelry in the town which is known to have closed in 1784. In that year the corresponding entry in the Assessments disappears but the tax quota was not added to neighbouring properties. The deficiency appears to have been made up by deliberate falsification.

Apart from a handful of random street headings which appear for a time in the 1790s, no topographical detail is incorporated in the Assessments until 1826, when brief descriptions of property were recorded, albeit haphazardly, usually simply as 'house' or 'house and garden'. However it is evident that the properties are arranged in topographical order street-by-street around the town up to 1814, when an alphabetical order by owner's name was introduced. Without this topographical order house repopulation would have been extremely difficult.[5]

(ii) *The Problem of Boundaries*

A critical problem with the study of the history of Ashbourne as an urban unit lies in the disposition of its administrative boundaries. The civil 'township' of Ashbourne at this period covered an area of only fifty five acres comprising the mediaeval core of the town. By the late eighteenth century this appears to have been well-developed with buildings on all the street frontages with gardens and outbuildings behind, leaving only one or two vacant crofts. The town possessed a considerable suburb of mediaeval origin called Compton, which was divided between the two townships of Clifton and of Sturston, each in a separate hundred. Apart from Compton

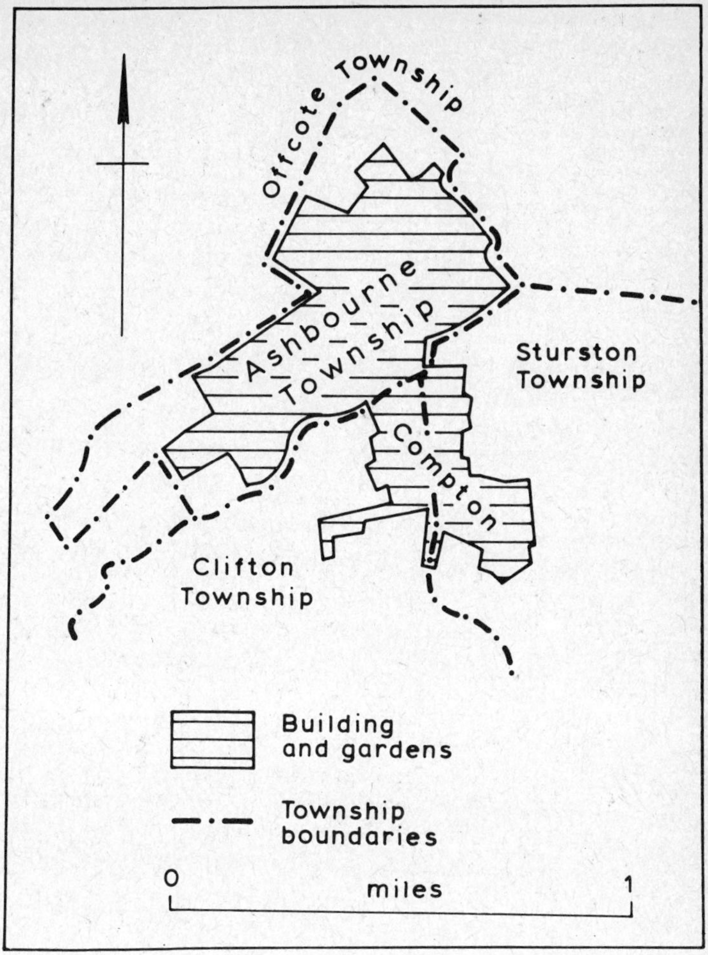

Figure 1. The Administrative Boundaries of Ashbourne, 1831.

both these townships were largely rural; Sturston was populated wholly with scattered farms and cottages, but Clifton included an entirely separate village. Each township has a separate series of Land Tax Assessments, but it is a major problem to isolate the suburban area of Compton from the rural areas. For this reason the house repopulation project had to be restricted to Ashbourne Township alone, but this has the advantage in that there is no confusion between urban and rural elements.

Table 1

Ashbourne Population Statistics, 1801-1831

	1801	1811	1821	1831
ASHBOURNE				
Population	2006	2112	2188	2246
Percent decennial increase	-	5.2	3.6	2.7
	Increase 1801-1831 = 12.0%			
CLIFTON				
Population	627	663	768	839
Percent decennial increase	-	5.7	15.8	9.2
	Increase 1801-1831 = 33.8%			
STURSTON				
Population	360	387	561	578
Percent decennial increase	-	7.5	45.0	3.0
	Increase 1801-1831 = 60.5			
ASHBOURNE, CLIFTON and STURSTON combined				
Population	2993	3162	3517	3663
URBAN ESTIMATE				
Population	2493	2662	3017	3163
Percent decennial increase	-	6.7	13.3	4.8
	Increase 1801-1831 = 26.8			

Note: The estimated urban population has been calculated by combining the census figures for the three townships and then subtracting 500 to represent the rural population of the combined area. This figure is only an approximation deduced from local topographical evidence and does not take into account any possible fluctuations over the period. However, there is no economic or topographical evidence for major change such as would significantly affect the estimate of overall urban population increase.

Source: Victoria County History, Derbyshire, vol II, 1907, pp. 194-205.

The boundary problem also means that it is difficult, if not impossible, to assess demographic movements in the eighteenth or even the nineteenth centuries. The ecclesiastical parish of Ashbourne included not only the three townships already mentioned but several other rural villages up to five miles distant. From the parish registers it is again impossible to isolate the urban population from the rural, and this also applies even to the population census figures from 1801 onwards for the individual townships. In Ashbourne Township there was a slow increase from 1801 to 1831, whereas in Clifton and Sturston there was a more rapid increase, especially from 1811 to 1821 (Table 1). If one estimates from the Census figures the approximate size of the rural population of these two townships combined, a crude estimate can be made of the movement of the urban population of all three townships. This reveals the greatest increase (13.3%) in the decade 1811–1821, largely accounted for by a remarkably steep increase of 45% in Sturston. The physical evidence of surviving buildings suggests that there was a considerable population expansion in the 1780s and 1790s also.

(iii) *Method*

Two preliminary measures were necessary before commencing the house repopulation project : photocopies of all the Ashbourne Assessments were purchased and a standard Property Record Sheet was devised. This was divided into vertical columns to record the year, owner, occupier, tax, and 'comments', and contained spaces for entering Land Tax data for each year from 1780 to 1832 as well as details from the 1846 tithe apportionment. One sheet was used for each property/tax unit, with subsidiary sheets to accommodate subdivisions or amalgamations.

Although in theory the project was concerned with working backwards through the Assessments from 1832, in practice it was found more satisfactory to work forwards from 1780 to 1832 and then to make the final identifications with the 1846 map. The 1780 Assessments were thus taken first, and 300–or–so Record Sheets completed for each separate property unit recording the names of owner, occupier, and amount of tax. The next year's Assessment was then processed similarly onto the same sheets and so on for each year to 1832. It was found essential to process each annual Assessment for the whole town before dealing with the next year, rather than trying to trace individual properties through the whole period. In this way any problems of property linkage could be worked out by processes of elimination. The successful linkage of an entry with the similar entry in the next year was of course crucial to the project, and linkages were made on the basis of one or more of the following criteria : (a) correlation of the personal names, (b) correlation of the amount of tax paid, and (c) the respective position of the entry in the lists. As an example, the changes recorded in four adjacent properties in Ashbourne between 1796 and 1797 are illustrated in Table 2. The first property has apparently remained in the same hands. The fourth has a new tenant. The second and third have changes of both owners and tenants but can be linked to each other by the correlation of their tenants' names, by their position in the Assessments, by the amount of their tax, and by the elimination of all other entries paying a similar tax.

A major problem was the abandonment of the topographical order in 1815, which meant that the position of the entry lost its significance. Although this made the establishment of relevant linkages more difficult and time-consuming, it was still possible by process of elimination. In a few cases where the names had changed totally and where there were two or more potential candidates each paying the same tax, identification was achieved by the use of information from the other record sources named

Table 2

Comparison of Ashbourne Land Tax Entries, 1796-97

1796			1797		
Owner	Occupier	Tax	Owner	Occupier	Tax
John Blore	Wm. Pidcock	1s 0d	John Blore	Wm. Pidcock	1s 0d
Mr. Buxton	Bourn, late Salt	2s 0d	Josh. Oakden	Mr. Burn	2s 0d
Do.	Bass, late Warin	4s 4d	Do.	Nath. Smith, Bass, etc	4s 4d
Mr. Brownson	Josh. Allen	8s 0d	Mr. Brownson	Mr. Spencer	8s 0d

Source: Derbyshire Record Office, Ashbourne Township Land Tax Assessments, QRL

below. Another difficulty was caused by the reassessment of all individual properties in 1799 and again in 1806, which meant there was no correlation of the tax paid in those two years with the previous years. Other problems were the occasional subdivision of properties, eg. a 12s property might become three of 6s, 4s 6d, and 1s 6d, but these could usually be resolved by simple arithmetic. More serious was the amalgamation of two adjacent properties, eg. two of 3s and 1s 6d would become one of 4s 6d, which was more difficult to trace.

With such a large project it was inevitable that there would be some mistakes in detail, but where possible checks were made from the other sources, and it was considered that any remaining errors were not of sufficient weight to upset the broad trends outlined below.

Once each Property Record Sheet was completed down to 1832 additional information was added to the 'comments' column derived from the other sources listed below, and the final linkage was made with the relevant property on the 1846 tithe map. Despite the time-difference between 1832 and 1846 this process was relatively straightforward as the Land Tax properties were arranged in street order. There was also a correspondence between at least half of the names of owners or occupiers between the two dates.

As there were between 280 and 312 property units listed on the Ashbourne Assessments over the fifty-two-year period, the project thus involved processing about 15,000 pieces of information. Without access to a computer a research group is probably the only answer to handling this quantity of data, although even then it is tedious and time-consuming work. It is tempting to take a five or ten-year sample, but then the property linkages become more problematical and for analytical purposes the *exact* year of change of owner or tenant is crucial.

(iv) *Other Sources*

The use of other contemporary record sources is vital both to confirm property linkages and to act as a control on the accuracy of the

Assessments. For Ashbourne these were as follows:
(a) The Ashbourne Township Tithe Apportionment of 1846.[6] The large-scale map accompanying the Apportionment shows property boundaries in detail.
(b) A Map of Ashbourne, drawn by 'the Pupils of Mr. Jones' Academy' in 1831.[7] The value of this is twofold. It shows that little building development had taken place within Ashbourne Township between 1831 and the date of the Tithe map in 1846. It also depicts the suburban area of Compton in greater detail than is shown on the respective tithe maps for Clifton and Sturston Townships.
(c) A Church Rate valuation of 1825, listing names of owners and occupiers, a brief description of the property, rateable value, and rate payable.[8] No addresses are given, but it is arranged in a discernable topographical order (although a different order to the pre-1815 Assessments).
(d) Church Rate Assessments of 1777 and 1781, listing names of occupiers only and the rate paid.[9] No property details or addresses are given but they are arranged in the same topographical order as the Land Tax Assessments. The 1777 list enabled the names of occupiers to be pushed back three years earlier than the first Land Tax record.
(e) Property sales advertisements in the *Derby Mercury* newspaper, 1732–1825.[10] As this was the only county newspaper, these provide what is probably a comprehensive coverage of property sales; used in conjunction with wills these should cover most transfers of property ownership. They usually include a reasonably informative description of the property, recording its function, but the locations are often vague and the owners' names rarely recorded. However it was possible to fix the precise locations of nearly all properties mentioned after 1780, and many before, by the evidence of the Land Tax and other sources.
(f) Wills of some 500 Ashbourne people between 1780 and 1825 are in the Lichfield Joint Record Office. Wills of non-residents owning property in the town are more difficult to trace.
(g) Title Deeds of individual properties dating back to the eighteenth century survive in local record repositories or in private hands, often deposited in banks or building societies. These provide essential details of transfer of ownership and shed light on family relationships, mortgages, and other financial settlements which may be reflected in changes of name on the Land Tax Assessments.
(h) Alehouse-keepers' recognizances, or bonds for the good behaviour of publicans, exist for Derbyshire for 1753–1827 and list annually the publicans' names but not the signs of their houses.[11] Most public houses in Ashbourne were identified by using these in conjunction with the Land Tax.

(i) Commercial directories listing the gentry and principal tradesmen in major towns are rare for the eighteenth century but for Ashbourne there is the *Universal British Directory* of 1793 and Pigot's *Derbyshire Directory* of 1822.

(j) Architectural evidence of surviving buildings. Ashbourne has fortunately escaped modern wholesale urban renewal and both the ancient property boundaries and a large number of buildings survive virtually intact from the Georgian period. An estimate of the dates of surviving buildings, based on documentary and architectural evidence, suggests a high level of building activity in the period between 1760 and 1820, especially in the 1760s, 1780s and 1800s.[12] The majority of the datable industrial buildings in the town and district, eg. cotton mills and malthouses, date from the 1780s and the terraced housing in the yards behind the main streets mostly from 1770–1815.

(v) *The Accuracy of the Assessments*

The accuracy of the Land Tax was tested at various points by comparison with other sources, especially the church rating records. Although the 1781 Land Tax Assessment is missing, comparison of the 1782 Assessment with the Church Rate Assessment of 1781 revealed a high degree of correspondence. As many as 94 per cent of the occupiers' names in the Land Tax were repeated in the Church Rate document. However, when the Church Rate Valuation of 1825 was compared with the 1825 Land Tax numerous discrepancies were found; only 71 per cent of owners' names agreed with each other. The Valuation appears the more accurate of the two sources, and there was a one-to-three year time-lag before the Assessments caught up with new changes. Much appears to have depended on the individual assessor or collector who compiled the Assessments; seemingly some were content simply to copy the previous year's list. Those after 1815 appear to have been increasingly prone to record out-dated information but, nevertheless, most changes of name were recorded eventually.

It is generally accepted that the actual Land Tax paid after 1780 was still based on a fossilized late-seventeenth century valuation, and this appears to be confirmed by a comparison between the 1781 Church Rate Assessment and the 1782 Land Tax Assessments. Although the date at which the church rating valuation was undertaken is not known, a rank order comparison of the highest-rated properties from the church rating list (ie. those paying 15s or over) with the same properties on the Land Tax document reveals some mismatch in rank order (Table 3).

Table 3

Rank Order Comparison
of Ashbourne Church Rate and Land Tax Assessments, 1781-82

Church Rate, 1781 £	s	d	Rank Order Position	Land Tax, 1782 s	d	Rank Order Position
1	3	9	1	16	0	1=
1	1	11	2	16	0	1=
1	1	9	3	10	9	9
	19	6	4	15	0	4
	17	9	5	16	0	1=
	17	0	6	8	0	12=
	16	6	7=	10	0	11
	16	6	7=	12	0	5
	16	6	7=	11	4	6=
	15	2	10	10	8	10
	15	0	11=	11	4	6=
	15	0	11=	11	4	6=
	15	0	11=	8	0	12=

Source: Derbyshire Record Office, Ashbourne Township Land Tax Assessments (QRL) and Church Rate Assessment, D.749/B

(vi) *Statistical Analysis*

The rate of turnover of property ownership can reflect the expansion, decline, or changing economy of a town. In her study of eight East Riding towns Margaret Noble has discovered decennial turnover rates between 30 per cent and 50 per cent over the period 1780–1830, with peaks in the 1790s and 1820s. A major problem with such studies is in distinguishing genuine turnover as a result of sales to new owners from turnover as a result of inheritance. In Noble's study

> 'family ties and inheritance were not assumed merely by surname, only when definite evidence existed to indicate that land was the subject of inheritance was such a tie recorded. This apart, all new names that appeared on the return were counted as 'new' property owners, although some of the property may have been the subject of unidentified inheritance'.[13]

From the Ashbourne study it would appear that 'unidentified inheritance' may well have played a larger part than is realized. Two common forms of inheritance would both have resulted in a change of surname appearing on the Assessments: the re-marriage of widows, and inheritance by sons-in-law. Before 1882 a married woman could not hold property in her own right, and so in both cases the husband's name would appear on the Assessments as the legal owners.[14] For example, the ownership of the Marquis of Granby in Ashbourne is recorded as follows:

1796–1800	Joseph Marshall
1801–1805	Ann Marshall
1806–1814	Thomas Hemsworth
1815–1827	Ann Hemsworth

The obvious inference is that the Marshall family sold the property to the Hemsworths in 1805–6, whereas in fact Ann Marshall, Joseph's widow, married Thomas Hemsworth in that year, but was again widowed in 1814. Ann Marshall and Ann Hemsworth are thus the same person and she in fact was the effective owner of the property throughout the period from 1796 to 1827.

For this reason *all* changes of owner's name, even where inheritance was obviously involved, were recorded in calculating the turnover rates for Ashbourne Township, even though this produces higher rates than actually occurred. The rates for three decades are remarkably consistent with figures around 33 per cent; the exception is the decade 1792–1801, which reaches nearly 60 per cent (Table 4).

Table 4

Decennial Property Turnover Rates, 1782-1821

1782-1791	1792-1801	1802-1811	1812-1821
32.5%	59.5%	32.0%	34.0%

Source: Derbyshire Record Office,
Ashbourne Township Land Tax Assessments, QRL

Decennial turnover rates are a somewhat crude indicator of property turnover, and one of the benefits of a house repopulation project is that it enables a more refined analysis to be made of the actual number of property transfers annually. The results of such an analysis for Ashbourne are illustrated in the graph in Figure 2 expressed as five-year moving averages, and these confirm the high level of change in the 1790s. A decennial analysis of the numbers of property owners together with the inter-decennial rates of change both for Ashbourne alone and for the suburban townships is shown in Table 5. The overall conclusions to be

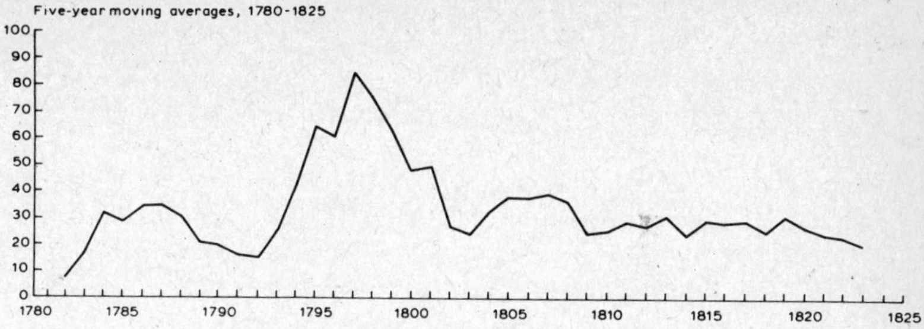

Figure 2. Ashbourne Property Transfers.

Table 5

Decennial Statistics of Property Owners, 1782-1822

Year	Ashbourne Owners No.	Ashbourne Owners Percent change	Clifton Owners No.	Clifton Owners Percent change	Sturston Owners No.	Sturston Owners Percent change	Combined Owners No.	Combined Owners Percent change
1782	115	-	58	-	50	-	223	-
1792	110	-4.4	61	+5.1	43	-14.0	215	-3.7
1802	120	+9.1	65	+6.5	47	+9.3	232	+7.9
1812	121	+0.8	64	-1.6	64	+36.1	249	+7.3
1822	134	+10.7	71	+10.9	80	+25.0	285	+14.5
1782-1822		+16.5		+22.5		+60.0		+27.8

Source: Derbyshire Record Office, Land Tax Assessments, QRL

drawn from all the above suggest that population pressure was, as would be expected, a major contributory factor to building development. This was accompanied by an increase in the numbers of landowners, many of them small men who initiated small building developments (Tables 1, 5). This was particularly marked in the period 1812–1821, which saw an overall increase of over 14 per cent in the number of owners in Ashbourne as a whole coinciding with a 13 per cent increase in population over a similar period. It was a particular feature of suburban Compton. A large increase, over 25 per cent more owners in Sturston, coincided with a very high increase in population of 45 per cent. However the two features did not always go hand-in-hand. The very large increase in owners in Sturston in

1802–1811 was matched by a very low population increase. In Ashbourne itself, there was no new building land available and the relatively small population rise was accommodated by the infilling of yards and gardens behind the main properties with rows of terraced cottages to form 'yards' such as Frost's Yard and Boot-and-Shoe-Yard. Here the increase in the numbers of owners was small and a study of the fourteen property units which accommodated these residential yards in the Assessments suggests that in nearly every case the development was carried out by one owner, who rented out the cottages as an investment. Only in three cases did development follow the division of the property as shown by fragmentation of the tax assessment. For example, after the closure of the Brick-and-Tile public house in Dig Street the property was sold as five separate units to different owners in 1811 and new building took place in the yard. Most of the property owners in the yards, who were presumably responsible for the residential development, were major or minor tradesmen in the town, and only two were members of the local gentry.

In Compton very little new development took place outside the mediaeval crofts either. Even here, where there were few large properties fronting the street and little competition for sites with a commercial or social position, it is notable that some development took the form of terraced housing in yards built on gardens or crofts. Indeed one row of eight terraced cottages known as Can Alley was erected at right angles to Clifton Lane in a rural field. This seems to suggest that lack of available building land was not a prime factor in the construction of what later became known as slum property, but simply the desire by speculative owners to develop their own small plots with the maximum number of houses.

The transfer of property within Ashbourne Township reached peaks in the mid-1780s, mid-1790s, and mid-1800s, and was particularly high in the 1790s. Indeed the decennial figures suggest that in 1792–1801 more property changed hands than remained in the same ownership (Table 5). Although population increase no doubt played a part, the pattern of property turnover seems to reflect more closely the cyclic changes in the national economy. These have been shown to affect building activities in larger towns.[15] A building boom in the late 1780s rose to a peak in 1792–3, but the outbreak of war in February 1793 caused financial panic. The remainder of the 1790s was marked by a spate of bankruptcies, a run on the banks, and high corn prices in 1795, 1799, and 1800. The economy, together with the building trade, did not recover until after 1801. The bankruptcies of three Ashbourne tradesmen are recorded in the pages of the *Derby Mercury* in 1794–6 and a further five in 1800–1802.[16] At the nadir of the recession in 1797 fifty nine of the principal inhabitants of the town signed a public declaration of confidence in the Bank of England.[17]

(vii) *Social Geography*

House repopulation also enables the social and functional geography of towns to be examined and displayed cartographically, for example the degree of segregation of the commercial and residential elements in the community. The situation in Ashbourne in 1780 is illustrated by Figure 3 which marks the distribution of the major private town houses, the major commercial properties, and all public houses.

Between c. 1690 and c. 1790 some twenty-three town houses were erected in Ashbourne as part of a major rebuilding which transformed it from a predominantly Tudor timber-framed town into a predominantly Georgian town in the space of a hundred years. These town houses were situated mostly in Church Street and in upper St. John's Street, with a marked polarization towards the eastern and western extremities of the town, perhaps attracted by the social magnets of Ashbourne Hall at the east and the parish church and the major charitable institutions at the west. Only one was in the Market Place and only two in Compton. House repopulation reveals both the names of the persons who built the houses in the 1780s and sometimes earlier, as well as the names of the tenants after 1780. One or two of the owner-occupiers were senior representatives of the local minor landed gentry, for example the Beresfords of Fenny Bentley. The town houses were, however, their *main* residence, the old country home often being reduced to a farmhouse; none of the local gentry seem to have kept a town house purely for residence during the social season. There were also several maiden daughters or younger sons of such families living in the town, usually renting their houses. Other residents were representatives of the professions, especially clergymen, attorneys, physicians, army officers, or private schoolmistresses. The clergy were often incumbents of neighbouring rural parishes. However, about half of the occupants of such houses were wealthy tradesmen, particularly mercers, tanners, maltsters, ironmongers, cheesefactors, or cotton spinners. Some men had retired from trade and were now regarded as property-owning 'gentlemen'.

Although some of the town houses remained in the same family throughout the whole period from 1780 to 1825 others changed occupancy every few years; advertisements for 'neat sashed dwelling houses' to let on short-term leases appeared frequently in the *Derby Mercury*. The Assessments show that the mean average period of occupancy of these houses as a whole over the period was 13.7 years. Towards the end of the Napoleonic Wars it became less fashionable to live in country towns, however, and fewer of the senior members of the gentry were resident in Ashbourne. For example, the large early-eighteenth century town house occupied in 1780 by Richard Beresford, esquire, was sold by the family in 1814 to a wealthy maltster who divided it into two.

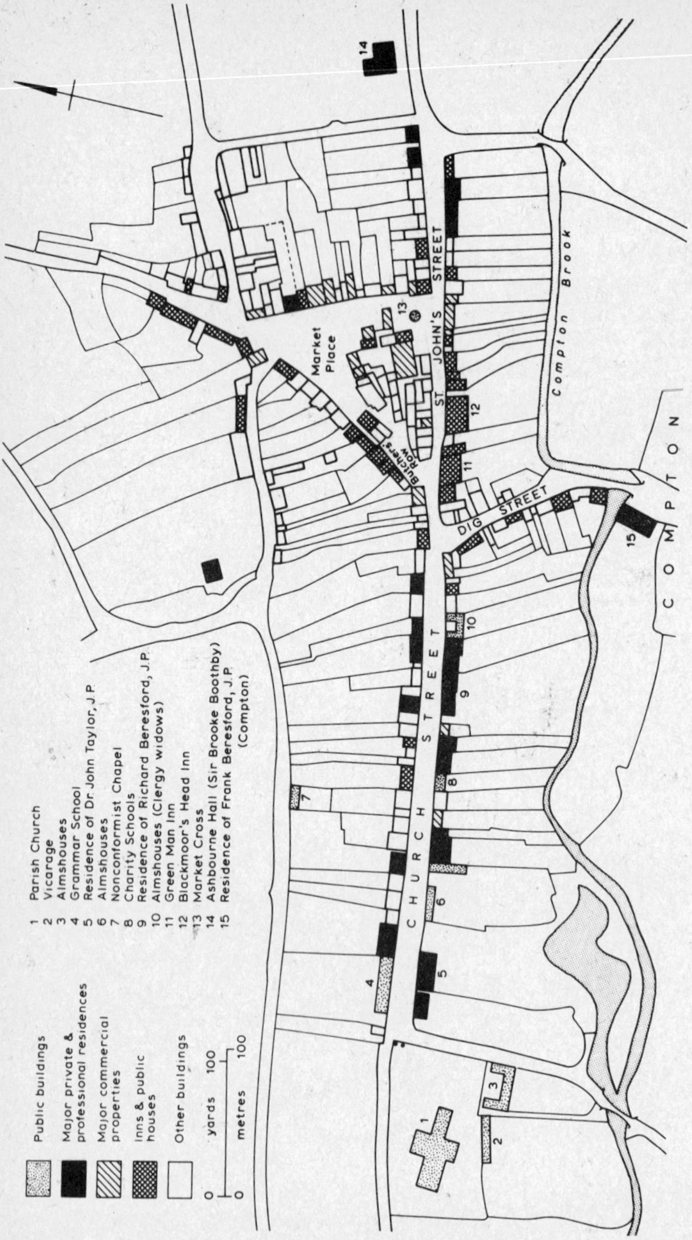

Figure 3. Ashbourne: Distribution of Building Functions.

The main commercial properties – chiefly representing food, clothing, hardware and other retail activities as well as public houses – were concentrated in the town centre, especially around the Market Place and in lower St. John's Street but with few in Church Street (Figure 3). Using the alehouse keepers' recognizances in conjunction with the Assessments, it is possible to name and locate all the forty-one inns, pubs and wine vaults existing in 1780. However, publicans moved frequently, often from one house to another; some changed the names of their signs and at one period there were two Nag's Heads in the town. There was a remarkable concentration of public houses on the south side of lower St. John's Street; in one block of ten adjacent buildings no less than eight were inns or pubs in 1780 (Figure 3).

Comparison of the situation in 1780 with that of 1825 reveals little overall change in the distribution of the various elements, although there were differences in detail. The Market Place and adjacent areas remained as the principal commercial quarter, and the dominance of Church Street as the main fashionable residential street was more marked.

The number of inns and public houses had been reduced by ten; of those present in 1780 thirteen had closed and three new ones opened. The rows of adjacent pubs in St. John's Street and in Butchers' Row had been reduced in length. Only one of the two major inns of 1780 – the Green Man – was still in existence. The evidence of the Assessments, confirmed by other sources, reveals how its proprietor bought up his rival – the Blackmoor's Head – in 1825, closed it down and added the sign to his own. One of the two Nag's Heads had been replaced by a private professional establishment (a private school founded in 1793 by Dr. Erasmus Darwin for his two illegitimate daughters), thus completing the dominance of the east end of the town by fashionable buildings. Several town houses had been rebuilt or enlarged in the 1780s, as well as Ashbourne Hall itself.

By 1825 the bulk of the working population was housed either in the several 'yards' behind the main streets or in groups of small cottages along certain of the lesser streets, especially Mutton Lane, Dove House Green and along both sides of Compton.

Although the various social divisions of the town can thus be expressed spatially, it would be dangerous to interpret these divisions too rigidly. Ashbourne was a small and compact town and the physical distances between different areas were slight. What is perhaps equally significant is the way in which different classes and functional groups were mixed together. For example, Hall's and Leason's Yards in St. John's Street were adjacent to some of the largest town houses, albeit behind and out-of-sight. A noteable cluster of poorer housing around Frost's and Smith's Yards half-way along Church Street appeared very much out-of-character with this fashionable street. In addition it is evident that many of the working premises of the wealthy tradesmen were situated behind their town houses. Robert Longden, a wealthy ironmonger and cheesefactor and also a J.P., had his warehouse immediately behind his house in the Market Place. The Hartshorne family erected a malthouse behind their residence in Church Street in 1785, next door to the garden of the Beresford family mansion. The home of another branch of the Beresfords in Compton was only a few hundred yards from a noxious tanyard.

(viii) *The Way Ahead*

The object of this paper has been to demonstrate how house repopulation can be achieved in a small country town back to 1780 through the medium of the Land Tax Assessments, providing a complete tenurial history of every property over a fifty-two year period. This can form the basis both for statistical analysis and for a study of the social geography of the community. Perhaps above all, however, house repopulation provides the skeleton around which a detailed analysis of the structure and operation of local society can be constructed, fleshed out by information from local newspapers and other sources. Such a wider study of Ashbourne is in the course of being carried out. It has been described in general elsewhere, and the detailed findings will appear in a forthcoming series of publications by the author and the Ashbourne Local History Group.[18] Some of the multifarious topics which are being investigated are as follows: the operation of the service trades such as grocery and ironmongery; the workings of markets and fairs; turnpike road construction and administration; the social functions of inns and pubs; fashionable lifestyles and their effect on local architecture and topography; the rise and fall of private schools; friendly societies and working class social organizations; and the local effects of national events such as the Napoleonic Wars. Without the basic framework of a house repopulation project to provide the additional topographical dimension to the study of these subjects, a very great deal of their significance would be missed.

NOTES

1 For the technique of house repopulation in relation to mid-nineteenth century censuses see Henstock, A., 'House Repopulation from the Census Returns of 1841 and 1851', *Local Population Studies*, volume 10, 1973, pp. 37–52; see also Mills, D.R., 'The Technique of House Repopulation: Experience from a Cambridgeshire Village, 1841', *The Local Historian*, volume 13, no. 2, 1978, pp. 86–94.

2 See, for example, Lloyd, D., *Broad Street: its Houses and Residents through Eight Centuries*, Ludlow Research Paper no. 3, Birmingham, 1979.

3 One of the first such projects using the Land Tax is described briefly in Iredale, D., *Discovering Your Old House*, Aylesbury, 1977, a revision of the same author's *This Old House*, Aylesbury, 1968.

4 For a description of the wider project see Henstock, A., 'Town Houses and Society in Georgian Country Towns', *The Local Historian*, volume 14, nos. 2–3, 1980, pp. 68–75, 149–55. The author would like to acknowledge the efforts of present and past members of the Ashbourne Local History Group who undertook the vast amount of work involved in this project. Special mention must be made of Mr. Ken Dadge who single-handed solved many problematical linkages in the Assessments.

5 Some Assessments do contain topographical detail throughout. In Nottinghamshire, for example, those for the towns of Mansfield, Newark, and Southwell all contain street names and property descriptions.

6 Derbyshire County Record Office (DRO), D.662A/P1590.

7 Derby Central Library (DCL), maps.

8 DRO, D.749B.

9 DRO, D.662A/PW11–12.

10 DCL, newspapers.

11 DRO, Quarter Sessions, Alehouse Recognizances.

12 The numbers of surviving datable eighteenth-century buildings in Ashbourne are as follows: 1700–1729: 15; 1730–1759: 6; 1760–1789: 20; 1790–1819: 26. For the chronology of rebuilding see Machin, R., 'The Great Rebuilding: a Re-Assessment', *Past and Present*, volume 77, 1977, pp. 33–56.

13 Noble, M., 'The Land Tax Returns in Investigations of the Building Process and Morphological Change in Small Towns', Conference Papers, September 1981.

14 The Married Women's Property Act, 1882.

15 Chalklin, C.W., *The Provincial Towns of Georgian England: a Study of the Building Process 1740–1820*, London, 1974.

16 *Derby Mercury*, 13th November 1794, 19th November 1795, 24th December 1795, 6th February 1800, 29th October 1801, 4th February 1802, 8th April 1802, 15th April 1802.

17 *Ibid*, 2nd March 1797.

18 See note 4 above.

Chapter 8

An Industrial Dimension to Land Tax Studies: The Barnsley Coalfield 1690–1830

ROBERT UNWIN

Introduction

Discussion of the uses of the Land Tax Assessments has usually concentrated on rural communities and small market towns, and less has been written of their possible value in looking at developing industrial regions. The following study employs the Assessments as one tool for looking at the development of an emerging coalfield. The choice of the coal industry, rather than other forms of industrial or manufacturing activity has been dictated primarily by the nature of the evidence for, although quarries, furnaces, forges, tanyards, brewhouses, brickyards, and mills are listed in the Assessments from time to time, the term 'coal mine' or 'colliery' was more frequently and consistently used than any other single term. The development of the Barnsley coalfield from a landlocked area with predominantly local markets in the seventeenth and early eighteenth centuries into an important industrial region transected by road, water, and colliery railway communications by the early decades of the nineteenth century raises a number of questions. Who were the principal personalities involved, and what were their motives? When, how, and why did the transformation take place? What were the main economic consequences and social effects?

In this paper attention will focus on the forty townships which constituted the wapentake of Staincross to observe, record, and explain the transformations which took place there during the period of early industrialisation. Dependent, to a greater or lesser extent, upon mixed economies of farming, crafts, trades, mining, and manufacturing, the observed inter-township disparities in economic structure can only be explained by examining a number of complementary factors and the necessary linkage of the Assessments and a variety of different classes of records. A key proposition is that nominal linkage of the Assessments with other documents, to record data about the same people and events, represents the most appropriate technique for interpretation and analysis. In the first section an early extant Assessment provides a framework for the interpretation of the local coal and charcoal iron industry within a well-known historical context, an approach that is particularly appropriate for the period before 1780 when the survival of Assessments is relatively rare. The second section, which covers the later eighteenth and early nineteenth centuries, a period that has plentiful survivals, permits a cumulative approach to the Assessments and intra-source nominal linkage. The third section also focuses on the years 1780–1830 but uses the technique of inter-source linkage between the Assessments and contemporary militia lists, census records, and the poll book of 1807.

(i) *The Land Tax and the Barnsley Coalfield*

Originally, the Land Tax was conceived as a pound rate which was to be based on the assessed value of a taxpayer's property. Within each township an attempt was made to assess wealth; land valued at rack rent, personal estate, the salaries or profits of public office, tithes, the value of houses, goods, and merchandise, and the fixed assets of industry. The extant Assessment for Cawthorne township in 1694 included land, woods, tithe, the furnace and furnace stock, mills, houses, crofts, coal pits, and Cannon Hall (Table 1).

During the period from about 1660–1750 the Spencer family of Cannon Hall, Cawthorne, who were at the centre of a combination of south Yorkshire ironmasters, acquired an interest in a constantly changing series of partnerships.[1] Many of the furnaces and forges, which dated from the late sixteenth and early seventeenth centuries, were located in Staincross wapentake. Initially, the iron industry had been attracted to the area because of large reserves of ironstone, together with three other important locational factors: limestone, water power and, above all, charcoal.[2] In the middle Coal Measures, between the Silkstone and Barnsley seams, Tankersley Ironstone outcropped in a zone commencing to the west of Barnsley in Hugset Wood and continuing through Dodworth, Broom Royd, Friar Tale, and West Woods to Tankersley Park.[3] Many of the leases for the seventeenth century included rights to dig coal and ironstone. Old field names, for example Coal Pit Close and Iron Pitts in Silkstone township provide one record of ancient workings; in Worsborough township 'Coal-pit Close' was leased in 1693 at an annual rent of £17.[4]

Table 1

An Early Farming-Industrial Community: Cawthorne Assessment 1694

Proprietor and Property Assessed	Land Tax Assessment £	s	d	Percentage of Township Land Tax Total (£98 7 4)
Mr Spencer for Cannon Hall; Linley Land and Gill Royds	6	12	6	6.74
Barnby Hall Land; tyths,furnace & Spring Wood	15	9	0	15.70
Mr Dickins for Furnace Stock	3	3	8	3.24
Jos: Goldthorp	2	14	5	2.77
more for Tyth	0	8	6	0.43
more for Springwood	1	4	2	1.23
Sir Matth: Wentworth for woods	6	1	1	6.15
his land in the Oxsp	1	16	4	1.85
Sir Matth: Wentworth for Tyth thereof	0	3	7	0.18
Jo: Butterworth for Colepits	0	3	6	0.18
Tyth of Rowleys	1	6	7	1.35
for Tyth	0	1	6	0.08
Tho: Dixon his owne; & Beanfars	1	2	9	1.16
for Milne	0	18	2	0.92
Jo: Webb for milne	0	10	0	0.50
Geo: Taylor for Simpson farme	0	9	11	0.50
house & Croft	0	1	2	0.06
Mr Wainwright for house & Shop	0	1	10	0.09
Mr Armitage for Norcroft	3	0	6	3.07

Source: Bradford City Library Archives Department, Spencer Stanhope MS 497, Assessment of Cawthorne for Land Tax, 8 March 1694.

The broken topography of the region, with the alternation of ridge and valley, provided a landscape characterised by many small swift flowing streams running down to the Don, more particularly the Dearne, the Dove, and their tributaries. The furnaces were conveniently located for the ironstone outcrop and were sited on streams for water power for the bellows. In the Cawthorne Assessment for 1694 the Barnby estate was assessed for almost sixteen per cent of the township total. Barnby furnace, on the site of an old bloomery, was erected by John Spencer in the mid-seventeenth century and it remained in operation for upwards of a century.[5] A number of the ironworks were held in partnership between the Spencer family of Cannon Hall, Thomas Dickin Senior and Junior of Overheaton and Kirkstall forges respectively, and William Cotton of Haigh Hall in Darton township, their joint interests embracing Barnby furnace and

Bank furnace between Barnsley and Wakefield, and the Wortley forges.[6] The partnerships also held the derelict Stainborough Smithies on the Wentworth Castle property and Rockley furnace near Worsborough in which they were associated with the Milner family of Rockley Old Hall. An extant Assessment for Worsborough township for 1708 included the sum of £3 17s 11d for Rockley furnace, representing 3.86 per cent of the township's Land Tax quota of £100 16s 0d per annum.[7]

The iron industry required large scale investment in the construction of furnaces, forges, and slitting mills, while long term credit often had to be given to customers, and additional capital was tied up in stocks of ironstone and charcoal. Many of the townships in Staincross wapentake were densely wooded particularly in Worsborough Dale, providing both large timber and the coppice or 'spring wood' which was used for charcoal. Significantly, the term 'Spring wood' was included several times in the Assessment for Cawthorne in 1694.

The combination of ironmasters, dominated by the Spencer family of Cannon Hall, seem to have made few innovations to their early furnace type, their concerns using processes and apparatus that were steadily being superseded in other districts. Although a number of attempts were made in other parts of the country to produce good iron using coal as fuel, none were really successful. While small quantities of 'pit-coal' were used in some districts for 'drawing out' the iron, the use of coal was mainly experimental and charcoal was usually preferred. With the increased use of coke-made pig iron during the course of the eighteenth century the decline of the charcoal iron industry was inevitable. The last Spencer to be interested in the trade sold his shares, and left iron-making for the life of a country gentleman. By the 1770s Barnby and Bank furnaces had been shut down on account of a lack of charcoal and only Bretton furnace was in blast.[8] Although the charcoal iron industry of Staincross wapentake could not offer a product suited to the general demands of the iron founders, the production of slit iron for the wire and nail trades represented a significant exception. A large quantity of iron passed through the wire mills, and then to the card-makers for wool combing. The increase in woolcombing and cloth dressing contributed to the growing scarcity of charcoal and its increased price in the eighteenth century.[9]

Whereas it seems unlikely that the 'Colepits' in the Cawthorne Assessment of 1694 were connected directly to the charcoal iron industry, there is evidence for the widespread working of coal in the region. The coal measures of Staincross wapentake – in particular the

Silkstone and Barnsley coal outcrops – form part of the Yorks-Derbys-Nottinghamshire coalfield. By the end of the seventeenth century, the Silkstone coal seam, later deemed as 'perhaps the most highly prized of the seams of the Yorkshire Coalfield', was being extensively worked.[10] A plan of 1697 included three coal pits adjoining Gawber Hall and a contemporary diarist recorded that:

> 'Near Gaubur (Gawber) Hall, a mile beyond Barnsley, there is a great coal-pitt which is on fire, and has burned many years.'[11]

In quality, Silkstone and Barnsley coal compared favourably with that of Newcastle and Sunderland but the absence of cheap transport precluded the widespread sale of the former.[12] Although numerous coal pits were worked, the undertakings remained small in scale and the markets essentially local, the coalfield remaining largely landlocked.

(ii) *Local Personalities and Industrial Development*

Although the Assessments for the period 1780–1830 rarely include detailed descriptions of industrial properties, the existence of coal mines was sometimes recorded (Table 2). The random inclusion of the terms coal mine, colliery or coal pit can do little, in themselves, to reveal the transformation of the Barnsley coalfield, but a careful analysis of the proprietors and leaseholders known to be engaged, or to have an interest in coal mining in the late eighteenth and early nineteenth centuries reveals something of the consolidation taking place at a time when the prospect of canals and colliery railways was enhancing investment propensities.

By the 1790s an upsurge in demand for coal brought about by a combination of demographic growth, nascent industrialisation, and urbanisation led to a mounting crisis in coal supply in Yorkshire and adjacent counties. With a growing need for more coal it was not surprising that attention should be focused on the rich, but under-exploited Silkstone and Barnsley seams. The Aire and Calder Navigation and the Don Navigation were the main waterway arteries for the development of the Yorkshire coalfield and the Barnsley and Dearne and Dove canal schemes were primarily promoted to provide more effective and cheaper links between the coalfield and a highly developed system of inland navigation. Not surprisingly, the proprietors who owned much of the land above the Silkstone and Barnsley seams, together with their tenants, played an important role in the promotion of the canal and colliery railway schemes in a period marked by intense local competition and rivalry.

In the late seventeenth and early eighteenth centuries, the Spencer family of Cawthorne had extended their landholdings in a number of the

Table 2

Distribution of Coalmining: Assessments in Staincross townships, 1780-1830

Date	Township	Description	Land Tax £	s	d	Proprietor	Occupier
1781	High Hoyland	Coal pits	0	5	10	Sir T.Blackett	Dyson & Thwaites
1781	Langsett	Coal pits	0	8	0	Lord Melbourne	Lord Melbourne
1785	Clayton	Coal pits	0	6	3	Sir G.Savile	John Ward
1790	Tankersley	Colliery	0	19	2½	Earl Fitzwilliam	Swallow & Co.
1791	Silkstone	Coal mine	1	10	0	Mrs Smith	Mrs Smith
1791	Silkstone	Coal mine	-	-	-	John Shaw	John Shaw
1791	Silkstone	Coal mine	-	-	-	Mr Bridges/or Mr	John Ellis
1796	Thurgoland	Coal mine	0	7	3	John Cockshutt	John Cockshutt
1796	Thurgoland	Coal mine	0	3	7½	(late) R.Elmsall	Ed.Marshall
1796	Thurgoland	Coal mine	0	3	7½	W.S.Stanhope	John Woodcock & William Beet
1799	Woolley	Coal pits and mills	1	6	0	G.W.Wentworth	G.W.Wentworth
1799	Cawthorne	Coal mine	0	1	0	W.S.Stanhope	Jarratt,Dawson and Hardy
1805	Cawthorne	Coal mine	0	12	0	F.Fawkes	Samuel Thorpe
1805	Kexborough	Colliery	0	4	8	Col.Beaumont	William Sellers
1805	Wortley	Colliery	1	6	3	J.A.S.Wortley	James Wilkinson
1805	Thurlstone	Coal pits	0	5	10	R.Milnes	T.Bradbury
1808	Barnsley	Coal mine	0	7	9½	Porter & Co.	Porter & Co.
1826	Darton	Colliery	0	8	3½	Col.Beaumont	Richard Mitchel
1826	Darton	Colliery	0	13	10	G.W.Wentworth	J.Charlesworth

Source: West Yorkshire Record Office, Land Tax Duplicate Returns, Staincross Wapentake.

townships in Staincross wapentake, partly with the intent of controlling charcoal supplies for the iron-making concerns. Their descendents, the Spencer-Stanhopes, reaped a rich return, not from the coppice timber but from the valuable seams of coal which lay under their estates in Cawthorne, Barugh, Silkstone, Barnsley, Thurgoland, Clayton, and other townships in Staincross. Son of a Leeds cloth merchant, Walter Stanhope (1749–1821) inherited, in 1770, the Horsforth and Thornton (Bradford) estates of his uncle John Stanhope; and shortly afterwards he added Spencer to his name when he succeeded to the even more valuable lands of John Spencer of Cannon Hall, Cawthorne.[13] Like many other landowners in traditional industrial areas, Walter Spencer-Stanhope made a positive contribution to early industrialisation. His estates comprised a vast complexity of farms, woodlands, manorial commitments, quarries, and mineral rights, but, on lands in the Pennine region, the subterraneous mineral wealth often proved more remunerative than rentals. At times of heavy direct taxation and stationary rents, investment in commercial, industrial, mining, and transport schemes permitted the Spencer-Stanhope estate to increase its income.

In addition to considerable land in Northumberland, Walter Spencer-Stanhope's marriage in 1782 also brought him a substantial shareholding in the Aire and Calder Navigation. In the years around 1790 he was a leading promoter of a new canal from the township of Heath, a little below Wakefield on the river Calder, southwards over a distance of fifteen miles to Barnsley and then on to Barnby basin in Cawthorne township, one and a half miles from Silkstone. A key section of the canal, between Barnsley and Barnby would run partly through the estates of Walter Spencer-Stanhope, who was permitted to subscribe £1,600 to the undertaking.[14] He stood to gain considerable benefits from the Barnsley Canal (1793–1802): the rents of his estates would be improved by cheap carriage and the introduction of Knottingley lime; as a large Aire and Calder Navigation share-holder he would gain from any traffic – most obviously the export of coal and manufactures from the Barnsley district – which the new canal might bring; and above all, it was below his land that the rich Silkstone coal seam was ready for large-scale exploitation.[15]

A comparison of the Land Tax Assessments levied on the Spencer-Stanhope estates in two different townships in Staincross wapentake, illustrated in Table 3, provides some indication of the importance of the transport factor in the development of the coalfield. Thus they focused particular attention on Cawthorne township close to the head of the Barnsley canal and within easy access of the colliery railways which linked Barnby basin to Banks Hall, Norcroft, Silkstone, and Silkstone Common; in contrast little attempt was made to consolidate in Thurgoland township where land and water communications were, in contrast, under-developed.[16] The turning point in the assured development of the Barnsley canal was the opening of the Silkstone colliery railway in 1810 and the enlargement of Barnby basin.

An important role in the development of the Spencer-Stanhope estates was played by John Hardy (1745–1806), the agent and land steward.[17] A keen advocate of the enclosure of both open and waste land, Hardy was responsible for the exploitation of the mineral resources of the Spencer-Stanhope lands. Fluctuations in prices, land values, wages, and rates of investment all affected the work of a land steward, who also had to concern himself with the complexities of taxation. Under the act of 1798, which made the amount voted for that year – at 4s per pound – a perpetual charge, proprietors were given the option of redeeming their tax incidence by the payment of a lump sum at fifteen years' purchase, thereby exonerating them from further payments.[18] In 1799 Hardy was in the throes of redeeming the Land Tax for Walter Spencer-Stanhope who was keen to be rid of the burden on his estates. However, it is also clear that the administration of the redemption procedures posed many problems for Hardy, who acknowledged to Spencer-Stanhope that:

Table 3

Land Tax Assessments for the Spencer-Stanhope estates in Cawthorne and Thurgoland, 1799-1820, distinguishing between owner-occupied and tenanted property

Date	Category of Property	Assessments CAWTHORNE £ s d	Category of Property	Assessments THURGOLAND £ s d
1799	Owner-occupied	12 9 9		
	42 tenants	29 18 2¼	5 tenants	11 9 9¾
	Total assessment	42 7 11¼		11 9 9¾
	As % of township total	42.09		16.52
1808	Owner-occupied	13 9 5	Owner-occupied	8 4
	55 tenants	29 3 9½	5 tenants	11 14 9½
	Total assessment	42 13 2½		12 3 1½
	As % of township total	42.35		17.48
1820	Owner-occupied	13 18 3	Owner-occupied	8 4
	58 tenants	45 19 9¼	5 tenants	11 14 9½
	Total assessment	59 18 0¼		12 3 1½
	As % of township total	59.46		17.48

Source: WYRO, Land Tax Duplicate Returns, Staincross Wapentake.

'I never was more puzzled than (by) the settling of your land tax.'[19]

Detailed township studies for Staincross wapentake suggests that re-assessment occurred in a number of instances and that such changes occurred hard on the heels of the statutory provision for redemption in 1798. For example, in Denby township the Assessment for 1799, which was very detailed, was divided into two sections, namely, 'original assessments' amounting to £46 9s 1½d and an additional section consisting of 'Property omitted in the original Duplicate' to a total of £3 18s 2½d to provide the township quota of £50 7s 4d.

In a number of townships, numbered schedules of properties assessed for Land Tax were drawn up in 1798–1800, a further indication that, in some instances at least, a degree of re-assessment was taking place. For example, in Silkstone township the Assessment for 1798 included a brief description for each of 55 sequentially numbered tax units, comprising 24 houses, 23 farms (messuages, outbuildings, land), 14 parcels of land, together with a foldstead, water corn mill, stable, barn, shop, orchard, woodland, vicarage and glebe land. In the detailed Assessment for that year the term 'coal mine' appeared once only and in this instance the assessment of £1 10s 0d to be levied on 'Messrs Moxon and Howcroft' was deleted from the final return. An analysis of the schedule shows that thirty-three different exactments were used, although seven of these were levied on almost half of the fifty five units. The lowest exactment – 1s 3d – was levied on houses with which parcels of land were not associated. The term 'farm of land' was used fourteen times in the 1798 Assessment, the total Land Tax on these properties amounting to £31 5s 2¼d or 55.8 per cent of the township total.

The Assessment for Silkstone in 1798 was more detailed than any of those for the township over the previous eighteen years. It was also the only numbered schedule, which permits easy comparisons with the later Assessments. By 1831, although the total Land Tax for Silkstone township was the same as in 1798, there were significant differences in the pattern of the tax exactments. The Assessment for 1831 included a brief description of each of the 139 tax units, comprising 'house and land' (forty-six units), 'land' (thirty-nine units), 'house' (thirty-four units), 'wood' (four units), 'estate' (three units), 'common land' (three units), 'hall' (two units), 'coal mines' (two units), 'mill' (two units), 'tithe' (one unit), 'house and garden' (one unit), 'waggoner's stables' (one unit), and 'land for the rail road' (one unit). The pattern of tax exactments of 1798 had been changed, and no fewer than eighty-three different assessments were used in 1831. In particular, a total of fifty-eight properties were assessed for less than 1s, principally on houses with which land was not associated. Nowhere in the Assessment for 1831 of Silkstone township was the term 'farm of land' used. In Silkstone and a number of other townships in Staincross wapentake – though by no means all – there is evidence of changes in the patterns of the Assessments, co-inciding with a period of rapid economic transformation with particular focus on the extraction of coal and the development of colliery railways and canal links. Yet the precise timing of such Assessment change seems to have been closely connected with the Act of 1798 rather than resulting from modifications in land use.

The exploitation of the Silkstone and Barnsley coal seams was marked by intense rivalry between a number of land stewards, industrial concerns, and coalmasters. The tendency for many land stewards to embark on entrepreneurial activities on their own account has been noted by at least one historian:

> 'Wherever natural resources permitted, coal seams and other minerals were mined and blast furnaces, iron manufacturing, quarries, lime-kilns, and brick-kilns were established. . . It was not therefore

merely by chance that some land stewards branched out as entrepreneurs on their own account.'[20]

With increased responsibility for the Cannon Hall estate, John Hardy was given a favourable lease of Barnby Hall near Cawthorne where he was able to realise some of his own industrial ambitions. In the 1790s he was one of the partners in the Low Moor Ironworks Company (Bradford), whose involvement in the Silkstone coalfield can be seen in the Assessment for Cawthorne in 1799:[21]

Proprietor	Occupier	Land Tax		
		£	s	d
Walter Spencer Stanhope	Jarratt, Dawson, Hardy	2	19	11
	ditto for Coal Mine	0	1	0

By 1801 the Low Moor Iron Company had won a new colliery at the long disused Barnby furnace and had constructed a short (one half-mile) tramroad to the Barnsley canal head at Barnby basin. In 1803, the year in which Hardy retired as steward to Walter Spencer-Stanhope, 7,230 tons of coal – one half of all the coal tonnage on the Barnsley canal – came from the Barnby furnace colliery; in 1804 output topped 10,000 tons, or one-third of all the canal tonnage. However the colliery failed in 1806–7 and remained closed for some years.[22]

The coal traffic, which the Barnsley and the Dearne and Dove canals were intended to encourage, was slower to develop than had originally been anticipated. The situation changed with the opening of a number of colliery railways in the townships of Cawthorne, Silkstone, Dodworth, Barugh, and Barnsley.[23] By the second decade of the nineteenth century the Silkstone coalfield may be considered developed, and coal tonnage on the Barnsley canal increased from 34,673 tons in 1808 to 114,353 tons in 1820. For many years about half the produce of the Silkstone coalfield was carried by way of the Barnsley canal into the Aire and Calder Navigation and its Ouse and Humber links; the remainder proceeded via the Dearne and Dove canal and the Don Navigation into Lincolnshire. Back carriage traffic included lime and limestone for land improvement and linen yarn for the textile mills in Staincross wapentake.

Many of the coalmasters had property interests in Barnsley itself, the principal and most populous township in Staincross. Four of the leading commissioners for the Land Tax in the wapentake resided in Barnsley, namely Joseph Beckett, a banker and linen manufacturer, Edward Taylor, a merchant, Samuel Thorp, a glass manufacturer and coalmaster, and Jonas Clarke, another coalmaster with a wide range of business and industrial interests.[24] In 1857 it was recorded that:

'the late Samuel Thorp of Gawber Hall . . . was the first person who worked extensively the Barnsley or Thick Coal in the neighbourhood of Barnsley.'[25]

Samuel Thorp, who succeeded to the Gawber Hall estate near Barnsley in 1774, owned some sixty-three acres of land in that township besides working coal on the estate of the Duke of Leeds, the lord of the manor. The timing and extent of Thorp's activities can be partly demonstrated by a detailed scrutiny of the extant Assessments. In 1782 he was assessed at £1 17s 10d for Land Tax as an owner-occupier in Barnsley township; rising to £2 4s 6d in 1795; and to £2 10s 3¾d by 1806 for himself and eight tenants, amongst whom was William Pickard who worked the coal pits near Barnsley Toll Bar.[26] By the 1790s the prospect of canal communications into the coalfield prompted the Barnsley coalmasters to acquire, either as proprietors or as tenants, lands in the townships west of Barnsley itself. In 1790 Samuel Thorp was assessed for 15s 2d as an owner-occupier in Barugh township and at £5 13s 4¼d as a tenant.[27] Samuel Thorp's name first appeared in the Assessment for Cawthorne in 1798, when he became a tenant of Francis Fawkes for the Bank Hall and Norcroft estates. Within two years Thorp had taken over a coal mine, also on the Fawkes' land, previously leased by the partnership of John Moxon and Howcroft for which the Land Tax Assessment was 12s. Already a large producer of coal in Barnsley township, Thorp worked the Bank Hall estate in Cawthorne until the 1820s, when it was acquired by the Spencer-Stanhopes.[28] Thorp's last years (1819–29) were marked by financial troubles so that he was forced to sell off part of his estates in Barnsley and Barugh to clear various mortgages; while the decline in his occupancy in Cawthorne township, illustrated in Table 4, provides further evidence of his changing fortunes. Samuel Thorp's most active competitor – though by no means his only one – in the coal trade was Jonas Clarke (1758–1822) of Barnsley and Silkstone, and the development of their rival coalmining estates in Cawthorne and Silkstone can be shown by a comparison of their occupancy Land Tax proportions in the Assessments of the respective townships.

The wealth of the Clarke family of Barnsley was partly derived from wire-drawing and by the 1780s they owned land, cottages and nailmakers shops in Hoylandswaine.[29] In the following decade, and no doubt prompted by the Barnsley and Dearne and Dove canal proposals, Jonas Clarke a Barnsley attorney and colliery owner embarked on a policy of land acquisition both in Barnsley itself and in the developing coal-producing townships to the west. In 1792 Clarke bought the Noblethorpe estate in Silkstone township for £2,220, being aware of the subterraneous beds of coal and of the potential profits to be made from enclosed land in the Silkstone Valley.[30] Between 1795 and 1812 Jonas Clarke spent

Table 4

Land Tax Assessments for Two Yorkshire Coalmasters

SAMUEL THORP: CAWTHORNE

Date	Property	£	s	d
1798	F.Fawkes, propr.			
	Samuel Thorp, occpr.	6	16	0
	Do: Norcroft	4	17	11¾
	Total assessment	11	13	11¾
	As % of township total		11.61	
1800	F.Fawkes, propr.			
	Samuel Thorp, occpr.	7	9	5
	Do: Norcroft	4	13	3
	Do: Coal mine		12	0
	Total assessment	12	14	8
	As % of township total		12.64	
1805	F.Fawkes, propr.			
	Samuel Thorp, occpr.	7	9	5
	Do: Norcroft	4	13	3
	Do: Coal mine		12	0
	Total assessment	12	14	8
	As % of township total		12.64	
1820	W.S.Stanhope, propr.			
	Samuel Thorp, occpr.	4	17	6
	Do: Coal mine		12	0
	Do: Hillhouse Farm	2	2	6
	Do: Norcroft Farm	4	4	10
	Do: Coal mine	1	16	0
	Do: Commonland		6	6
	Total assessment	13	19	4
	As % of township total		13.86	
1826	Late W.S.Stanhope, propr.			
	Samuel Thorp, occpr.			
	House, land and colliery	10	7	3¾
	As % of township total		10.29	

JONAS CLARKE: SILKSTONE

Date	Property	£	s	d
1797	Jonas Clarke, propr.			
	Self, occpr.	3	19	6
	As % of township total		6.97	
1798	Jonas Clarke, propr.			
	Self, occpr.	3	19	6
	Tenant		13	6
	Total assessment	4	13	0
	As % of township total		8.15	
1805	Jonas Clarke, propr.			
	Self, occpr.	6	1	6
	Tenant		8	7
	Total assessment	7	8	1
	As % of township total		12.98	
1820	Jonas Clarke, propr.			
	Self, occpr.	11	18	11
	Nine tenants	8	4	2
	Total assessment	20	3	1
	As % of township total		35.34	

Source: WYRO, Land Tax Duplicates, Staincross Wapentake

approximately £3,672 on thirteen different pieces of land, and in 1810 he was left the Bullah Hall estate adjacent to Noblethorpe.[31] Clarke's purchase of the various freeholds was primarily related to the opportunities for exploiting the Silkstone seam and the necessary access rights, and he seems to have had very little interest in the agricultural aspects of his enlarged holdings in Silkstone.[32] Jonas Clarke was particularly eager to purchase land in the vicinity of the Bullah Hall and Noblethorpe estates, retaining the mineral rights but leasing off the agricultural interests to tenant farmers. When Jonas Clarke died in 1822 his eldest son, Joseph, appears to have inherited the family concerns and properties in Barnsley, Dodworth and Cawthorne; Robert Couldwell Clarke his second son took over the estates in Silkstone. Between 1822–41 R.C. Clarke purchased twelve different parcels of land in Silkstone, the overall purchase price of land being in excess of £3,200.[33] Although such a policy of land acquisition was still practical, it became increasingly difficult to sustain due to competition from other colliery companies for land and mineral leases which pushed up prices. In 1831 R.C. Clarke's property, occupied by twenty tenants in Silkstone townships, was assessed for Land Tax at £8 12s 5d. This was levied on Woolley estate, part of Bullah Hall, eighteen small parcels of land, thirteen houses, and the waggoners' stables. As owner-occupier, Clarke was assessed at £9 19s 9½d, comprising coal mines (£3 0s 0d), three estates (£6 6s 9½d), a mill (10s 1½d), woodland (2s 4½d) and one small house (6d).[34]

The Clarke family preferred to own the mineral rights of their estates rather than to lease them, their collieries representing only part of their expanding industrial interests. By the beginning of the nineteenth century Jonas Clarke was operating two small pits in Noblethorpe Park and, when the Barnsley canal reached Barnby basin in 1802 he opened a small mine called Basin colliery. Clarke also owned lime kilns at Barnby basin and made coke at Cross pit yard.[35] in 1805 clarke made arrangements for a trial cargo of Silkstone coal to be shipped to the London market, but the overall cost of carriage – by colliery railway, canal boat, and coasting vessel – proved too expensive at that time.[36]

Until 1810 the coal traffic passing through Barnby basin was largely in the hands of Samuel Thorp and Jonas Clarke. However, shortly afterwards new competitors appeared. When Thomas and Daniel Wilson succeeded the Low Moor Iron Company as tenants on the Spencer-Stanhope estate in Cawthorne, they re-opened the Barnby colliery and developed the coal to the east side.[37] In 1820 Daniel Wilson's tenancy was assessed at £2 8s 6½d for Land Tax and he was one of the leading tenants of Walter Spencer-Stanhope. In the neighbouring township of Silkstone, John and Joseph Popplewell had developed an important coal-working estate, as tenants of a number of proprietors (Table 5).

Table 5

Land Tax Assessments of the Popplewell Family in Silkstone, 1831

Rental £ s d	Proprietor	Occupier	Description	Assessment £ s d
40 0 0	Rev.R.Affleck	Popplewell & Co.	Coal mines	1 0 0
17 13 6	Rev.R.Affleck	Popplewell & Co.	Land	8 10½
39 0 0	Jno. and E.Ellis	Popplewell & Co.	Land	19 6
7 16 6	J.Wilkinson	Popplewell & Co.	Land	3 11
6 3 8	Trustees of School	Popplewell & Co.	Land	3 1
3 6 10	Joseph Popplewell	Himself	Land	1 8
3 0 0	J.Wadsworth	Joseph Popplewell	House	1 6
1 8 0	W.Vickers	John Popplewell	House	8½

Total rental = £118 8s 6d Total assessment = £2 19s 3d

Source: WYRO, Land Tax Duplicates, Silkstone Assessment

Table 6

Silkstone Colliery Railway: Toll Revenue and Estimated Coal Tonnage

Name of Coalmaster	1810 Toll £	1810 Estd. Tonnage	1811 Toll £	1811 Estd. Tonnage	1823 Toll £	1823 Estd. Tonnage
Samuel Thorp	532	14,364	377	10,179	453	12,204
Jonas Clarke	173	4,671	256	6,912	648	17,500
Thomas and Daniel Wilson			244	6,588	698	18,846
John and Joseph Popplewell					371	10,017

Source: Wakefield Metropolitan District Library Headquarters: John Goodchild Loan Collection, Coal Notes.

The coal mining activties of the Thorps, Clarkes, Wilsons, and Popplewells depended on the developing transport network, and some idea of the scale of their activities can be gauged from extant toll details from the Silkstone colliery railway and its branch lines (Table 6).

Given the importance of railway and canal communications in the development of the coalfield in Staincross wapentake, the lacunae of descriptions in the Assessments is striking, and is more marked than in the case of terms associated with coalmining. That the assessments for canal property were not completely fixed may be evidenced in the case of the 80-acre reservoir in Wintersett for which the assessment rose from £1 11s 1½d in 1799 to £2 11s 4d in 1826. (Table 7)

Table 7

Staincross Wapentake: Land Tax Assessments for Canals and Colliery Railways, 1799–1831

Date	Township	Proprietors and Description	Assessment £	s	d
1799	Wintersett	Barnsley Canal for reservoir	1	11	1½
1799	Barnsley	Canal Company		3	9½
1808	Ardsley	Dearne and Dove Canal		4	6
1808	Monk Bretton	Barnsley Canal for canal banks and land		3	9½
1808	Carlton	Barnsley Canal for water		8	3
1820	Ryhill	Proprietors of the reservoir		12	6
1828	Notton	Barnsley Canal		4	11
1831	Silkstone	Canal Company for railroad	2	9	7

Source: WYRO, Land Tax Duplicate Returns, Staincross Wapentake

A careful study of the Assessments for Staincross wapentake can assist in explaining the motives of landed proprietors and their tenants in the promotion of transport schemes. At the same time the Assessments may assist in explaining why other proprietors were anxious to promote alternative routes. For example, one of the principal landowners in Staincross wapentake was Colonel Thomas Richard Beaumont (1758–1829), who, despite serving as a member of the Barnsley canal committee in 1792–93, opposed the Barnsley Canal Bill and promoted a competing scheme which would have utilized the Don Navigation and the river Dearne together with an extension from Haigh through a tunnel to the Calder and Hebble Navigation at Horbury. In this rival scheme

Beaumont was supported by Godfrey Wentworth of Woolley Hall and it has been suggested that their stance was prompted by pecuniary opportunism and their anticipation that they would be bought off by the Barnsley Canal promoters.[38] However, a scrutiny of the Assessments reveals that the alternative scheme would have had considerable benefits for the Beaumont and Wentworth families by permitting the extended exploitation of coal in the townships of Darton, Woolley, and Kexborough. Since Beaumont also owned land in Barugh and Cawthorne – and even a small parcel in Barnsley itself – his stance seems to have been entirely consistent with his proprietory interests, which stand revealed from a scrutiny of the Assessments.

(iii) *Exercises in Nominal Linkage*

Descriptions of property in the Land Tax Assessments cannot, in themselves, provide a fully comprehensive picture of coal mining activity in Staincross Wapentake. Inter-source linkage also presents difficulties for the terms 'coalowner' or 'coalmaster' were rarely used in contemporary sources. For example, in the 1807 poll book for the county of York Samuel Thorp was recorded as a glass manufacturer and Jonas Clarke as simply 'gent.' The extant militia list for Staincross wapentake in 1806 provided more discrete occupational details but only included men aged between 18 and 45 years. Nevertheless, it is not inappropriate to link the Land Tax Assessments of 1806 with the near contemporary poll book and militia lists as a basis for analysing the landholding structure at township level. In Silkstone township, where coal mining was developing rapidly in the late eighteenth and early nineteenth centuries, the absence of the coal mining community either as proprietors/owners or as occupiers of property assessed for Land Tax is striking. (Tables 8 and 9)

A comparison of the Assessment for Silkstone township with the 1806 militia list suggests that certain occupations were under-represented in the Land Tax schedule and the tax was less likely to be paid by the poorer sections of the community (Table 10). The absence of the coal mining community from the Silkstone Assessment was not untypical. A check of the names of the 152 coalminers included in the 1806 militia lists for Staincross wapentake against the occupiers names in the Assessments for the townships showed that fewer than half a dozen miners were included and that the largest amount for which their occupied property was assessed was 2½d. Thus problems of record linkage exist at both ends of the social scale: at the top end the proprietors and tenants working coal on their estates are rarely referred to as coal owners; at the lower end it is possible to identify the labouring miners in the militia lists although they only rarely appear in the Assessments.

Table 8

Analysis of Proprietors in Silkstone Land Tax Assessment, 1806

RESIDENT PROPRIETORS

Occupations and Numbers		Assessments of owner-occupied properties £ s d	Tenanted Properties: No. of tenants	Tenanted Properties: Assessments £ s d
Farmers	2	1 3 3		
Labourers	1	3 0		
Non-provision dealers	1	13 6		
Craftsmen	4	1 4 0	1	12 0
Professions	2	6 0 0	5	1 10 0
No stated occupations	2	1 6	4	7 6
Totals	12	9 5 3	10	2 9 6

NON-RESIDENT PROPRIETORS

Occupations and Numbers		Assessments of owner-occupied properties** £ s d	Tenanted Properties: No. of tenants	Tenanted Properties: Assessments £ s d
Gentry/Landowners	7	12 6 9	14	17 13 7¼
Farmers	3	3 1 6	2	16 6
Non-provision dealers	1		1	2 3
Iron manufacturers	1	1 6		
Professions	1		1	13 6
No stated occupations	8	3 9 0	8	6 1 1½
Totals	21	18 18 9	26	25 6 11¾

Source: WYRO, Land Tax Duplicate Returns, Silkstone Assessment

**These were properties 'in hand', belonging to persons who did not reside in Silkstone. '...it was not unusual for farms to have land in two parishes, or for shopkeepers to live away from their shops, while woodland was often "occupied" by members of the gentry whose mansions were many miles away'. (Gibson, J. and Mills, D. (eds) Land Tax Assessments c.1690–c.1950, Stourbridge, Federation of Family History Societies, 1984, p. 8.)

Table 9

Analysis of Occupiers in Silkstone Land Tax Assessment, 1806

RESIDENT OCCUPIERS Occupations and Numbers		Assessments of owner-occupied properties			Assessments of properties occupied as tenants			Totals		
		£	s	d	£	s	d	£	s	d
Farmers	16	1	3	3	21	12	9	22	16	0
Labourers	4		3	0		17	2¾	1	0	2¾
Provision dealers	1					3	0		3	0
Craftsmen	7		12	0		17	3	1	9	3
Nailmakers	1					12	0		12	0
Labouring stonemasons	1					3	0		3	0
Professions	3	6	0	0		16	6	6	16	6
Estate (land) agents	1				2	5	0	2	5	0
No stated occupations	7	3	10	6	1	12	3	5	2	9
NON-RESIDENT OCCUPIERS Occupations and Numbers		Assessments of 'in-hand' properties								
		£	s	d						
Gentry/Landowners	4	9	8	3				9	8	3
Farmers	2	6	0	0				6	0	0
Ironfounders	2		4	6					4	6
Total(all occupiers)	49	27	1	6	28	18	11¾	56	0	5¾

Source: WYRO, Land Tax Duplicate Returns, Silkstone Assessment

The distribution of coal mining and other extractive industries in Staincross wapentake, as shown in the Assessments, is confirmed in almost every instance by the militia lists of 1806. Although the lists are not totally comprehensive, and while the extent of evasion is unknown, the age range (18–45 years) represented a significant part of working life and provides a useful comparative source for the different sectors of the regional economy. Coal mining was carried on in sixteen of the forty Staincross townships; the primary stages of iron production in three, wiredrawing in five, and nail making in twelve of the townships. Textile manufacture – linen, woollens, worsteds and even a little cotton – was carried on in more than half of the Staincross townships, though this was the manufacturing activity least represented in the Assessments. In the north-east of the wapentake, mining and manufacturing industry had not developed in the townships of Ryhill, Brierley, Chevett, Hemsworth, and Shafton, which were farthest removed from the coal and ironstone outcrop. More surprisingly, in view of the industrial occupations in all of the surrounding townships by 1806, there were no coal mining, iron, or textile making activities recorded for Stainborough township in the militia

Table 10

Silkstone Township in the 1806 Militia List

Occupations	Men aged 18–45	Per cent of Silkstone list
Farmers	2	2.7
Labourers/Farm servants	20	27.0
Gardeners	2	2.7
Butchers	1	1.4
Building craftsmen	7	9.5
Clothing craftsmen	13	17.6
Other craftsmen	5	6.8
Nailmakers	2	2.7
Coalminers	11	14.9
Labouring stone miners	9	12.2
Professions	2	2.7
Total	74	100.2

Source: Wakefield Metropolitan District Library Headquarters: Staincross Wapentake Militia Lists, 1806

lists.[39] The occupational pattern is confirmed in the early census returns, the detailed enumeration of 1831 including particular reference to coalmining in the townships of Barnsley, Barugh, Darton, Silkstone and Tankersley.[40]

Conclusion

The eighteenth and early nineteenth centuries witnessed an acceleration of economic change in many parts of the country, particularly in the half century, 1780–1830, for which the Land Tax Assessments are most plentiful. In looking at the mechanics of industrialization and the structure of local communities, the extant Assessments, if handled appropriately and linked with other sources can play an important part. In the first instance, the choice of a broad area for study must be recommended, for parishes and townships cannot be studied in isolation from each other, especially with respect to the economic and social standing of individuals at the forefront of industrialisation. The technique of nominal linkage may be employed for a variety of manufacturing or extractive activities and the few published studies using Assessments in this way suggest that coal mining may provide opportunities for worthwhile inquiry.[41] Detailed scrutiny of a wapentake or a hundred using the Assessments over a decade or more may permit the precise location of coal mining, township by township, and provide indications of the timing of development as revealed in estate consolidation. The township quotas in Staincross wapentake, which became fixed in the 1690s, hardly changed in the eighteenth century. An analysis of the forty townships also reveals direct and close correlation between the Assessments and the Book of Rates which was used for local taxation, county estreats, and the poor law. Thus the process of estate consolidation (or disintegration) can be examined against a number of fixed baselines and, in the case of the larger proprietors and tenants it is possible to compare the rate and timing of the consolidation process in a number of townships. Changes in individuals' Land Tax Assessments, whilst not in itself conclusive, may provide a basis for inquiry and questioning on the rise or decline of family fortunes. At a broader level, a careful scrutiny of the Assessments can assist in deepening understanding of the important relationship between estate consolidation, transport undertakings, and industrial activity.

NOTES

1 Raistrick, A. and Allen, E., 'The South Yorkshire Ironmasters, 1690–1750', *Economic History Review*, 1st series, volume 9, 1939, p. 168.
2 Hopkinson, G.G., 'The Charcoal Iron Industry in the Sheffield Region, 1500–1775', *Transactions of the Hunter Archaeological Society*, volume 8, 1963, pp. 122, 125.
3 ibid., p. 123.
4 Wilkinson, J., *Worsbrough*, Barnsley, 1872, p. 247.
5 Raistrick and Allen, loc. cit., p. 170.
6 Hopkinson, loc. cit., p. 123. In 1676 Thomas Dickin Senior and William Cotton entered into a partnership with John Spencer concerning Barnby furnace and Kirkstall forge near Leeds, Spencer paying £836 11s 9d, 'this being one-third part of the stock'.
7 ibid., p. 124.
8 ibid., p. 133. Of Spencer's other partners by that time, two transferred their energies to the newly introduced steel trades, the main part of the concerns being sold and the forges only carrying on after dramatic reorganisation.
9 Raistrick and Allen, loc. cit., p. 177.
10 Green, A.H. and others, *The Geology of the Yorkshire Coalfield: Memoirs of the Geological Survey of England and Wales*, London, (1878). In the mid-seventeenth century, Robert Thwaites, who held the manorial rights of Silkstone, was working coalmines valued at £26 13s 4d per annum, Wakefield Metropolitan District Library Headquarters (WMD), John Goodchild Loan Collection, Coal Notes. I should like to express my thanks to Mr Goodchild for his most helpful advice and assistance.
11 *Diary of Abraham de la Pryme* (edited by C. Jackson), Surtees Society, volume 54, 1870, p. 147.
12 Unwin, R.W., 'The Aire and Calder Navigation, Part 1: The Beginning of the Navigation', *Bradford Antiquary*, New Series, Part 42, 1964, p. 20.

13 Firth, G., 'The Roles of a West Riding Land Steward, 1773–1803', *Yorkshire Archaeological Journal*, volume 51, 1979, p. 105.
14 The Barnsley Canal was initially estimated to cost £50,000 and there were eighty five subscribers, of whom sixty put up £800 each.
15 Slatcher, W.N., 'The Barnsley Canal: its first twenty years', *Transport History*, volume 1, 1968, p. 51. Estimates for the canal quickly rose to £72,000.
16 West Yorkshire Record Office (WYRO), Land Tax Duplicate Assessments for Cawthorne and Thurgoland.
17 Firth, loc. cit., pp. 105–15.
18 38 Geo. III, c.5 and c.60.
19 Firth, loc. cit., p. 108.
20 Mingay, G.E., 'The Eighteenth-Century Land Steward', in Jones, E.L. and Mingay, G.E. (eds.) *Land, Labour and Population in the Industrial Revolution*, London, 1967, p. 4.
21 Firth, loc. cit., p. 112. In 1789 the Low Moor estate was purchased by three Bradford partners – John Jarrett, John Preston, and Richard Hird – for the low price of £33,000. Shortly afterwards, they were joined by a former Independent minister, Joseph Dawson, and the land steward, John Hardy. In the nineteenth century, the Low Moor Company was to become the leading Yorkshire ironworks.
22 Hadfield, C., *The Canals of Yorkshire and North East England*, Newton Abbot, 1972, volume 1, p. 176.
23 Slatcher, loc. cit., pp. 60–63.
24 Other local commissioners were William Garlick, Esq. of Dodworth and Thomas West.
25 WMD Library HQ, John Goodchild Loan Collection, Coal Notes. William Thorp, a grocer of Glasshoughton near Castleford settled at Gawber Hall near Barnsley in the 1730s and worked the Gawber glasshouse. In 1774 he was succeeded by his two sons, Samuel and Richard.
26 In December 1773 the trustees of the Doncaster-Saltersbrook turnpike road paid Samuel Thorp £4 11s 6d 'for Coals', for brick making.
27 WYRO., Land Tax Duplicate Returns, Barugh Assessments. In the 1790s Samuel Thorp was one of the tenants of Francis Sitwell, Esq., and also the tenant of John Bowden and Company.
28 Thorp's colliery railway connected with the main Silkstone line, Slatcher, loc. cit., pp. 62–63.
29 Roberts, R.A., *The Clarkes of Silkstone and their colliers*, Barnsley WEA, 1981.
30 In 1791 Jonas Clarke married Elizabeth Ann Gace of Stixwould, Lincolnshire, by whom he had five sons and one daughter. The Noblethorpe estate was ninety two acres in extent.
31 WMD Library HQ, John Goodchild Loan Collection, Coal Notes. Jonas Clarke was left Bullah Hall estate in the will of Mary Sykes of Mirfield. In addition, in 1807, Clarke purchased Pye Greave Farm for £670 and Sunny Bank Farm, which were immediately mortgaged to raise capital for expanding industrial interests.
32 Prince, J.F., *Silkstone*, Penistone, 1922, p. 98.
33 WMD Library HQ, John Goodchild Loan Collection, Coal Notes.
34 WYRO, Land Tax Duplicate Returns, Silkstone Assessment, 1831.
35 Prince, op. cit., p. 104.
36 The opening of the London market for Silkstone coal occurred in the late 1820s, Slatcher, loc. cit., p. 63.
37 Daniel Wilson, who died in 1825 aged sixty four, was a descendant of a Featherstone family and became a tenant of Spencer-Stanhope at Barnby furnace.
38 Slatcher, loc. cit., p. 53.
39 WMD Library HQ, 1806 Militia Lists, Staincross Wapentake.

40 *Census of Great Britain, Enumeration Abstracts*, volume 2, London, 1831 (published 1833), pp. 816–17.
41 Wilson, G.J., 'The Land Tax and West Derby Hundred, 1780–1831', *Transactions of the Historic Society of Lancashire and Cheshire*, volume 29, 1979, p. 68.

PART IV: LAND TAX ADMINISTRATION AND THE EARLY LAND TAX

Chapter 9

Land Tax Administration at the Local Level 1693–1798

J.V. BECKETT

Introduction

The use that historians have made of Land Tax Assessments implies an acceptance of their value as an historical source, and, by implication, that their compilation was generally objective as between individuals appearing in the lists and as between the lists for different places. But was this the case? In this paper the LTAs will be viewed within the overall context of the Land Tax administration, in the belief that this is a necessary foundation for an objective assessment of their value. The primary study of the subject, W R Ward's book *The English Land Tax in the Eighteenth Century*,[1] is largely based on central records and concerned with the political history of the tax. Ward has little to say on local administration, but some of the issues outlined in the book can only be fully examined by reference to what was happening out of sight of Westminster. A major aim of this paper is to provide insights of this kind. Most of the examples are drawn from Cumberland and Westmorland, which, as will become clear, were not entirely representative. However, this evidence, together with a number of comparative examples, helps to open up several lines of enquiry designed to demonstrate the credibility gap between theory and practice. By looking first at the theory – what was supposed to happen according to the annual acts of Parliament – and then at what actually took place in the localities, it should be possible to hint at some of the inconsistencies pervading the administration. The contention advanced is that these *might* be significant when considering the LTAs: they might, for example, raise such questions as just how far were the lists objective? How often were they updated? How far was compilation affected by bias and prejudice as a result of pressure exerted on both commissioners and assessors, and how far are these likely to invalidate the use of the source? The conclusions will necessarily be tentative, but also, hopefully, suggestive.

(i) *The Land Tax Acts and the Administrators*

The eighteenth-century Land Tax is normally taken to date from the annual legislation passed in the Spring of each year between 1692 (1693 n.s.) and 1798, after which the tax was made permanent, but redeemable on payment of a lump sum. Between 1693 and 1696 it was levied as a pound rate of four shillings in the pound; in 1697 as a four shilling assessment supplemented by a Poll tax; and from 1698 until 1798 on the principle of the Interregnum and Restoration Monthly Assessments, whereby each county was apportioned a quota. Despite these changes the procedure laid down in the original legislation was repeated throughout with only minor modifications.[2] Commissioners were named for each county to supervise the assessment and collection procedures laid down in the acts. They were instructed to hold a general meeting on a set date, and then to divide into groups which would act for smaller areas. At the general meeting they made an order to the High Constables

> to issue out your warrants to the several petty constables within your ward, requiring them to summon four able and sufficient inhabitants . . . that two or more of them for every constablewick respectively may be appointed assessors.[3]

Within a few days the assessors met and were told the amounts that they were required to charge. A week or so later they reported back with the assessments for each individual. The commissioners then heard appeals, and if they could not agree on the proportions the matter was referred to the Exchequer, although such a course was generally avoided: one northern gentleman was under no illusion that 'it might be of dangerous consequence'.[4] Payments took place quarterly or half-yearly (depending on the tax rate), and collectors were summoned by the receiver-general half-yearly to pay over their balances. From then onwards superintendence of the revenue passed into the hands of the Tax Office and Treasury, who exercised direct control over the receiver-general.

These arrangements were not novel in 1692; they represented tested means honed on previous post-Restoration 'extraordinary' taxation. Many of the administrators had acted in similar roles before; most of the receivers-general, for example, had served in a similar post since the Revolution.[5] The employment of established procedures enabled central government to request speedy execution of its demands. The commissioners were to meet before 15 February 1692/3, and the assessment was to be completed in time for them to certify a true copy of it into the Exchequer before 20 March (or within thirty days thereafter). The first quarterly payment was to be levied by 10 March, and paid by 20 March (or within twenty days of either date), and receivers-general were to pay the money into the Exchequer before 25 March or within twenty days. Similarly strict details were given for the three other quarterly payments, so that all four were to be paid into the Exchequer by 14

January 1693/4, just eleven months from the first meeting of the commissioners. The procedure having been laid down it was repeated with only minor amendments in subsequent acts. Thus in 1702 the commissioners were to meet by 1 May, assessments were to be made by 20 May, and payments by 24 June, 29 September, 12 December and 25 March. Quarter days became standard payment times by 1711, except that when the rate was reduced to two shillings in 1713 only half yearly payments were required.[6] Anyone reading the legislation could be forgiven for thinking that here was a smooth, well-oiled machine for efficient annual assessment and collection, but it was one thing for central government to lay down rules and regulations, and quite another for it to enforce them.

Each act named commissioners for the individual counties of England and Wales and for the county boroughs. Usually the men appointed were drawn from the landed gentry, although lawyers and parsons increasingly appeared in the lists during the course of the eighteenth century. In 1699 commissioners were required to have an income from land of £50 a year, and this was doubled two years later. By nominating the local gentry to the commission central government was adhering to the principle that property incomes could only be taxed successfully by obtaining the consent of the landed classes. This normally meant involving them in the process of supervising assessment and collection. Such a situation was not ideal, since no one could control the commissioners, who worked without remuneration, although they did enjoy the services of a paid clerk. The most that the Treasury could do was to ascertain which members of the commission actually participated. Andrew Hudleston, receiver-general for Cumberland and Westmorland, was asked in 1697 'forthwith as privately as you may to transmit to us a list of the names of such persons as you have observed to be the most active commissioners for the taxes in the counties of Cumberland and Westmorland'.[7]

Commissioners were nominated by MPs, who paid careful attention to their choices, commonly engaging in list 'fixing'. In effect, this was a tactical battle reflecting the efforts of different interest groups to avoid disproportionate assessments. William Fleming, local MP and Westmorland gentleman, took pains to ensure that only sympathetic 'friends' were nominated: he informed his father in 1698 that 'I have already a list of commissioners which includes my own relations'.[8] In West Cumberland the Lowthers were anxious to protect the growing town of Whitehaven from being overassessed by jealous assessors and commissioners. James Lowther wrote to his father in 1699.[9]

> Sir George Fl[etcher] tells me he is desired by Mr Latus to put him and his son in for commissioners of the land tax which may be

> prejudical to your part of the country they being like to side with the commissioners who are for laying a greater proportion upon Whitehaven.

If all other means failed MPs could invalidate appointments by misspelling names, though even this was not fail-safe since in the 1697 Westmorland list Mr Baynes's name was 'writ Raynes very plainly, whereof I took notice, but both he and the other gentlemen present were not willing that any notice should be taken of it, so Mr Baynes was sworn as well as the rest'.[10] Sufficient care was taken in 1708 to ensure that a misspelling could only have been by design according to one local commentator, but even so 'they have put in two dead men; they have murdered the names of thirteen others, and the clause of £100 per annum for every commissioner will exclude many of those that are spelt as they ought to be'. Since Roman Catholics, and other men who lived outside the area, were also included despite not being qualified, it was far from clear that there would be enough commissioners to perform the task adequately.[11] Nor did the situation improve: as late as 1772 the local receiver-general was complaining that many of the named commissioners were either dead or had moved from the area.[12]

The position of receiver-general was also something of a political football. Major purges took place following swings in party fortune, in 1706, 1711–12 and 1715–16 for example, while some of those dropped sometimes found themselves restored to favour with a change in the political climate.[13] Appointments were effectively the preserve of local magnates, particularly as the men who filled these positions tended to be small landowners with a sprinkling of merchants, bankers, town clerks and others looking for positions of patronage. In Cumberland and Westmorland – the two counties had a single receiver except for the years 1716–21 – the dominant Lowther family came to control the position. Sir James Lowther, of the Whitehaven branch of the family, was partly responsible for the appointment of his distant cousins Charles and Benson Highmore in the 1720s, and John Fletcher in 1727. When Fletcher went bankrupt in 1742 Lowther was at a loss for a suitable replacement: his estate steward did not know 'of any other of your friends that will care for the trouble and hazard of it'. The position eventually went to local tobacco merchant Peter How, with Lowther's blessing.[14] At his bankruptcy twenty years later William Brownrigg was appointed. Brownrigg was personal physician to Sir James Lowther of the Lowther branch of the family (created Earl of Lonsdale 1783), who also had contact with the Atkinson brothers – appointed receivers in 1777. Thomas Denton, receiver in the 1790s, was a steward on Lonsdale's Westmorland estate.

(ii) *The Assessments: who paid?*

According to the terms of the first act of 1692/3 fixed and movable property was to be taxed in due proportion. Four shillings in the pound was charged on the rack rent of real estate and the profits of office, while personal property was liable at 6 per cent of capital value. This attempt to raise a realistic pound rate on income reflected a long held desire on the part of central government to tap the country's wealth for tax purposes. The fourteenth century 'fifteenths' and 'tenths' had been designed as a wealth tax, as had the sixteenth century 'subsidy' and the 1601 Poor Law. As recently as 1671 an attempt had been made to renovate the 'subsidy' in order to make it a tax on real values, and in the first two Parliamentary sessions following the Revolution three pound-rate taxes had been levied.[15] Since the fourteenth century, however, governments had found that pound rate taxes seldom yielded as much as was estimated, and that they tended to decline after the first year. It was therefore easier and more lucrative to accept the county quota system embodied in the Monthly Assessments, whereby government settled the sum a county had to raise but did not interfere with the collection procedure.

Commissioners were less likely to connive at inefficient assessment to a county quota, because the total had to be achieved somehow, than they were to a pound rate, where it was the government which suffered. At the same time it was recognized that taxes collected on the Monthly Assessment principle were essentially land taxes. Once the government resorted to county quotas in 1698 the 'Land Tax' proper was born, although the quota was supposed to be raised by a pound rate levied in the county – a unique amalgam of the two chief methods of post-Restoration direct collection methods. Tacit acceptance that the government had surrendered control of the assessment and collection procedure is apparent from 1702 when the annual legislation came to be known as the Land Tax Act, although the personal property clause remained in the legislation until 1833.[16]

Whilst some counties may have continued to use a pound rate principle within the county after 1698, as the legislation demanded, in practice it is clear that the situation was open to local interpretation. Most eighteenth-century writers seem to have been of the opinion that the tax fell on the *owners* of land, and this was largely true of freehold tenancy land in Cumberland. John Christian, the Duke of Somerset's agent in the county, explained to his opposite number at Petworth in the 1740s that 'for the land tax and other rates and assessments, the farmers expect that they are to be paid, as they have always hitherto been, by the landlord and which is the general usage in this county.'[17] In 1759 it was still common in Cumberland 'when an estate is let to farm for the owner to agree to pay all the taxes'.[18] However, such generalizations obscure a multitude of variety in practice. The third viscount Lonsdale transferred responsibility to many of his tenants during the 1730s, as did the earls of Suffolk and Carlisle. By the 1760s tenants were paying the tax on the Pennington estate in west Cumberland.[19] Officially Roman Catholics were supposed to pay double tax, but this rarely happened in practice. Cumberland and Westmorland were charged £1218 to the special tax laid on Catholics in 1723, although only £618 was accounted for in the two counties.[20] On the other hand it was not unknown for non-Catholics to be rated double to the Land Tax: Sir John Lowther of Whitehaven had been assessed as such to the first four shilling tax, although two neighbouring Catholics, Mr Curwen and Mr Fletcher, were not.[21] When the Tax Office enquired in 1792 as to how many Catholics were paying Land Tax in Cumberland the answer was that:

> there are few Catholics in this county, and only three of any Property who are not double rated to the Land Tax, as I was informed by a late agent of Mr Howard of Corby that he is only rated in proportion with his neighbours and he believed the other two are the same.

The Westmorland reply was in a similar vein.[22]

This was freehold property but the vast majority of real estate in Cumbria was held by customary tenure, with the additional complication of fines and services. The question of who should pay the Land Tax on these properties was widely debated. Until 1705 customary tenants were held responsible, but thereafter only for particular properties where the rent was less than twenty shillings. This was the opinion of Sir John Cheshire, a noted Carlisle attorney, who based his argument on the clause in the Land Tax acts which referred to deductions out of Fee Farm rents amounting to twenty shillings. Thus, in his opinion, the landlord was liable for each individual payment of more than twenty shillings customary rent, but the tenant was responsible when smaller sums were involved. It was not permissible for properties to be grouped together in order to make the total rent exceed twenty shillings.[23] In general, this opinion seems to have been followed, although it did not solve all the difficulties. Quit rents of under twenty shillings had to be excluded because they were liable to be taxed by both tenant and lord, and some customary tenants tried to lump their rents so that the total exceeded twenty shillings. A few succeeded: in 1717 the Earl of Thanet complained to his steward that he was the only landowner in Westmorland paying his tenants' small taxes, despite twelve years of repeated demands to the agent to end the allowances, 'for lumping is a way I approve not'.[24]

Any attempt to demonstate the relationship of theory and practice with regard to customary rents and Land Tax payments is extremely hazardous. Odd copies of LTA lists survive prior to the 1780s, and by comparing these with customary estate fine books it ought to be possible to show who was paying tax.[25] However, the exercise produces disappointing results. Manor and constablewick boundaries did not necessarily coincide, and it is obvious from the amount of tax paid that many customary tenants had more than one holding. Conceivably some had freehold as well as customary property, which further complicates any attempt to correlate the amount of tax paid with the amount of customary rent. The manor of Kennyside on the Leconfield estate in Cumberland shows the nearest apparent relationship, but even here the amount of rent constituting one penny of Land Tax varied between 10d and 1s 4d.[26] A further test is derived from the nature of the assessment and collection procedures. For reasons to be outlined shortly, anyone rated to local taxes should have appeared in the LTAs. Comparison of a poor rate assessment and LTA for the parish of Dalston in Cumberland in 1761 shows an almost identical relationship in names, but some were paying different proportions for Land Tax from their poor rate, indicating a different set of assessments.[27] Usually only cottagers were not rated to the poor, since their rental would not normally exceed one shilling. On the Earl of Thanet's manor of Mallerstang in Westmorland the indication is that no tenant paying less than one shilling rent appeared in the LTA of 1791.[28] Not only is it impossible to be sure how many customary tenants were rated in the LTA lists, but it is equally difficult to draw any conclusions concerning those who paid in excess of twenty shillings customary rent. Sums such as this were unusual, but in the twenty-five examples found, only seven of the tenants do not appear in the LTA lists. This is not entirely surprising, since twenty shillings rent indicated a substantial holding,[29] and the tenants were likely to have additional property elsewhere, either customary or freehold. However, practice certainly varied. At Holme Cultram in Cumberland full Land Tax had been allowed for Fee Farm and copyhold rents above and below twenty shillings when John Spedding inspected the estate in 1731 with a view to purchasing it for Sir James Lowther. Spedding noted in 1744 that 'Land Tax at four shillings in the pound makes a great hold in the copyhold rents'.[30] At Troutbeck, in Westmorland, there were sixty-two entries in the 1706 LTA. Benjamin Browne was one of them, even though his rent exceeded twenty shillings.[31] Overall, the difficulties involved in using LTAs alongside other pieces of evidence are such as to ensure that any correlation is tentative. Cheshire's judgment may have been sound in legal theory, but in practice in Cumberland and Westmorland considerable variation existed. Many tenants did indeed appear in tax lists, and in some cases the assessments were a true reflection of property value difference, or at least would seem to have been, given the decision of several Westmorland parishes to divide the commons at enclosure on the basis of Land Tax Assessments.[32]

(iii) *The Assessments: how much was due?*

The decision to adopt a pound rate assessment in 1692/3 was the outcome of heated argument as to the best method of raising money to maintain the war against France, and the recognition that the Monthly Assessment principle was unequal. The question of whether to use a pound rate or Assessment was raised in Parliament during the supply debate of 1691, and according to Narcissus Luttrell, 'a great debate' ensued. MPs for Norfolk and Suffolk argued that they were overrated to an Assessment and suggested a pound rate, 'but the majority of the House, especially the western and northern members being for a Land Tax by a monthly assessment, it was carried for the same'.[33] Twelve months later the issue was again under debate, and once again the members for Norfolk and Suffolk argued that their counties were paying between 6s and 10s in the pound whilst other counties contributed only 2s or 3s. According to Luttrell:

> There was a long debate about it. The north country gentlemen as Yorkshire, Northumberland, Durham, Cumberland, Westmorland, Lancashire, Derbyshire etc [and] those gentlemen who have estates here in houses in Middlesex, etc. were for the tax by way of a monthly assessment. But Norfolk, Suffolk, Essex, Wilts, Bucks, Bedford, Kent, Surrey etc, were for that of a pound rate because in this they paid less than to a monthly assessment.

In the end the decision favouring a pound rate was carried by 226 votes to 148. It took several more debates to iron out the clauses, during which, according to Luttrell, the north country members continued to take exception 'to anything that was proposed to have an equal tax throughout England'.[34]

These Parliamentary tactics were a well rehearsed performance. According to Luttrell's account, in the 1692 debate the first MP to propose the Monthly Assessment rather than the pound rate was Sir Christopher Musgrave, MP for Westmorland. This role of watchdog fell on the shoulders of successive generations of northern MPs. Sir James Lowther, sixty years a backbencher in the lower house, much of the time representing the interests of his native Cumberland, believed that if the Land Tax was really levied at four shillings in the pound it would mean the ruin of the northern counties. For him the reassessment of the Window Tax in 1747 epitomized the disastrous consequences of electing outsiders to represent the three boroughs: as he told his steward, 'nobody spoke to show the great hardship it would be on such poor counties as ours next Scotland but myself . . . the two Cockermouth members were there but said not a word'.[35] After Lowther's death in 1755 the mantle of defender of the north fell on Sir Wilfrid Lawson of Isel. When the question of a more equal assessment was raised in 1764 Lawson helped to forstall positive action by the dramatic gesture of taking to the House of Commons 'a loaf of barley bread, a pair of wooden shoes &c in order to evince the poverty and low manner of living in these northern counties'.[36] However accurate the poverty argument there can be little doubt that it was exaggerated on occasion for form's sake. Sir James Lowther even admitted to his steward on one occasion that 'it is our interest to have it thought a poor county as it really is'.[37]

Although the northern MPs lost the debate in 1692 this did not mean that a full four shilling pound rate was immediately levied through the region. As early as 1694 'great remarks were made upon Westmorland (Cumberland was touched upon) that it paid not 9d in the pound', and when in 1698 the government returned to a county quota system using the figures for money collected in 1693 local MP William Fleming wrote that 'Cumberland will fare easily about the Tax in consequence of the prudent act of the commissioners in the first four shilling aid'.[38] Since these figures were never altered the inequalities became inbuilt. Charles D'Avenant noted in 1695 that 'the Land Taxes by monthly assessment seem unequally laid; and the pound-rate of four shillings in the pound, does seem unequally levied upon the nation . . . the north and west have not born their due share and proportion of the common burthen'.[39] An anonymous pamphleteer of 1732 claimed of the Land Tax that

> when it is at four shillings, a man perhaps in Kent or Essex shall pay the full, or sometimes more; in Norfolk or Lincolnshire he shall pay three shillings; in Staffordshire and Shropshire two; in Devonshire and Yorkshire fifteen pence; in Cornwall and Wales nine pence.[40]

Perhaps most interesting of all about this argument was that although the northern MPs had argued for a monthly assessment rather than a pound rate tax in 1692, a comparison of what was actually paid on the first Land Tax with the Monthly Assessment raised during 1692 (on the 1691 legislation) reveals that the north actually did rather well. Overall the Land Tax produced an increased yield of 16.4 per cent, but it was London and the Home Counties which footed the bill. Even Norfolk paid more, despite the arguments of its MPs, whilst Cornwall, Cumberland, Lancashire, and Westmorland, all made an absolute contribution lower than ever before.[41]

Unfortunately no papers have survived from which it can be established how Cumberland and Westmorland reached the figures that they settled upon. The sum raised in Cumberland was £3713 16s, approximately £150 more than the equivalent used for the three shilling aid of 1689. If the calculations behind the original figure cannot be established, the pattern of falling assessments in the 1690s was a national phenomenon. In 1693 the two counties were charged with £6742. A year later £15 less was assessed, and another £17 was taken off in 1695.[42] No duplicate has survived for 1696, although West Ward in Westmorland reduced its contribution by £7.[43] In 1697 £6842 was collected, but this reflected the decision to collect part of the tax as a pound rate and part as a Poll Tax.[44] When, in 1698, the government resorted to quotas based on the 1693 figures Cumberland was rated at £3713 and Westmorland at £3045. According to local MP William Fleming in the latter case a slightly lower figure might have been achieved but 'for want of timely information'.[45]

The quotas remained in force for as long as the tax itself, thus enshrining the inequalities in the subsequent legislation. It was another hundred years before the Board of Taxes even attempted to find out how the localities assessed and collected their assessments, and the replies to their circular in 1798 revealed a considerable array of practices.[46] As a tactical measure, the decision to leave the counties to their own devices reflected the overriding consideration in the locality, the need to assess and collect efficiently, without fuss, and without the possibility of having to pay more than a minimal amount. It was usual for the inhabitants of a township to take on the roles of assessor and collector by turn, and in the interests of local harmony they were generally unwilling to change existing ratings.[47] From the beginning Cumberland apparently raised Land Tax as an ordinary county rate, according to a method of taxation known locally as the purvey.[48] In the early years an effort was made in Westmorland to conform to the terms of the legislation. The 1695 duplicate mentioned '£ rate charged in manors, messuages, lands, tenements and hereditaments', as well as 'sums rated on personal estates, offices and employments'.[49] It is impossible to be sure whether this distinction was more than a purely nominal one, but from 1698 the county reverted to using its usual form of assessment, the Book of Rates. The advantages were stressed by Lord Lonsdale in a letter to Sir Daniel Fleming:[50]

> I am entirely of opinion with you that the Book of Rates is the best way to raise the three shillings in the pound, for as much as I have heard of it, tis the most equal way, but were it less so than it is I should think that the practice and custom of it should recommend it to our choice, rather than the best new projected experiment whatever.

During the course of the eighteenth century the inequalities were exacerbated because it was established that while parish assessment levels might alter, within the county rates were fixed. A writer of 1745 examined the power of commissioners to alter quotas assessed within the hundreds and wards of different counties, and argued that certain parts of Westminster were being grossly unfairly treated by comparison with the rest of Middlesex, with newly developed areas contributing very little. Commissioners with a vested interest in maintaining the status quo had argued that the quotas were fixed by Parliament, and as a result the Land Tax varied between different parishes from a true four shillings in the pound to only 1s 8d in one of the newly improved parishes.[51] In Cumberland and Westmorland the Land Tax was simply an extension of a system which included county rates. Occasional changes were made in the intra-county levels of responsibility, but the County Rates Act of 1739 was taken to imply that quotas as between hundreds should be regarded as fixed. Thus changes in proportional wealth between different areas could not be reflected.[52] In addition, vested interests worked against any change in assessments because, for example, land prices and values had come to be at least partially determined according to the rate of tax to which they were liable. Cross-county comparisons of price and value became increasingly meaningless. Nationally this was recognised by no less an authority than Sir John Sinclair. Writing in his *History of the Public Revenue of the British Empire*, he noted that calls for an equal Land Tax would not be relished by those who had recently purchased estates on the understanding that no change was likely.[53] Cumberland landowner Sir James Lowther often stressed the significance of a change in tax rates for land prices: 'the prospect of having Land Taxes at four shillings in the pound will keep down the price of land in Cumberland',[54] and just how great the difference could be is illustrated by the case of Charles Pelham. He bought land in Lincolnshire in 1744 for 26½ years' purchase, but reckoned the same land would have been worth thirty years' purchase in Cumberland where the Land Tax was so much less.[55]

The inequalities, coupled with the use of customary procedures, makes it extremely difficult to calculate the amount of tax actually paid. However, in 1699 the Whitehaven branch of the Lowther family paid about 4.3 per cent of their income in Land Tax, some 10.3d in the pound. By 1744, however, Sir James Lowther was paying only about 1.8 per cent of this rental income in Land Tax, the equivalent of about 4.3d in the pound on a four shilling rate. On Richard Honywood's Westmorland estate in 1746 Land Tax amounted to 1s 6d on a four shilling rate.[56] These figures may help to give a general impression of the extent of the underassessment, but they may not be entirely accurate since it is clear that the nature of the rating system made for differences between properties. On the Earl of Thanet's Westmorland estate, for example, Land Tax accounted for 10 per cent of the rental of Brougham Castle and demesne, but only 5 per cent of that for Appleby Castle, while ten shillings Land Tax was paid on both Brougham Mill (rent £14) and Brough Sowerby Mill (rent £6 10s).[57] Lord Berkshire's tenants at Long Sleddall in Westmorland also paid a variety of rates. Different tenants paid 16s 8d Land Tax on rent of £11 and £13, while two others paid 16s 4d on rents of £10 and £11 10s.[58] On the Queen Dowager estates in the manor and forest of Ennerdale 22.4 per cent of the rental was deducted for Land Tax in 1703 and 19.5 per cent in 1705. It is unclear, however, whether this money was actually paid or merely deducted.[59] Certainly it was normal practice to deduct four shillings in the pound from all Fee Farm rents before payment, although Sir John Lowther, for one, preferred to keep on friendly terms with the Bishop of Chester by not deducting the full amount. His son, Sir James, had more difficulty with a later bishop who wished to discontinue the normal allowance.[60] Perhaps the most telling evidence, however, as to just how much tax Cumbrians avoided paying, was provided by Sir Wilfrid Lawson who died in 1704. Lawson, ironically a forebear of the later defender of Cumbrian poverty, was so struck by the deficiency of his taxes that at his death he bequeathed £600 to the crown to make up the difference between what he had actually paid in Land Taxation, and what he regarded himself as having been liable for.[61] The contemporary figure of ninepence in the pound may have been a slight underestimation for the heavily assessed years of the 1690s and 1700s, but it was probably not far wrong by the early 1730s.

(iv) *Collection*

Once the assessments were laid they still had to be collected and remitted to London. Both stages proved to be sources of delay and sometimes of outright losses to the government. Collectors received 3d in the pound commission,[62] but this did not prevent misdemeanours. In 1714 it was alleged that more money was collected in the Barony of Kendal each year than was remitted to the Exchequer, and the residue of £20–£30 was divided between the deputy-receiver and 'the officer'. Westmorland MP Daniel Wilson was said to be privy to the affair.[63] Some collectors simply did not pay up. The commissioners were supposed to compel them on pain of a £20 fine, but this depended on whether they could be persuaded to act.[64] In March 1713/14 three of the Westmorland commissioners instructed the High Constable of Kendal and Lonsdale wards to summon the Land Tax collectors to find out why £277 was outstanding from the area on the 1712 tax.[65] Not all commissioners were so obliging, and such action did not guarantee the appearance of the money. Collectors were sometimes abused while performing their duties, which did not speed the collection process, while the receivers' efforts to extract money from them often ran into considerable difficulty. In 1738 the Shropshire receiver prosecuted a local collector for forging a receipt of Land Tax money he had not paid, but the issue was lost in court and a mob gathered 'crying they'd humble the King's Receiver'.[66] William Brownrigg, receiver-general for Cumberland and Westmorland 1763–77, had great difficulty recovering arrears from Leath Ward, Cumberland, and in particular from the parish of Hutton John. He wrote several letters to Andrew Hudleston, lord of the manor and a local commissioner, in the hope of persuading him to act. Hudleston considered that some of the accusations had arisen from misconceptions and poor accounting, but helped Brownrigg by sending bills of exchange to London to replace the money he was out of pocket.[67] In the 1790s Thomas Denton found his thorn-in-the-flesh was Whitehaven. Richard Oyes, the local collector proved to be extremely tenatious at holding on to the money. Denton visited the town in 1792 to collect debts, and persuaded the acting commissioners to summon Oyes. Even the threat of exchequer process had little effect, and he was eventually replaced.[68]

Once the collectors paid over their receipt to the receiver several factors combined to ensure that the remittance to London was delayed. On the receivers' part a legitimate claim was that they were expected to meet certain charges from their collection and that they needed to retain cash in hand until this was completed. The practice of paying local bills from tax revenue was long-standing and sensible. Much of the extraordinary taxation raised after the Revolution was spent in the provinces to support campaigns in Scotland and Ireland. In addition, from 1722 receivers were made responsible for paying rewards for the arrest of army deserters, and with the reorganization of the militia in 1759 they became the financiers. On occasion other responsibilities were also added to their burden, including the hemp and flax duties in 1783.[69] A second delaying factor was the difficulty of transferring money to London. The demand in the legislation that receivers pay receipts to the Exchequer within twenty days was quite impractical. Remitting money in specie was both dangerous and slow. Even from Somerset, let alone the more distant counties, it could take more than the alloted number of days. In addition, local communities were reluctant to see large quantities of scarce cash removed to London. The obvious means of transfer was the bill of exchange, but the receiver had to compete with excise, and, in the maritime counties customs' collectors, quite apart from estate stewards remitting money to London. As late as the 1780s it was still not possible for some receivers to obtain good bills of exchange, making it necessary for them to send quantities of specie.[70]1 A third factor delaying the return was the poor reward offered to receivers. The twopence poundage allowance (plus a further 3d in remote counties)[71] was hardly a lucrative reward. The Cumbrian receiver earned an allowance of just £55 5s 4d when the rate was four shillings in the pound and less when lower tax rates operated.[72] Some flexibility allowing receivers to make use of the money proved to be necessary. Peter How, for example, took on the post in Cumbria to help facilitate his Whitehaven tobacco business. He made a fortune during the 1740s when the French tobacco purchasers began buying their requirements from his Whitehaven firm. To meet the demand he bought tobacco from fellow merchants for cash, but the French paid him in London. To avoid having to move large sums of money How sought and obtained receiverships of excise, in 1739, and land and window taxes, in 1743. He used the cash collected in Cumbria to pay his fellow merchants, and the balances accumulating in London from his French clients to pay the tax.[73] The danger for central government of allowing such practices was amply demonstrated when How went bankrupt in 1763. More than a third of the 1762 Land Tax was paid only in 1767. In this case the Treasury received the money but in other instances it was less fortunate; between 1715 and 1770 over £82,500 was lost as the result of default by receivers.[74]

For central government the main problem was to persuade receivers to pay in their collection. Although it was accepted that they needed to retain some money in hand – to pay militia expenses, for example – slow returns were costly since Exchequer Bills issued on the security of the annual legislation could only be paid off when the revenue was received. Periodic attempts were made to hasten collection. Lord North brought in a bill to this effect in 1781, which was dropped in committee. A report from the Commissioners of Accounts in 1782 also suggested the need for statutory regulation. It was calculated that £13,262 was lost annually, in terms of potential interest on capital retained by the receivers. As a result, the commons resolved in June 1782 that 'regulations ought to be adopted in the manner of collecting and receiving the duties arising from the Land Tax, and on Houses and Windows, and in the Payment of the said Duties into the Exchequer.' Nothing further came of this plan, however, and five years later William Pitt made further efforts to speed up remittance.[75]

The ineffectiveness of these measures stemmed from two sources. The first was the lack of muscle available to the Treasury. It could threaten process against a recalcitrant receiver, and make reappointment dependent upon a reduction of balances. William Brownrigg told his deputy John Moore in July 1774 that 'I am called upon by the Treasury to make up and clear my account for the year 1772 before I receive my commission for the present year, according to a rule established three years ago, which I cannot any longer avoid complying with'. Thomas Denton was informed in April 1794 that 'your re-appointment will depend on your accounts for 1792 being cleared, and your balances for 1793 appearing as low as possible'.[76] But such threats could not always be enforced, and the Treasury found it expedient not to push the receivers too far or too fast. In fact, and this was the second reason for the slowness of remittance, the receivers' view was tacitly accepted that the poundage of 2d in the pound was insufficient, and the job only became worthwhile if they were allowed to use the balances for their own benefit. This admission led directly to a working arrangement whereby the impression was allowed to take root that receivers might retain half a year's receipt in hand. By the 1790s the Tax Office was instructing receivers informally as to how much they were to remit in a particular year.[77] For their part the receivers' took some pains to keep the size of this figure low; Thomas Denton, for example, sent regular gifts of six Cumberland hams to George Goodenough in the 1790s, originally 'as a small token for the many civilities shown to me by you since my appointment'.[78]

The problem of assessment and collection, and the nature of the machinery of remittance, were such as to ensure a prolonged decline in efficiency of tax collection. The receivers managed to remit 45 per cent of the 1693 assessment within six months of the first act, and most of the rest within eighteen months. But this proved exceptional, and normally during the eighteenth century less than 5 per cent was paid within six months. The bulk was remitted between six and eighteen months after the act, and, from the 1730s perhaps 20 per cent even later.[79] Return times gradually lengthened, although even by eighteenth century standards the 1725 two shilling aid created something of a record when the last payment was received in 1790. By the 1780s in Oxfordshire collection did not normally begin until two and half years tax was due.[80] The use of tried and tested methods of assessment ensured that the culprit for arrears was usually an inefficient collector. On Robert Lowther's Westmorland estate, for example, in January 1699 quarterly Land Tax was paid within three days of becoming due, but by the 1730s payments could be up to six months late.[81] In periods of financial necessity the Tax Office attempted to speed up remittances, but rather than reform the tax various ministries sidestepped the root problems, preferring to supplement the revenue with additional assessed taxes. Overall between 1693 and 1798 mean return time for each levy was 1.64 years through the country, with Cumbria slightly slower at 1.75 years.[82]

Conclusion

As conceived in 1693 the Land Tax was an attempt to tax equitably on the basis of income, to ensure that those capable of paying contributed to the war effort of William III's reign. In practice, the ideal could not be maintained in the face of administrative inefficiency and abuse. Central government accepted the reality by reverting to the old Assessment principles in 1698. At the heart of the problem was the amateur administration. Counties such as Cumberland ignored the rules from the outset, preferring to utilize customary procedures which, if they did not obey the law and were not necessarily a true reflection of any one man's worth, were accepted as representing the differences between individuals. Like Westmorland, other counties doubtless followed suit in 1698, although this is an area in which detailed local research is needed. Thus, only for five years was the Land Tax assessed on incomes, and for one hundred it was fixed as between counties, and between the larger units within them, but it was generally collected – if rather late – without much difficulty. Furthermore, in an ironic sense, the longer it survived the more popular it became. As a fixed rent charge the tax became a progressively lighter burden because of rising prices and rents. The situation arose where considerable hostility existed towards the idea of reform, and apart from occasional wartime attempts to speed up remittance, government ministers found it convenient to sidestep the question. Only when a major crisis arrived in the form of the French wars was Pitt able to introduce a professionally organized and administered income tax, and commit the antiquated Land Tax to a slow death.

NOTES

1 Many of the book's findings have stood the test of time. See Beckett, J.V. and Smith, D.K., 'The Land Tax Returns as a Source for Studying the English Economy in the Eighteenth Century', *Bulletin of the Institute of Historical Research*, volume LIV, 1981, pp. 54–61.

2 The Acts are printed in *Statutes of the Realm* until 1714, but thereafter survive only randomly. I have consulted the earlier Acts, and several later ones, from which it appears that the rules and regulations changed only slightly.

3 K(endal) R(ecord) O(ffice), WD/TE i, 22.

4 C(arlisle) RO, D/Lons/W, James Lowther to Sir John Lowther, 8 Apr. 1699.

5 Ward, W.R., *The English Land Tax in the Eighteenth Century*, Oxford, 1953, pp. 4–5, 11.

6 These details are taken from Acts printed in *Statutes of the Realm*.

7 KRO, WD/Ry 5101, Commissioners of the Treasury to Andrew Hudleston, 25 Feb. 1696–7.

8 ibid., 5236, William Fleming to Sir Daniel Fleming, 10 Mar. 1697–8.

9 CRO,/D/Lons/W, James Lowther to Sir John Lowther, 18 Mar. 1698–9. He was still worrying in 1738 when he informed his local steward that his 'one objection to the dispensing so many prints to show the greatness and increase of buildings at Whitehaven which should be considered of' was 'that it may draw an increase of taxes on the town both for the Land Tax and window lights', Lowther to John Spedding, 7 Oct. 1738.

10 KRO, WD/Ry 5119, James Bird to Sir Daniel Fleming, 9 Mar. 1696–7.
11 CRO, D/Lons/W, James Lowther to William Gilpin, 24 Jan., 12 Feb. 1707–8.
12 KRO, WD/RGL, William Brownrigg to John Moore, 2 Apr. 1772.
13 Ward, op. cit., p. 51.
14 CRO, D/Lons/W, John Spedding to Sir James Lowther, 28 Jan. 1743, Lowther to Spedding, 8 Feb. 1743.
15 1 William and Mary c.20, s.2; c.1, s.2; c.5. The first of these was for 12d. in the pound, the second for 2s. and the third for 1s. The third was specifically stated to be a supplement to the second, and in most areas the two were collected together as a 3s. rate. On the 1671 new subsidy see Chandaman, C.D., *The English Public Revenue, 1660–1688*, Oxford, 1975, pp. 149–50.
16 British Library, Harleian MSS 4226, folios 4, 45. In Cumberland £191 7s. was assessed as the 'personal' property element, just 0.05 per cent of the combined total for real and personal income. See also Chapter 12 on personal assessments.
17 CRO, D/Lec/170, John Christian to Thomas Elder, 2 Jan. 1742.
18 ibid., 8 Jan. 1759.
19 Beckett, J.V., *Landownership in Cumbria 1680–1750*, University of Lancaster unpublished PhD, 1975, pp. 73, 309; CRO, D/Pen Agents' letters, L. Herbert to Sir John Pennington, 1 Mar. 1765, 28 Sep. 1764; D/Lons/W, Estate memoranda papers, bundle 23; Durham University, Howard of Naworth, C/170/53.
20 P(ublic) RO, E/183/4, f. 37.
21 CRO, D/Lons/W, William Gilpin to Sir John Lowther, 26 Mar. 1694.
22 CRO, D/Lons/L, Land Tax 1790–1805, Thomas Denton to George Goodenough, 7 Mar. 1792.
23 Horwitz, H., ed., *The Parliamentary Diary of Narcissus Luttrell 1691–1693*, Oxford, 1972, p. 139; KRO, WD/TE iv, 173.
24 KRO, WD/Ry, box 19, 'Mr Minchell's opinion about taxing Quit Rents'; WD/Ho, box 23, 'The burgage account for nine years ended at Lady Day 1717'.
25 The following conclusions are based upon evidence from 20 manors taken at random in Cumbria, and belonging to the Earls of Egremont, Thanet and Lonsdale, the Musgrave family of Edenhall and the Wilsons of Dallam Tower.
26 CRO, D/Lec/297, 1773 General Fine. 1773 Land Tax Assessment.
27 CRO, Dalston Poor Rate Assessment 1761; D/Lons/L, Land Tax list 1761. Also Q/6/2, f. 136.
28 KRO, WD/Ho, 1790 Court book, WQR/PLT 1791.
29 Jones, G.P., 'The Decline of the Yeomanry in the Lake counties', *Transactions of the Cumberland and Westmorland Antiquarian and Archaeological Society*, new series, (CW2) volume lxi, 1961, p. 204. In Grasmere customary rents were approximately one-fifteenth of the real annual value.
30 CRO, D/Lons/W, Misc. estate papers, no. 24, Holme Cultram, John Spedding to Sir James Lowther, 24 Aug. 1744. The example is unusual in that the copyhold tenure was rarely found in the north west.
31 KRO, WD/TE, ix, 49–50.
32 Evidence from Kent suggests that there was usually a high degree of correlation between tax paid and the acreage of a holding. This suggests that while reassessment at the hundred and county level was unusual, at the parish level changing land values could be reflected in tax assessments, or that changes were not sufficient to upset the original correlation, Mills, D.R., *Lord and Peasant in Nineteenth Century Britain*, London, 1980, p. 25. See also Chapters 2 and 3 above and 10 below for discussion of reassessment and correlations.
33 Horwitz, op. cit., pp. 61–2, 311–13, 321, 340–1, 348–9, 353–5. Luttrell sat for a Cornish seat, so it is likely that he supported the Assessment principle.

34 ibid., p. 311.
35 CRO, D/Lons/W, Sir James Lowther to John Spedding, 20 Jan. 1747.
36 Hutchinson, W., *History of Cumberland*, London, 1794, volume II, p. 684. For a further example of propoganda designed to prevent a reassessment of Cumberland because of its poverty see *Gentleman's Magazine*, volume XXVI, 1766, pp. 581–2.
37 CRO, D/Lons/W, Sir James Lowther to John Spedding, 11 May 1742.
38 KRO, WD/Ry 4692, Sir Christopher Musgrave to Sir Daniel Fleming, 29 Jan. 1694; 5236, William Fleming to Sir Daniel Fleming, 10 Mar. 1697–8.
39 Charles D'Avenant, *An Essay upon Ways and Means*, London, 1695, in *Works*, ed. C. Whitworth, 1771, volume I, pp. 23,38.
40 *The Case of the Salt Duty and Land Tax offered to the Consideration of every Freeholder*, London, 1732, pp. 16–17.
41 Ward, op. cit., pp. 7–8.
42 PRO, E/360/28.
43 Levens Hall MSS, box 3/31. The total amount collected in East and West wards was not reduced in the 1690s, but the money returned was, so that each year a greater surplus accrued, which was presumably used for local expenses.
44 E/360/28.
45 KRO, WD/Ry, 5235, Sir Daniel Fleming to William Fleming, 2 Mar. 1698; 5244, William Fleming to Sir Daniel Fleming, 31 Mar. 1698.
46 PRO, Chatham Papers, 30/8/278. Ward, op. cit., p. 142.
47 On the general unwillingness to alter assessments see Beckett, J. V., 'Local Custom and the "New Taxation" in the Seventeenth and Eighteenth Centuries: the Example of Cumberland', *Northern History*, volume XII, 1976, pp. 118–19, and KRO, WD/Ry, box 82, bundle 'Sir William, 3rd bart., Window Taxes'.
48 Beckett, ibid., pp. 114–15.
49 KRO, WD/Ry, Sir Daniel: Public Office.
50 ibid., 5259, Lord Lonsdale to Sir Daniel Fleming, 3 May 1698. Beckett, J.V., 'Westmorland's "Book of Rates"', *CW2*, volume LXXVII, 1977, pp. 127–37.
51 *An Enquiry how far the Commissioners . . . Have Power to Alter the Quotes*, London, 1745.
52 Beckett, 'Local Custom', pp. 118–19; idem, *Local Taxation: National Legislation and the Problems of Enforcement*, London, 1980, p. 18. Such a conclusion must raise serious doubts about the validity of inter-county comparisons on the basis of Land Tax figures.
53 Part III, 1790, pp. 111–12. According to a correspondent of the *Gentleman's Magazine*, volume XXXVI, 1766, p. 581, nine-tenths of the land of England had been bought and sold on the assumption of fixed rates since the 1690s.
54 CRO, D/Lons/W, James Lowther to John Spedding, 2 Feb. 1727, 17 Dec. 1734.
55 ibid., Spedding to Lowther, 11 July 1744.
56 For Lowther the calculations are based on CRO, D/Lons/W, Estate memoranda papers, bundle 21, and Estate Ledger 1738–57 (figures for 1744 on a loose sheet). For Honywood, see KRO, WD/Ho, box 35, H. Holme to R. Honywood, 19 May 1746. Since many landlords in the region were not paying tax for their tenants, this may have made the *actual* rate of shillings in the pound of genuine land value artificially low.
57 KRO, WD/Ho, box 19, bound volume of rentals and dropping fines; box 23, parchment accounts 1694.
58 Levens Hall MSS, box 10.
59 Nottinghamshire RO, Portland MSS DD4P/54/105.
60 CRO, D/Lons/W, William Gilpin to Sir John Lowther, 1 June 1693, 2 July 1696, Sir James Lowther to John Spedding, 8 Jan. 1754. The Fee Farm rent clause was probably applied to copyhold property in other areas, although further research is needed to ascertain whether or not this was the case.

61 PRO, T/27/18, f. 47.
62 PRO, E/369/4.
63 KRO, WD/Ry, Sir William 1st bart., unsorted file.
64 CRO, D/Lons/L, Land Tax 1790–1805, J Sanderson to G Wheatley, 12 Nov. 1794.
65 KRO, WD/TE i, 23.
66 Ward, op. cit., pp. 86–7.
67 CRO, D/Hud/ A7, letters of Brownrigg and Hudleston.
68 CRO, D/Lons/L, Land Tax 1790–1805, letters of T. Denton to G. Goodenough, 11 Nov. 1791, 7 Mar., 5 May 1792, to Mr Graham, 19 Oct. 1790, C. Dering *et al.* to Land Tax Commissioners, 15 Nov. 1791, G. Wheatley to R. Oyes, 12 Sep. 1792, to Mr Harriman, 24 Aug. 1796, T. Harriman to G. Wheatley, 9 Nov. 1795.
69 Ward, op. cit., pp. 46–7; Western, J.R., *The English Militia in the Eighteenth Century*, London, 1965, p. 130; PRO, E/183/4; Beckett and Smith, loc. cit., p. 59.
70 PRO, T/1/564, f. 228.
71 Ward, op. cit., p. 108. This conduct money was paid to the receivers for Cumberland, Westmorland, and the Welsh counties, but unlike the normal twopence poundage it was not deductable at source.
72 PRO, E/183/1, 5a. In practice, with the conduct money this would have risen to £138 on a 4s. rate.
73 Beckett, J.V., *Coal and Tobacco: The Lowthers and the Economic Development of West Cumberland 1660–1760*, Cambridge, 1981, pp. 106–8, 116–17.
74 PRO, T/22/6, f.73. At his failure, How had £10,129 outstanding on the Land Tax; Ward, op. cit., p. 110; Binney, J.E.D., *British Public Finance and Administration 1774–1792*, Oxford, 1958, p. 57.
75 Binney, ibid., pp. 54–6; William L. Clements Library, Ann Arbor, Michigan, Marquis of Lansdowne (Shelburne) Papers, volume 166; *Commons Journal*, volume XXXVIII, 1782, p. 1113.
76 KRO, WD/RGL, William Brownrigg to John Moore, 8 June 1774; CRO, D/Lons/ Land Tax 1790–1805, G. Goodenough to T. Denton, 2 Apr. 1794.
77 ibid., 22 Nov. 1792 (and other examples); Binney, op. cit., p. 54.
78 CRO, D/Lons/ Land Tax 1790–1805, T. Denton to G. Goodenough, 10 May 1791.
79 Beckett and Smith, loc. cit., p. 56.
80 PRO, T/30/20, f. 33; Ward, op. cit., p. 139.
81 CRO, D/Lons/L, AM2, AM58. Land tax for Ravenstonedale park and mills for 1733 was paid only on March 20 1734, although this may have been exceptional because of the 1s. rate in 1732 and 1733.
82 Beckett and Smith, loc. cit., p. 56; Beckett, 'Local Custom', p. 107.

Chapter 10

The Incidence of Revaluation[1]

DONALD E. GINTER

Those who wish to use the Land Tax for historical analysis must recognize and accept a number of constraints which arise from the way in which the tax was assessed. The constraints which have normally been mentioned in the literature are those which are due to the quota system. In 1698 the government abandoned any further attempts to levy taxation on real and personal property by a poundage rate and instead imposed a quota on each county. These county quotas never varied thereafter. The county land tax quotas were in turn subdivided by local authority into quotas for each individual parish or township. These local quotas also became traditional and ossified, and in 1798 the redemption act made them permanent.[2] Thus the total amount of Land Tax which each township owed to meet the annual county quota – barring a change in the national statutory rate[3] – never altered during two and a half centuries of land tax administration. But land values did change, and quite dramatically by the later eighteenth century. Rents did not rise equally in all parts of the country, however, nor in all regions of a single county. The rental history of each township must in fact be considered as unique and to have pursued its own peculiar pattern of development. Thus by the years 1780 to 1832, when Land Tax duplicates are most generally available for analysis, the proportional distribution of township quotas no longer bore any consistent relation to the distribution of real land values. They could not do so, since the quotas had become ossified and could not respond to fluctuations in any of the factors affecting land values.[4]

In one sense, then, the Land Tax never underwent revaluation, since the quotas and thus the proportional regional distribution of the burden of the tax and its relation to current land values were never revised. And the failure to revalue by revising quotas imposes the most widely recognized constraint upon the use of the Land Tax: the tax quotas of the various parishes and townships are not equivalent departures from either rack or actual rent – or at least they are not so by the 1780s after nearly a century of differential movements in rent – and thus individual tax entries in the later returns are not comparable in their absolute values across townships.[5] One cannot select, let us say, a series of £10 tax entries in several different townships and expect them to represent equivalent land values. To some degree each tax entry, while appearing to represent the same property value, will represent holdings of quite different values, and precisely because the valuational base of the tax will have developed uniquely within each township. The lack of comparability among entries of different townships poses hazards of great seriousness for anyone wishing to undertake comparative analyses employing individual tax entries grouped by class interval. For some other and statistically more sophisticated forms of analysis the problems are surely fatal.[6]

But while no one doubts that all or most apparently equivalent tax entries in different townships represent different real property values, there persists a long standing debate over the likely magnitudes and seriousness of such differences. This debate, which centres on only one aspect of the problem of revaluation, I shall engage at more length elsewhere. Suffice it to say here that my own findings suggest that the magnitudes of differences in valuational base between townships is by the early nineteenth century far greater than any of us might have expected.[7] But in the remainder of this essay I wish to turn to an equally important aspect of the topic, and one which has not hitherto been systematically studied, namely, the incidence and nature of revaluation within individual townships. If it could be shown that the townships themselves failed to undertake continuous or at least reasonably periodic revaluations, or failed to accompany such revaluations with proportionate internal redistribution of the burden of the tax, then the Land Tax entries would indeed be perfectly useless to historians – except as examples of a most remarkably inequitable and oppressive system of local government. Internal revaluation and reassessment had to occur if the tax entries were to maintain any relation whatever to actual land values or even – given the continual parcelling off and engrossment of fields – to any real configuration of landed holdings within the community. Internal revaluation is thus an even more critical issue in estimating the reliability of the Land Tax than are those issues revolving around the consequences of the quota system.

The data base for the conclusions which follow are the valuational 'rents'[8] and tax entries reported in the Land Tax duplicates of the twenty nine townships of the wapentake of Gilling East in the North Riding of Yorkshire. Alterations in rent and tax entries were examined for each township at five yearly intevals from 1785 to 1830. Gilling East is an almost wholly agricultural wapentake lying just to the east of the Great North Road in the Vale of Mowbray, and no significant enclosures occurred within these townships during that period. The wapentake thus offers a relatively normal and undisturbed rural area for testing the incidence of revaluation, isolated from the processes of urbanization, industrialization, and enclosure where the literature has taught us to expect that revaluation might sometimes occur.

Internal revaluation and reassessment for the Land Tax may be expected to occur in one of four ways. The first mode would be a general revaluation in which every property bundle[9] in the township would be reassigned its rental value and tax assessment. Such revaluations might be undertaken by professional valuers, in which case the expense to the township would be considerable, or it might be completed by local assessors on the basis of local knowledge. Such general revaluations should produce a rise in the aggregate total of valuational rent assigned within the township. A second mode of revaluation would also be one in which the total amount of assigned rent would rise, but in this case the rise would be wholly attributable to a restricted number of properties within the township. No general revaluation or reassessment would have occurred, and the rise in total rent would be a reflection of more limited adjustments in the distribution of the burden of the tax quota. A third mode of revaluation would similarly involve only a restricted number of property bundles, but in this case the adjustments would be made without altering the aggregate total of rent assigned within the township. A fourth mode, in which all property bundles would be revised without increasing the total rental, I have found to be quite rare.

It is crucial to note that under the quota system it is irrelevant to the administration of the tax whether the total valuational level of a township rises or remains constant. If the level rises, the only administrative consequence is that the general ratio of valuational rent to tax within the township also rises, and the individual tax assessment entries will depart proportionately further from current valuational rents. Such departures, while of considerable importance for historical analysis, had no consequences for the collection of the Land Tax as such, and there was nothing in the administration of the Land Tax which should either have inhibited or encouraged the rise of valuational totals whenever revaluation occurred. Historians who are tempted to employ Land Tax 'rents' instead of tax values, however, should first determine whether total rents were rising or remaining constant in their townships. Land Tax rent should not be construed as actual rents in any case and must be assumed to depart from actual and rack rents to some degree. But Land Tax rents in townships with constant totals should depart from current actual and rack rent values to a greater degree than rents in other townships where totals vary. Such departures introduce further elements of incomparability into intertownship analyses when rents are employed.

The evidence from Gilling East suggests that internal revaluation was usually an intermittant but an almost universal process during the later eighteenth and early nineteenth centuries. General revaluations, in which the total rent rises and all properties are at risk, is a readily encountered but comparatively unusual phenomenon. It is the second mode of revaluation, in which total rent is allowed to rise while only a few properties are affected, which is more commonly found within the wapentake. Only eight of the twenty nine townships failed to alter their valuational rent totals significantly during the half century under observation. The total rent to total tax ratios of some of those remaining eight townships, by approaching the wapentake mean, suggest that they too had experienced substantial revaluation during the years prior to 1785.

In ten of the townships the valuational totals increased by more than thirty percent between 1785 and 1830. In the wapentake as a whole the increase following 1801 (when the series becomes fuller) was almost twenty-two percent, with virtually all of that increase (20.8%) occurring by 1815. By the end of the Napoleonic wars overall growth in total rental values had virtually ceased in the wapentake as a whole. The pattern of valuational change is entirely plausible in the shape of its curve, then. But the magnitudes of change are all wrong. Evidence at the national level suggests that actual rents on large estates increased during the war years by ninety to one hundred percent, falling off between 1815 and 1835 by ten to fifteen percent.[10] The records of some of the larger North Riding estates similarly suggest that the magnitude of rise in valuational rents in that region during the war years was substantially below that of actual rents. If valuational rents were to any degree responding to movements in actual rents, as they appear to have been, the response was not a simple one. While it may be reasonable to conclude that revaluation for tax was widespread and was to some degree a response to changing land market values, it would clearly be unwise to estimate the magnitude of change in either series from the other.

The evidence from Gilling East also makes it clear that measurements of change in total valuational rents will substantially underestimate the incidence of revaluation. The third mode of internal revaluation, in which the values for a limited number of property bundles are altered without adjusting the total township rental, was common to all of the townships of the wapentake, even to those which on other occasions adjusted their total rentals upward or downward. Revaluations of this type were almost invariably in response to transactions in the land market. Most Land Tax duplicates record some small number of alterations in its property bundles almost annually. Tenants come and go, giving occasion perhaps to adjustments in actual rents. Fields are transferred among tenants or are purchased by other proprietors, causing the total number of property bundles to fluctuate. Entire properties are sold. Cottages are built or torn down, thus altering the number of tax units. It should be remembered that under the quota system any addition or diminution in tax units must add to or diminish the tax burden of the remainder of the township. If the township chooses not to alter the valuational total, ripples of alterations may be expected throughout the township in both rent and tax entries. Minor revaluations of this third mode were virtually incessant throughout the wapentake, but more especially in those townships where the land was held by large numbers of proprietors or tenants and the land market was commensurately more active.

Revaluation seems in fact to be more clearly attributable to activity in the land market than to any other factor; and indeed it is difficult to imagine how any society could either endure or operate a tax system which failed to reflect such propertied transactions. Other factors seem also to have been at work, however. The movements in valuational rent do seem to have mirrored movements in real rents, in direction if not in magnitude. But while secular trends in real rent may in broad terms have been influential, a more strict interpretation should perhaps view commodity prices as a constraint on movements in valuations, which were more directly being driven by activity in the land market and by pressures from other local rates.

Direct evidence for the relationship between Land Tax valuations and those of other rates is difficult to find, but there is little doubt that throughout the country a large proportion of parishes and townships employed a common valuation in assessing the Land Tax and such local rates as the poor and constable's rate. Many townships in the industrial West Riding collected the Land Tax and constable's rate simultaneously and listed only the aggregate of the two assessments on the Land Tax duplicates. In other townships there is a clear statistical correlation between the valuational totals for the Land Tax and the poor rate, and Eden's *State of the Poor* offers abundant evidence that these two and other taxes share valuational bases in many parishes throughout the countryside.[11] Moreover, most townships listing rent in the Land Tax duplicates report it after 1798 for redeemed as well as unredeemed properties, and the redeemed rentals are revalued as well as the unredeemed. Since the redeemed tax entries had become permanently frozen by the very act of having them redeemed, there is no administrative purpose serviceable to the Land Tax in either recording or in revising the rentals of redeemed entries. The widespread recording and revision of redeemed rent entries can only be explained if the process of valuation for the Land Tax is itself part of a larger process of valuation for one or more local rates. If this hypothesis is correct, then Land Tax revaluations, and in particular the propensity to raise and lower the total valuation assigned to a township, must have been to some degree impelled by pressures from other forms of taxation than the Land Tax itself. A rise in valuational total would not result in an increase in the total Land Tax raised, because of the quota system. But if it were necessary to increase the amount to be raised for the poor rate, for example, then it would indeed be useful to permit the valuational total for the township to rise. Not that the total must rise to meet the full deficiency in the rate, since the local poundage rate can also be adjusted upward. Local patterns suggest that both of these mechanisms were being interactively employed in revaluations, and I suspect quite often to solve arithmetic complexities in computing assessments.[12]

Certainly the administration of the Land Tax looks very odd to the modern observer. The more closely one examines the administration of the tax, the more it appears a crazy quilt of inequalities and anomolies, and particularly in the distribution of its burden among townships and regions. Yet this most inequitable of taxes remained a popular bulwark of traditional government, for reasons which are too complex to explain here. Something should be said about larger pressures for revision, however. None of the major fiscal events of the later eighteenth and early nineteenth centuries made a significant impact on the distribution of the burden of the tax or on the process of revaluation. The incidence of revaluation increased only marginally in Gilling East during the decade following redemption. The publication of township valuations for the 1815 property tax, which were almost uniformly higher than Land Tax valuations throughout the North Riding, caused no embarrassment among local assessors of the Land Tax and no flurry of revaluations – on the contrary, the incidence of revaluation slackened at that point. When in 1824 the North Riding quarter sessions required that each overseer revalue his township so that the county rate quotas might be redistributed, they were vexed to find that the valuations returned were generally higher than the Land Tax but still lower than the valuations for the 1814 property tax; and, even worse, the new valuations departed from the property tax in a disproportionate manner. The justices, after a year's efforts, were unable to secure a genuinely equitable system of new county rate valuations, and they gave up trying. They simply imposed the proportions of the property tax.[13] All of this effort and fuss made not the slightest impact on the incidence of Land Tax revaluation. Nor was revaluation in any way a peculiar feature of the war years. It is clear from prewar examples, as well as from the rent to tax ratios found throughout the riding, that revaluation, and particularly in the third mode, was an almost continuous and intractable – and unflappable – feature of the local administration of the Land Tax. Movements in rent should not be viewed as causing movements in valuation. The extent and direction of revaluation – and of revisions in rent – were substantially determined by movements in commodity prices. But the process of revaluation had its own inner dynamic, centring on the land market and local rates.

All of this is of course very good news to those of us who wish to use the Land Tax for historical analysis. Tax entries within townships were indeed being regularly revised and, to some degree, in a manner reflective of transactions in the land market. But is this all of the news? Unfortunately it is not. Lack of comparability between townships will continue to impose serious constraints on the use of the tax, and those constraints arise from incompatabilities of greater magnitudes than any of us had previously realized. But there are other serious deficiencies which can now be identified internally within the returns of each individual township. Although reassessment may regularly occur, it may not necessarily result in an equitable distribution of the tax burden within the township. Even more importantly, the examination of reassessment procedures has revealed new problems of extraordinary gravity for redeemed entries. In short, the problems of the Land Tax are far more complex than earlier debates have suggested. These complexities are associated with the valuational basis of the tax, a topic which has been strangely neglected and which I am presently treating at greater length elsewhere.

NOTES

1 The author is currently completing a larger study of the valuational basis of the Land Tax and the local and regional distributions of its burden in the later eighteenth and early nineteenth centuries. The chapter which follows briefly reports conclusions reached on one aspect of that topic, revaluation.

2 The early history of the Land Tax is most fully treated in Ward, W.R., *The English Land Tax in the Eighteenth Century* London, 1953. An excellent account for the later eighteenth century may be found in Binney, J.E.D., *British Public Finance and Administration 1774–92* Oxford, 1958, pp. 49–60.

3 Alterations did occur in the national statutory rate during the eighteenth century, and such alterations changed the quotas. For example, a 4s. rate would double quotas owed under a 2s. rate. But such alterations in the statutory rate do not constitute revaluation, since the proportional distributions of the burden of the tax were not thereby altered among townships or regions. See chapter 11, footnote 12 for a table of rates.

4 The quotas might have maintained a consistent relation to the distribution of land values if one could believe fluctuations in land values varied consistently across space and time. But such consistency in fluctuation did not occur on a large national or regional scale, and is unlikely to have occured even on a small or local scale. Certainly evidence for inconsistent patterns of fluctuation is easy to find.

5 Beckett, J.V., 'Local Custom and the "New Taxation" in the Seventeenth and Eighteenth Centuries: the example of Cumberland', *Northern History*, vol. XII, 1976, pp. 105–126 has shown that in at least one county the 1698 parish quotas were merely those compounded for purveyance in 1617. Much more work needs to be done on the origins and equitability of the 1698 quotas.

6 Studies of the impact of enclosure and of the disappearance of the small landowner have commonly employed class intervals across townships, although usually by first coverting

tax values to acreage equivalents. Soltow, L., 'Wealth Distribution in England and Wales in 1798' *Economic History Review*, vol. XXXIV, 1981, pp. 60–70 has attempted a statistically more sophisticated use of the Land Tax values by computing gini coefficients of wealth inequality. For criticisms of that attempt by myself and Wilson, G.J., and for Soltow's reply, see *EcHR*, second series, vol. XXXV, 1982, pp. 416–433.

7 I noted in my reply to Soltow that in the North Riding ratios of total valuational rent (as reported in the Land Tax duplicates) to total tax per township varied from the statutory ratio of 5:1 to as high as 80:1. Since writing that reply I have found ratios many times higher than 80:1.

8 For the years 1826 to 1832 'rents' are commonly reported on the Land Tax duplicates throughout the country. In some counties they are widely and regularly reported from the 1780s. In most counties they appear only rarely before 1826, however. In the North Riding they appear irregularly before that date in only a scattering of townships, except in the wapentake of Gilling East were the level of reporting rents is unusually full from an early date. These 'rents' must not be construed as actual rents. They should be strictly viewed as the valuational basis for the individual tax assessment, and they must be assumed to depart to some degree from both actual and rack rents unless direct evidence proves the contrary. It can be shown that Land Tax rents generally fall below contemporary valuations for other purposes. One should therefore be particularly careful not to assume that Land Tax ratios of rent to tax reveal actual burdens of the tax. By the later eighteenth century actual burdens should in general be considerably lighter than such ratios indicate, and to different degrees within each township. Ratios of 5:1 should be viewed with peculiar suspicion. They almost certainly result from a long standing failure to increase the valuational total of the township – although the proportional contributions to that total by individual properties may have changed.

9 A great deal of confusion and some error has been caused by misinterpretations of the nature of line entries in the Land Tax duplicates. Each proprietor entry, and even each tenant entry, should not be characterized as 'a property' and most certainly not as 'a farm.' The first term is misleading in that discontiguous agricultural holdings and multiple cottages are often lumped together in a single line. Portions of the holdings assigned to a single line may be split off in subsequent years, suggesting that to some degree the properties assigned to that line were not a single unit. Nor are the line entries necessarily uniform in character. Some are merely land, others are land and cottages, while still others are only one or more cottages. Returns after 1826, when the nature of the property is specified, make it clear that many line entries with moderate to small tax values are silently lumping together more than one cottage. Tithes and mines are also incorporated into the returns, often without designation as such. Customs and excise officer salaries are commonly found, as are taxes on stock in trade in many urban centers, though all of these are normally identified as such. For all of these reasons I prefer the term 'property bundle' when designating line entries in the duplicates.

10 Chambers, J.D., and Mingay, G.E., *The Agricultural Revolution 1750–1880*, London, 1966, pp. 112, 118, 167.

11 The valuational basis for the poor rate in 1803 can be calculated from *British Parliamentary Papers*, 1818, volume XIX, ff. 235; Eden, F.M., *The State of the Poor*, London, 1797, in 3 volumes. [See also chapter 11 below, in the discussion of Cambridgeshire LTAs. It is also worth noting that the series for many Cambridge parishes ran on long past the usual final date of 1832, with apparently full sets of names, etc. This practice may have facilitated rates collections as well as the collecting of Land Tax from non-exonerated properties. (Editors)]

12 Revenue from local rates was also frequently increased by simply collecting multiples of a fixed rate. This third mechanism need not in any given year entail any alteration in valuation or local poundage rate, although over the long run valuations had to be

altered for the reasons given above. This mechanism could substantially relieve pressures to revalue for periods of time in those townships where it was employed, to the extent that the land market was stable.

13 North Yorkshire County Record Office, North Riding Quarter Sessions Special Order Book, 1823–5 passim, QSM; idem., County Rate Valuation Returns, 1824–5, QFR 1/1–18.

Chapter 11

Early Land Tax Assessments Explored (1) Rutland, Cambridgeshire, and Lincolnshire

DENNIS MILLS

Introduction

This chapter,[1] together with the following one and the appendix, represents an attempt to open up the use of those Land Tax Assessments which survive from the period between the inception of the tax in 1692 and the beginning, in 1780, of the Quarter Sessions collections of Assessments. The appendix shows that about 5,000 parishes possess at least one Assessment from this period. It is also clear that these documents are more plentiful for years at either end of the period 1692–1779. Given the thinning out in the mid-eighteenth century, attention has been concentrated in both chapters on the earliest returns available in the five counties studied.

This concentration of effort has the advantage that it allows use to be made of Assessments which are much more likely to represent true rental values than do later Assessments, owing to the geenral absence of revaluation of properties. More important, a study concentrating on the years around 1700 opens up the possibility of throwing some light on the evolution of landownership structures which have been observed in detail from the second half of the eighteenth century, when enclosure awards, Assessments and tithe awards provide plentiful data. There are two distinct levels of analysis, one focussing on individual landowners, the other on the landownership structures of whole parishes or townships.

In the latter respect there is an extensive literature which has used the open-closed model of rural social and landownership structures during the period circa 1780 to circa 1914. Many writers of that period, as well as later historians, distinguished between parishes owned by a very small number of proprietors (close, or clsoed) and those in which property was much divided (open parishes). The context of discussion frequently revolved around problems of poor law administration since the tightly controlled closed parishes were able to draw labour from neighbouring villages without responsibility for seasonal unemployment, ill health and the like. As it is generally agreed that the model has greater applicability in the corn growing areas of eastern and southern England and in areas of declining industrial employment, it has particular significance for the areas discussed in these two chapters.

A simple dichotomy between open and closed parishes is however inadequate on its own. It should be amplified by a careful consideration of the long continuum of parochial variability which stretched in some counties from the single owner in some parishes to over 100 owners per parish in others and from averages of over 1,000 acres per owner down to less than twenty acres. In particular it is necessary to distinguish among closed parishes between those owned by an absentee and those in which the principal proprietor resided (estate villages). Among open parishes some distinction is also desirable between the divided and the much subdivided (peasant) parishes. The use of early Assessments should help historians to examine the evolution of the pattern here described in outline and it is of some interest that the first use of the term 'close parish' appears in a text thought to date before 1690 and reissued in 1753.[2]

Any analysis which focusses on individual owners should be related to the debate on the supposed disappearance of the small landowner. The conclusion of Johnson, who was one of the first historians to make use of Land Tax Assessments, including a few for the period before 1780, was 'that the closing years of the seventeenth century and the first years of the eighteenth century were fatal to the small owner.'[3] Since then, only the work of Holderness[4] has made significant use of early Assessments in order to check and amplify Johnson's very general discussion. It is therefore appropriate that Holderness's area of study (south-east Lindsey, Lincolnshire) should be included among the five areas selected for use in these two chapters, which have similar basic aims.

In addition to a geographical division of labour, the two chapters have other distinctive objectives. The present chapter tackles the basic problem which applies to most early Assessments – that of distinguishing between proprietors and occupiers. It also offers a possible basis for comparative analysis. Consequently actual analysis is relatively modest given the large territory studied. The next chapter is able to take the technical discussion further by looking at such problems as those presented by personal estates, industrial property, and papists. It does this within a smaller geographical area and the analysis goes more deeply than this chapter, concerning itself with farms as well as estates, and leads on to some of the ways in which the Assessments can and should be used in conjunction with other documents.

Table 1

Ashwell, Rutland, Land Tax Duplicate for 1712

Spelling as in the original

Assessors: Jno. Cole and Jno. Pawlet

	Yearly payments		
	£	s	d
The Lands of Bart Burton Esqr.	155	10	01
Mr Alcock	006	12	02
Mr Mason	026	12	01
Doctor Willson	021	02	09
Mr Blake	002	19	04
Mr Rose	003	10	11
Mr Storgis	001	00	08
	217	08	00

Source: Leicestershire Record Office, Finch MSS, DG 7/4/1

(i) *Rutland*

The Rutland Tax Assessments of 1712, covering all fifty five 'land tax'[5] parishes, survive in a single document in the Finch Manuscripts.[6] The Finches were large landowners in Rutland, having a seat at Burley Hall, and held the earldom of Nottingham. Internal evidence suggests that the document owes its survival at least partly to its use of reference purposes up to 1808.[7] Although the 1712 text in the document was written by only one scribe, he was clearly dependent on parochial assessors who did not keep to a uniform format. Nevertheless, there were only two main formats in use, one represented here by the Ashwell duplicate, the other by the Market Overton duplicate. It will be argued that in the first format, followed in forty four duplicates, mainly owners' names appear, while in the second format, followed in eleven duplicates, there is definitely a mixture of both owners' and tenants' names, although there is still but one single column of taxpayers.

The Ashwell duplicate (Table 1) plays an important part in supporting the assertion that, except where there is evidence to the contrary, one should assume the names of taxpayers in these early Assessments are those of the owners. In a parish of 1,835 acres there were only seven taxpayers and the smallest payment was well above the level of four shillings commonly charged on the smallest property units in Rutland, probably cottages with a little land. The styles of address indicate that all seven taxpayersheld at least the status of minor gentry, perhaps including some yeomen farmers, but excluding tenantry, for whom the style 'Jno. Cole' was probably reserved. The internal evidence of the Ashwell document, therefore, points to the strong probability that all the taxpayers were proprietors.

The Market Overton format will be considered next, before a return is made to the Assessments set out like the Ashwell duplicate. The Market Overton duplicate was selected to represent the eleven documents which certainly include tenants' names, because itcontains the most unambiguous evidence that some of the taxpayers' names were those of tenants. The extract in Table 2 shows the seven sets of payments bracketed together by the assessor, indicating the responsibility of one taxpayer for each set. For example, in the first set Mr Nix paid on the three properties he occupied, the first belonging to Mr Wingfield, the second to Mr Roberts and the third to himself. The assessor clearly thought that it was important to distinguish the properties by means of identifying the owners. Other duplicates in this group of eleven also contain the occasional bracket, but more common is the format used by the Bisbrooke assessor when he indicated John Vine's responsibility for the tax on three properties:

	Quarterly payments		
	£	s.	d.
Jon. Vine his freehold		9	9
The Lord's land		8	8
Yelsmore		3	6
John Cant	1	10	4

First we have Vine's owner-occupied land, followed by rented land in two parcels, one identified by its owner, the other by a topographical name, followed again by an entry for the next taxpayer.

The contrast between the two Rutland formats, as illustrated in Tables 1 and 2 will now be evident. The status of the documents set out in the Ashwell format can also be appreciated by comparing them with early Assessments from other parts of the country. The Kent and Sussex documents selected for use in the next chapter are set out like late eighteenth century Assessments, with separate columns for occupiers and proprietors. Some of the Lincolnshire Assessments discussed in section iii of this chapter contain unambiguous headings such as 'Lord Monson's

Table 2

Extract from Market Overton Land Tax Duplicate for 1712

Spelling as in the original

	Yearly payments		
	£	s	d
Mr Nix pt. of Mr Wingfield's	08	00	00
And pt. of Mr Roberts	03	08	00
Mr Will: Nix	05	16	00
Jno. Christian	00	12	00
pt. of Mr Wingfield's	01	00	00
pt. of Mr Roberts	02	00	00
Will: Pawlett	00	16	00
pt. of Mr Wingfield's	02	16	00
pt. of Mr Roberts	01	12	00
Edwd. Ireland	02	04	00
Jno. Hardy	02	04	00
William Brownsworth	01	12	00
for Jno. Martin	00	08	00
Tho: Walker	00	08	00
pt. of Mr Nicks	00	13	00
Widow Draper	00	12	00
pt. of Mr Wingfield's	00	14	00

Source: as for Table 1

tenants' and/or make use of a format similar to many of the single entries like the following examples taken from a Cambridgeshire Assessment discussed in the next section:

James Maddy for his Landlord's
Ambrose Koe for Mr Crane's.

Perhaps more than any other evidence mentioned here, these two lines support the view that contemporaries themselves often regarded tenants as paying on behalf of the owners. It was the real estate which attracted the tax, not the activities of the occupiers upon that property (except where specifically levied on stocks of goods). A number of features of these early Assessments, therefore, lead up to the assertion that historians should, for the time being at least, regard the names of taxpayers as those of owners, unless there is evidence to the contrary. It is essential, both to settle the general argument and in order to take full advantage of these documents, that they should be used in conjunction with other documents which offer possibilities of nominal linkage and the unambiguous identification of owners and occupiers.

Nevertheless, it is significant that an analysis of the forty four Assessments of the Ashwell type, which are asserted to contain only owners' names, produces a distribution of tax which is broadly consistent with that assertion, and hardly credible if one assumed that all the names were those of occupiers. Table 3 gives a good general impression of the parochial differences which summarise the distribution of tax. In ten parishes there were less than ten taxpayers, in fifteen there were 12–25, in a further fifteen there were 26–50, while in the remaining four parishes there were between sixty and 130 taxpayers. On the reasonable assumption that most of these taxpayers were owners, the distribution seen in Table 3 is broadly similar to that obtained from the Leicestershire Assessments of 1780–1832.[8]

Variations in the mean figures of tax paid were also considerable, despite the fact that this calculation eliminates variations which are the result of differences in parish size. This problem is also confronted in column 4, which gives mean acreages per taxpayer. The situation at Burley was exceptional, the Finches and the Church sharing over 3,000 acres. Leaving Burley on one side along with the market town of Uppingham, there was still a ratio of 1:34 between the most subdivided parish (Barleythorpe, mean acreage per taxpayer = 19) and the most concentrated parish (Tickencote, mean acreage = 647). The figures in column 4 are again broadly comparable with Leicestershire in 1832,[9] but with a significant tendency towards higher average acreages per owner (taxpayer) in Rutland. In a county well known for its large estates and lost

Table 3

Rutland: analysis of 44 Assessments of 1712 where names of taxpayers are assumed to correspond to owners

Name of 'Land Tax' parish	Taxpayers Number	Mean tax £	s	Mean acreage*
Ashwell	7	31	1	262
Ayston	24	2	2	38
Barleythorpe	66	1	0	19
Barrow	16	3	17	64
Barrowden	50	2	4	36
Brooke	21	4	19	69
Burley	2	126	0	1,526
Caldecott	40	2	0	29
Casterton, Great	21	7	12	110
Casterton, Little and Tolethorpe	19	2	10	65
Clipsham	26	3	8	62
Cottesmore	27	4	3	93
Egleton	14	2	17	66
Glaston	40	2	9	29
Greetham	37	2	12	83
Gunthorp	5	10	0	95
Hambleton	16	11	6	179
Langham	70	3	2	42
Leigh Forest	44	4	10	54
Luffenham, North	25	4	13	81
Luffenham, South	19	4	15	76
Lyndon	6	16	13	152
Manton	30	2	6	39
Martinsthorpe	2	35	0	27
Morcott	45	1	13	30
Normanton	3	12	10	240
Pickworth	18	6	9	138
Pilton	6	6	3	58
Preston	33	9	11	37
Ridlington	36	4	8	58
Seaton	40	3	8	36
Stoke Dry	15	9	2	66
Stretton	9	9	3	220
Teigh	27	4	13	48
Thistleton	27	1	12	51
Thorpe	21	3	0	33
Tickencote	2	22	10	647
Tinwell and Ingthorpe	24	2	16	71
Tixover	7	6	14	120
Uppingham	130	1	0	9
Weston, Edith	19	3	10	98
Whissendine	90	2	2	49
Whitwell	14	4	0	45
Wing	37	1	15	30

*Mean acreage has been calculated by dividing the parish acreage by the number of taxpayers, on the assumption that parish acreages did not change between 1712 and the end of the nineteenth century. Acreages from the Victoria History of the County of Rutland, vol II, 1935, pp. 231-2.

Source: as for Table 1.

villages this is unsurprising, but the value of the 1712 Assessments is that this general impression of great variations between neighbouring parishes is based on a single source at a single date. The early Assessments can, therefore, be seen as potentially an important supplement to the estate papers and the relatively sketchy records of enclosures, on which so much history of landownership has been written for this period. They are one of the very few means of obtaining something approaching a comprehensive assessment of great and small landowners alike.

(ii) *Cambridgeshire*

Of the four Cambridgeshire parishes with early Assessments, Comberton and Meldreth have been chosen for discussion because they possess documents which make a more consistent distinction between owners and occupiers than the other two, Linton and Orwell. In all four cases the Assessments have survived in parochial records,[10] thus making it possible to study the relationship between the two kinds of document. Discussion here is, however, almost wholly directed at an analysis of landownership at the level of the individual owner.

Table 4

Cambridgeshire: Two Long Term Comparisons of Landownership Structure

		COMBERTON				MELDRETH			
		1707		1829		1699		1815	
Size group	Tax bracket	No. of owners	% tax paid	No. of owners	% tax paid	No. of owners	% tax paid	No. of owners	% tax paid
10	£20+	2	40.3	2	38.4	3	37.5	3	35.1
9	£10+	2	18.0	2	17.3	4	26.7	4	23.7
8	£8+	1	6.7	1	5.9			2	7.6
7	£5+	4	18.4	4	19.9	4	10.7	4	10.6
6	£4+					2	3.7	1	1.9
5	£2+	4	6.9	5	9.5	6	8.0	11	13.3
4	£1+	6	6.5	5	5.4	11	6.6	7	4.0
3	10s+	5	2.4	5	2.3	13	3.9	7	2.2
2	4s+	4	0.8	5	1.3	23	2.9	10	1.5
1	under 4s			1	0.1	2	0.1	1	0.04
	TOTALS	28	100.0	30	100.1	68	100.1	50	99.94

Note: This table is standardised on a tax rate of four shillings in the pound; to obtain rentals multiply the tax brackets by five. It is also uniform with Table 5 below, and the size groups and tax brackets correspond to those used by Grover in Tables 3-6 in the next chapter.

Sources: Cambridgeshire Record Office, for Comberton P47/18/2 and Q/RPL3; for Meldreth R78/29 and Z94/0121

The analysis shown in Table 4 is based on the same size groups of owners as used by Davies in the 1920s.[11] These have been used partly as a means of making comparisons, but when comparisons are made between parishes (as opposed to intra-parochial comparisons at different dates), it is important to recognise that Land Tax rates were effectively different in different parts of the country, while rentals also varied considerably. The main reason for adopting Davies' system is that with ten size groups it makes finer distinctions than any later system of analysis. It is always possible to bracket size groups together to obtain a more generalised picture, as is done below, but without a large number of groups more detailed analysis is impossible.

In principle it is also convenient and desirable to work with rentals rather than tax payments, since rentals eliminate problems arising from variations in Land Tax rates,[12] and allow direct comparison with other documents giving rents. In the case of Comberton, however, the 1707 Assessment gives no rentals while that of 1829 gives rentals which do not bear a consistent relationship to the amounts of tax paid. Consequently, Table 4 has been set out with levels of tax paid at the frequently used rate of four shillings in the pound, which applied in 1707 and 1829. To compare this table with a set of rentals would only involve multiplying each bracket by a factor of five.

At Meldreth, however, the rentals provide the only clear common denominator, because not only were the rates of tax different in the two years, but also in 1699 the assessor did not quite keep to the standard rate of three shillings in the pound which was levied in that year. Indeed the document is headed with the phrase 'the Assessment upon the parish of Meldreth for the raising the sum 187.16.9.3 in one year.' (This figure is taken to be £187.16.9¾d). The need to raise this quota was probably more important to the assessor than the official rate and there is strong internal evidence that he made direct use of the previous year's parish rate to save himself time and trouble, both documents being in the same hand.

At Comberton the 1707 document is the only early Assessment, while at Meldreth the 1699 document is the earliest of a series. These are compared in each case with the earliest Assessment available after 1780 in the Quarter Sessions collection. The results in Table 4 can now be discussed. At Comberton there was very little difference between the structure of landownership at the two dates. If the possibility of significant fluctuations between 1707 and 1829 is ignored, the Comberton data support Johnson's assertion. As early as 1707 the 1,954 acres[13] were concentrated in twenty eight pairs of hands, giving a mean of 69.8 acres, a figure well up the continuum seen in Rutland in 1712 (Table 3). The top four owners controlled over half the property, but with the biggest owner paying only twenty per cent of the tax, Comberton could hardly be classified as a closed parish.

At Meldreth the situation was different in two major respects; this was a much more open parish than Comberton and the eighteenth century did witness significant change, though its precise nature and timing are left uncertain by the gap of 130 years between documents. In 1699 there were sixty eight owners on 2,000 acres, a mean of only 29.4 acres and a figure comparable with those for the category of much sub-divided or peasant parishes in Leicestershire in 1832.[14] Even here the seven top owners paid 64.17 per cent of tax in 1699 and 58.79 per cent in 1815, but they did not share in the consolidation between the two dates, which occurred at lower levels. There were eighteen (26.4 per cent) fewer owners in 1815 than in 1699, all of them disappearing from the four groups which paid less than £2 each in tax (rentals below £10). Most of their property had been absorbed by owners of properties in the next (fifth) group, who nearly doubled in both their number and the amount of tax paid. In terms of capitalist agriculture very little had happened, but in a period of rapidly rising population the chances of owning a cottage and a modest few acres had receded considerably.

(iii) *Lincolnshire*

For the Candleshoe wapentake we have available the earliest set of Lincolnshire Land Tax Assessments, with varying survival rates between 1695 and 1747. The twenty three parishes stretch from the lower slopes of the Wolds north of Spilsby across the Marsh as far as the coast at Wainfleet, Skegness, and Ingoldmells. Like those in Rutland, the Assessments are contained in private records, in this case those of the Massingberd family whose Gunby Hall residence is situated in Candleshoe. Their Lindsey Deposit[15] shows that they had been connected with local administration since before 1600, one of the consequences being that these Assessments are closely associated with returns relating to the poll tax, window (houses) tax, and the taxes on births, burials, bachelors, and widows. Taken in conjunction with other records, the Lindsey Deposit has considerable potential for studies of late seventeenth century taxation, of the distribution of wealth, and of socio-demographic structure.

Attention is here concentrated on six parishes possessing some of the most legible and unambiguous Assessments, all for the year 1709, which are compared in Table 5 with those for 1780. Driby, a Wold parish was already completely owned by squire and church in 1709, but in the other five parishes there was a fall in the total numbers of owners of almost exactly forty per cent, from 242 in 1709 to 146 in 1780. None of these parishes was disturbed by parliamentary enclosure between the two dates.[16]

Table 5

Candleshoe Wapentake, Lincolnshire: Six Comparisons, 1709-1780

		ASHBY-by-PARTNEY				BRATOFT			
		1709		1780		1709		1780	
Size group	Tax bracket	No. of owners	% tax paid	No. of owners	% tax paid	No. of owners	% tax paid	No. of owners	% tax paid
10	£20+			1	43.3	1	26.0	1	34.0
9	£10+	1	30.7	1	24.6				
8	£8+					2	21.2		
7	£5+	4	49.9	1	12.2			3	24.6
6	£4+	1	8.4	2	16.6	2	10.8	2	11.1
5	£2+	1	5.9			6	18.6	4	15.2
4	£1+	1	3.5	1	2.8	6	10.6	5	8.2
3	10s+	1	1.2			8	6.8	5	3.9
2	4s+	1	0.4	1	0.4	15	6.0	8	3.0
1	under 4s (none)								
	TOTALS	10	100.0	7	99.9	40	100.0	28	100.0

		CROFT				DRIBY			
		1709		1780		1709		1780	
Size group	Tax bracket	No. of owners	% tax paid	No. of owners	% tax paid	No. of owners	% tax paid	No. of owners	% tax paid
10	£20+	5	54.8	4	81.8	1	86.7	1	89.6
9	£10+	8	19.0	1	2.1				
8	£8+	3	4.5	2	2.7				
7	£5+	7	7.1	4	4.0				
6	£4+	3	2.2	4	3.1	1	13.3		
5	£2+	19	8.4	9	3.7			1	10.4
4	£1+	13	3.2	9	2.2				
3	10s+	4	0.5	3	0.4				
2	4s+	5	0.3	2	0.1				
1	under 4s (none)								
	TOTALS	67	100.0	38	100.0	2	100.0	2	100.0

		FIRSBY				WAINFLEET			
		1709		1780		1709		1780	
Size group	Tax bracket	No. of owners	% tax paid	No. of owners	% tax paid	No. of owners	% tax paid	No. of owners	% tax paid
10	£20+					3	30.2	4	69.9
9	£10+			1	39.8	4	16.0	1	5.0
8	£8+					6	14.6	1	2.3
7	£5+	1	11.3			8	12.8	5	9.1
6	£4+	1	9.0	2	18.4	6	7.1		
5	£2+	8	53.0	3	16.0	13	9.3	6	4.8
4	£1+	6	18.3	7	20.4	15	5.5	12	4.8
3	10s+	2	3.2	3	4.2	11	2.1	15	3.0
2	4s+	7	5.2	2	1.3	32	2.4	11	1.0
1	under 4s					2	0.1		
	TOTALS	25	100.0	18	100.1	100	100.1	55	99.9

Note: see under Table 4 for further explanation

Source: Lincolnshire Archives Office, Lindsey Deposit 35/2

Here, then, is evidence to challenge Johnson's conclusion mentioned above about change in the eighteenth century, on a parallel with the case of Meldreth in Cambridgeshire. Fortunately the work of Holderness makes it possible to draw stronger inferences than would be possible from Table 5 alone.[17]

Although there was a common downward trend in the numbers of owners in these parishes, other circumstances varied considerably. Ashby-by-Partney, situated in the Lymn valley just below the Wold slopes was a parish of 1,026 acres and a population of 120 in 1801. The ten Ashby proprietors in 1709 owned about 120 acres each, but the Assessment shows that this was concentrated in the hands of the five largest owners who paid eighty per cent of the tax. In 1780 the number of owners had gone down to seven and the concentration had increased to eighty per cent of the tax paid by the top three owners, the lower groups being less affected by agglomeration. In the mid-nineteenth century Ashby could be described as an absentee landlords' parish.[18]

Bratoft, in the inner Marsh, contained 1,833 acres and a population of 131 in 1801, but was much more divided in terms of landownership than Ashby, having forty owners with an average of 45.8 acres in 1709, the top three just failing to reach fifty per cent of the Assessment. The loss of twelve owners by 1780 was confined to groups paying less than £4 tax, the gain being made by the topmost owner whose share increased from twenty six to thirty four per cent. In the seventeenth century the Massingberds had had a seat at Bratoft, but in the nineteenth century one could probably have described it as a divided parish and there was no gentleman of any kind in residence in 1856.

Croft, in the outer Marsh, had a population in 1801 of 379 and a late nineteenth century acreage of 5,539. However, it had gained land by reclamation in the eighteenth century, so the average acreage of seventy acres for its sixty seven owners of 1709 is a rough estimate, but is good enough to show that a larger parish could contain both large and small owners more easily than a smaller one. Thus, although over half of the tax was paid by the five top owners in 1709 and over eighty per cent by the four top men in 1780, Croft could be described as a divided parish in terms of landownership differentials at both dates. In the band of tax from £1 to £4, representing rentals of £5 to £20, there were thirty two owners in 1709 and eighteen even in 1780.

Driby was a Wold parish of 1,370 acres and a population in 1801 of only sixty six. It was bought from Sir John Bolles by the Massingberds in 1714 and was enclosed by them privately in 1780. The latter event possibly explains the slightly different tax responsibilities of the church and absentee landlord at the later date.[19]

Firsby, in the inner Marsh, again demonstrates the drift of property from the medium and smallest owners towards the largest landowner, who paid nearly forty per cent of the tax in 1780, compared with a little over ten per cent in 1709. The Group 5 owners, paying between £2 and £4 fell from eight paying over fifty per cent of the tax to three paying sixteen per cent. Nevertheless, at the later date Firsby could still be described as a divided parish, with eighteen owners on 1,107 acres and an 1801 population of 117.

Our last example is Wainfleet, a port and market town of declining fortunes, but with the large acreage of 8,538 in its two parishes. Like Croft, it could accommodate both large and small owners, but suffered a fall in total numbers of very similar proportions, despite a population of 927 in 1801, many of them tradesmen and craftsmen who would tend to inflate the numbers of small owners. The loss of owners was, however, not confined to the lowest groups, those paying from £4 to £20 tax declining from twenty four to seven between 1709 and 1780, their share falling from fifty per cent to seventeen per cent.

This brief survey has demonstrated two main points. Firstly, parochial circumstances varied considerably in a very small compass, demonstrating that a fairly sophisticated form of the open-closed classification of parishes is necessary for descriptive purposes, yet is relevant as early as 1709. Secondly, nevertheless the decline in the number of owners was general and some evidence marshalled by Holderness suggests that it may have occurred mostly before 1747. It is, however, overshadowed by a much larger rise in numbers between 1790 and 1810, mainly because of agricultural prosperity and again between 1810 and 1830, mainly because of fen drainage leading to the conversion of common rights to real property. Concurrently with the decline in small owners and owner-occupancy in the first half of the eighteenth century, there was also a decline in the number of tenants. The subsequent rise in owner occupancy in 1790–1810 lends itself to the interpretation that the most important factor in the fluctuations of landowning fortunes throughout the whole period was not, with certain obvious exceptions such as Dalby, aristocratic and gentry aggrandisement, but rather changes in the strength of demand for land from practising farmers.[20] In particular, Holderness notes that almost all owner-occupiers were simultaneously proprietors and tenants,[21] an observation which implies that historians should use the technique of nominal linkage in order to view from as many angles as possible the *dramatis personæ* with whom they are concerned. The Land Tax Assessments have an important role to play in this process.

NOTES

1 I would like to acknowledge the help I have received from discussions with Dr J.V. Beckett, Mr R.J. Grover, and Dr M.E. Turner. The Open University has given financial assistance in respect of photocopying the Assessments. More especially it made possible the work of Mrs Hannah Burt on the Candleshoe documents, through a grant awarded to Dr K.P. Wilson and myself. I would like to thank Mrs Burt for evaluating a complete set of Assessments for Candleshoe and for producing the results shown in Table 5. Following this, Dr B.A. Holderness generously allowed access to his Ph.D. thesis and permitted me to draw on his conclusions. It is reassuring that his evaluation and our evaluation of the reliability of the Candleshoe assessments narrowed down on to almost exactly the same group of parishes.
2 Mills, D.R., *Lord and Peasant in Nineteenth Century Britain*, London, 1980, especially pp. 25 and 84.
3 Johnson, A.H., *The Disappearance of the Small Landowner*, Oxford 1909, reissued by Merlin Press, London, 1963, p. 136.
4 Holderness, B.A., *Rural Society in South East Lindsey, Lincolnshire, 1660–1840*, University of Nottingham, unpublished Ph.D. thesis, 1968.
5 The term 'land tax' parish is used here and in the next chapter to indicate that such units did not always correspond to other administrative areas, though in Rutland they appear to have been more or less synonymous with agricultural townships, which were usually also ecclesiastical parishes.
6 Leicestershire Record Office, Finch MSS, DG 7/4/1.
7 Except for one or two eighteenth-century documents, there are no further Assessments for Rutland in the county archives. However, it would be possible to make comparisons with the 1798 Assessment at the Public Record Office, Kew, reference IR 23/70.
8 Mills, D.R., *Landownership and Rural Population with special reference to Leicestershire in mid-nineteenth century*, University of Leicester, unpublished Ph.D. thesis 1963, appendix 4.
9 Mills, *Lord and Peasant*, pp. 73–77.
10 Cambridgeshire Record Office: Comberton 1707 CRO P47/18/2; Linton 1674 Rate and 1694 Land Tax Assessment CRO L95/24; Meldreth 1698–1720 CRO R78/29. The 1698 document is a parish rate, but follows a very similar pattern to the Land Tax Assessments for 1699–1720; Orwell 1736 CRO L. 63.55.2. The reference for Comberton 1829 is CRO Q/RPL3 and for Meldreth 1815 it is CRO Z 94/0121.
11 Davies, E., 'The Small Landowner, 1780–1832, in the light of the Land Tax Assessments', *Economic History Review*, 1st series, volume 1, 1927, pp. 87–113.
12 The rates of the Land Tax were as follows (shillings in the pound rental value):

1693–97	4	1722–26	3	1750–52	3
1698–99	3	1727	4	1753–55	2
1700	2	1728–29	3	1756–66	4
1701–12	4	1730	2	1767–70	3
1713–15	2	1731–32	1	1771	4
1716	4	1733–39	2	1772–75	3
1717–21	3	1740–49	4	1776 onwards	4

13 Acreages are taken from the *Victoria History of the County of Cambridge*, Volume II, 1973, pp. 131–8.
14 Mills, *Lord and Peasant*, p. 75.
15 Lincolnshire Archives Office, Lindsey Deposit 35/2.
16 Tate, W.E., *Domesday of English Enclosure Acts and Awards*, ed. M.E. Turner, University of Reading Library, 1979.

17 Holderness, B.A., op. cit., especially chapter 5. Dr Holderness's work is independent confirmation that the choice of these six parishes is historiographically acceptable.

18 The most reliable acreage figures, generally, are those provided by the Ordnance Survey to the Census authorities. The figures appearing in the 1891 Census have been used here, except for Croft, where an estimate has been made to take account of land reclamation, Holderness, ibid., p. 432. *White's Directory of Lincolnshire* 1856 has been consulted for resident gentry at that date.

19 Holderness, ibid., p. 48 and idem., 'The agricultural activities of the Massingberds of South Ormsby, Lincolnshire, 1638–c. 1750', *Midland History*, volume I, 1972, p. 15.

20 Holderness, *Rural Society*, Chapter 5, especially pp. 324–31 and 346, Chapter 6, especially pp. 423, 432–4, 477–8. On the last pair of pages he records a variety of arrangements made between landlords and tenants as to who should pay the Land Tax, including shared responsibility. Dalby suffered a decline in landowners from about ten in 1747 to three in 1790, through the land acquistion of the Bownes family, p. 328.

21 Holderness, ibid., p. 606.

Chapter 12

Early Land Tax Assessments Explored (2) Kent and Sussex

RICHARD GROVER

Introduction

The previous chapter introduced some of the basic features of the early Land Tax Assessments and offered a standardised method of analysing the data they contain. In this chapter[1] the scene shifts to south-east England and therefore presents a different regional perspective on the issues previously raised. It introduces some of the complications which arise from the provision in the Land Tax acts for the double taxation of papists and the inclusion in the Assessments of sums levied on industrial premises and personal estates as well as agricultural property. These problems can be solved within the general framework of analysis as used in chapter 11, thus providing an opportunity for overall conclusions to be drawn from the two chapters.

Kent and Sussex are relatively well-endowed with surviving Land Tax Assessments, including significant numbers from the period before 1780. This chapter utilises those from two divisions, St. Augustine East in Kent, and Hastings Rape in Sussex.[2] The former was in north east Kent. Its south western boundary was formed by a line of parishes lying west of the Dover-Canterbury road. It included four of the Thanet parishes but most of the division lay south of the River Stour. The liberties of Dover and Sandwich, although contiguous with the division, were not a part, being responsible for their own tax administrations. Hastings Rape lay in the extreme eastern part of East Sussex. Its north east boundary was the Kent-Sussex border and its western one passed through Ticehurst, Heathfield, Herstmonceux, and Bexhill. Hastings, Winchelsea, and Rye, though lying within the boundaries of the Rape, administered their own tax affairs. Both divisions were traditional administrative areas and of some antiquity when the Land Tax was introduced.

Large numbers of both early and later Assessments survive for most parishes in both divisions. Assessments for selected parishes from the first decade of the eighteenth century are compared with ones from circa 1780 so as to illustrate changes in landownership and occupancy during this period. The parishes have been chosen because their Assessments at both dates clearly differentiate between proprietors and occupiers. As little previous use has been made of the early Assessments, their quality is first compared with the more familiar later ones.

(i) *Quality of the Early Assessments*

The early Assessments have two principal deficiencies when compared with the later ones. Firstly, a smaller proportion of them have survived so that their temporal and geographical coverage is more restricted. In consequence they constitute a less comprehensive record of landownership and occupancy. The sizes of estates and farms computed from the early Assessments is subject to a downward bias as those parts of holdings which lay in parishes for which Assessments have not survived can obviously not be included. Thus the computed range of estate and farm sizes is more compressed than that which actually existed, which gives the appearance of a more egalitarian distribution of landed wealth. The restricted temporal coverage limits analyses which require continuous runs of Assessments, such as turnover studies of estates and farms.[3] Moreover the areas with surviving Assessments may not be wholly representative of eighteenth century parishes. For example Kent and East Sussex were scarcely touched by the parliamentary enclosure movement. Table 1 shows the proportions of the Assessments made in each decade to have survived for the two selected divisions. Almost all the later Assessments for both divisions are available. The proportion of the early Assessments to have survived increases during the period but Assessments survive for only certain of the early years.

As the previous chapter showed, a second major difference between the early and later Assessments is in terms of the quantity of information recorded by the assessors. The proportion of early Assessments recording both the proprietor and occupier of each property is much lower, with many just identifying the taxpayer, who might be either party. However a significant number of Assessments do record both parties, permitting computation of estate and farm sizes and analysis of tenure. The Assessments that record taxpayers only are not without value. For example they may be used to classify parishes according to the degree of concentration in terms of the access to the land. Table 2 summarises the information contained in the early Assessments for the two selected divisions.

The character of the Assessments changed during the life of the Land Tax so that there are some important differences between the information contained in the early and in the later Assessments. Where the introduction of the tax resulted in new valuations rather than the

Table 1

The Proportion of the Assessments which Survive for Each Decade, 1690s-1780s, for Each Division

Decade	Hastings Rape %	St. Augustine East %
1693-99	7.1	28.6
1700-09	22.0	59.8
1710-19	64.5	98.2
1720-29	81.0	99.3
1730-39	74.7	99.6
1740-49	87.8	98.2
1750-59	87.8	99.5
1760-69	85.7	99.8
1770-79	87.5	80.5
1780-89	98.3	99.8
No. of 'land tax' parishes	40	55

Sources: Kent Archives Office and East Sussex Record Office, Land Tax Assessments

Table 2

The Quality of the Land Tax Assessments

	Hastings Rape c.1702*	St. Augustine East 1699
Number of parishes	40	55
Number of surviving Assessments	32	55
Number of Assessments -		
listing occupiers and proprietors	13	45
levying a rate in excess of 4s in £	11	0
listing industrial properties	13	4
listing personal estates	16	5

*Where Assessments for 1702 have not survived, those for 1706 or 1707 have been taken instead.

Sources: as for Table 1

application of established methods of apportionment,[4] the Assessments reflected the actual annual value of the property. Once parish quotas were introduced no subsequent revaluations occurred, though examples can be found of the reapportionment of quotas within parishes in accordance with changing relative values. Thus the Assessments ceased to bear a direct relationship to the annual value of properties and may only be used to indicate *relative* physical size of properties. The Assessments made in the early years can be used to study the distribution of wealth.[5] Those for Hastings Rape include ones made in 1693, before the introduction of quotas, and at a time when the Land Tax acts contained directions to assessors as to how to value property as opposed to how to apportion a quota.[6]

In its early years the Land Tax could more properly be regarded as a comprehensive income tax rather than as a 'land tax'. The assessors included personal as well as real property in their assessments, and these must be excluded from computations of landed property. Assessments on personal property amounted to almost three per cent of the total number in Hastings Rape circa 1702, principally accounted for by stock in trade and money at interest. As table 2 shows, fewer such assessments were made in St. Augustine East. This may reflect a different assessment policy which was pursued by the divisional commissioners or, more likely, the more highly developed industrial base of Hastings Rape and its related capital market. Over time the number of personal assessments declined as taxpayers moved or died, or the assessments became consolidated into those on real property.[7] Hastings Rape contained a part of the Wealden iron industry so that the early Assessments include significant sums levied on industrial property. The Assessments for circa 1702 record ten forges and furnaces.[8] As the industry declined these assessments disappeared along with those on the personal property of the ironmasters. Industrial, like personal property, must be identified and excluded from any computation of estate and farm sizes.

The Land Tax acts provided for the double taxation of papists. Several major estates in Hastings Rape were owned by persons subject to double taxation and twelve of the Assessments for circa 1702 contain properties on which double taxes were collected. This provision can distort the calculation of the relative sizes of properties as those belonging to papists appear to be twice their real size.[9] Fortunately the assessment policy in Hastings Rape was to levy a double poundage on the 'rents' or annual value assessed, the rents being computed in the same way as for other proprietors. Thus the papists may be identified and their properties treated in the same way as those of their protestant neighbours. Complications arose when the property was sold to a protestant or when an heir renounced the family's faith. Sometimes a small remission might be made in the parish quota so that neither the new proprietor nor the parish would have to bear the burden of the previous double taxation.[10] In Hastings Rape the scale of the problem resulted in the reapportionment of the excess tax amongst all the proprietors within a parish. The tax paid on each property increased but there was not an alteration in their physical sizes. As landed property was assessed so as to meet that part of the quota not raised from other taxable items, similar changes in the tax payable on agricultural property could occur as a result of changes in personal or industrial property, or offices in a parish.

The introduction of quotas in 1697 and their revision in 1698 on the basis of the 1693 Assessments led to problems for certain parishes whose tax base declined between the two dates. Some eleven parishes in Hastings Rape circa 1702, including Whatlington, were obliged to meet their quotas by levying a rate poundage in excess of four shillings. The maximum rate was four shillings and sixpence. The tax base could decline due to the removal of personal property or the closure of industrial property, or due to a decline in the annual value of landed property.[11] At Worth in St. Augustine East there were also difficulties in meeting the assessed quota. Until 1705 the commissioners reapportioned a part amongst the other parishes in Eastry hundred.[12] The scale of the problem in Hastings Rape was such as to prevent a similar solution.

In the tables that follow the annual values or 'rents' have been taken as the appropriate indicator of relative size and the annual tax payment has been computed by applying a rate of four shillings in the pound to these rents. A discrepancy therefore exists between the annual amounts of tax payable on certain properties as listed in the Assessments and those used in compiling the tables. This practice has been adopted to overcome the problems presented by papists and those parishes where rates in excess of the statutory poundage were levied. As noted in chapter 11, such a practice is necessary for comparisons between years in which parliament varied the rate poundage from one to four shillings.[13] It should be noted that each parish has been treated in isolation even though a few proprietors and occupiers had interests in more than one parish within the group. The bias towards a more egalitarian distribution in landed wealth noted earlier is slightly exaggerated by this treatment which results in holdings spread over two parishes being treated as two distinct units.

(ii) *Analysis of Land Ownership and Occupancy*

Tables 3 to 6 set out the numbers and sizes of the farms and estates in fifteen selected parishes within the two divisions. They comprise four frequency distributions setting out the numbers of and percentage of tax paid by estates and farms by ten categories of size for 1702/5 and 1780/1.

Table 3: Numbers of Proprietors by Size Groups

	Size Groups	2	3	4	5	6	7	8	9	10	Total
HASTINGS RAPE PARISHES											
East Guldeford	1702	0	0	1	3	4	5	5	4	2	24
	1781	0	0	0	2	4	4	3	6	6	25
Iden	1702	6	5	10	4	2	3	1	6	4	41
	1781	8	4	7	4	4	3	1	4	3	38
Ninfield	1702	12	8	5	9	3	3	0	1	1	42
	1781	11	8	5	2	1	1	3	2	1	34
Ore	1702	4	3	8	5	1	0	2	0	1	24
	1781	4	0	7	6	1	2	0	2	1	23
Pett	1702	5	1	3	0	0	6	3	3	2	23
	1781	3	1	2	0	0	2	5	3	1	17
Playden	1702	6	4	8	4	2	2	1	2	0	29
	1781	5	4	7	2	1	4	0	1	1	25
Whatlington	1702	2	3	4	10	4	1	0	2	0	26
	1781	4	5	6	5	1	3	2	2	0	28
ST AUGUSTINE EAST PARISHES											
Adisham	1705	5	8	4	4	2	1	0	3	1	28
	1780	7	4	4	3	1	2	0	3	1	25
Guston	1705	4	0	2	3	0	0	1	1	1	12
	1780	5	1	2	1	1	0	1	0	1	12
Lydden	1705	8	2	4	4	0	1	1	1	0	21
	1780	6	4	5	2	0	0	0	2	0	19
Monkton	1705	14	4	2	5	1	1	1	2	3	33
	1780	5	13	8	4	1	1	0	3	2	37
Stonar	1705									1	1
	1780									1	1
Sutton	1705	6	2	1	7	1	0	1	1	0	19
	1780	4	3	0	7	0	0	2	1	0	17
Womenswold	1705	6	2	1	3	0	0	1	3	0	16
	1780	10	2	3	2	0	0	1	3	0	21
Worth	1705	7	4	14	3	3	4	0	9	4	48
	1780	8	8	9	7	5	2	3	5	5	52
TOTAL	1702 & 1705	85	46	67	64	23	27	17	38	20	387
	1780 & 1781	80	57	65	47	20	24	21	37	23	374

Size Groups, with annual tax payments at four shillings in the pound:

1. under 4/- (none above)
2. 4/- and up to 10/-
3. 10/- and up to £1
4. £1 and up to £2
5. £2 and up to £4
6. £4 and up to £5
7. £5 and up to £8
8. £8 and up to £10
9. £10 and up to £20
10. £20 and over

Sources: as for Table 1

Table 4: Percentage of Tax Paid by Proprietors in Each Size Group

Size Groups		2	3	4	5	6	7	8	9	10	*ATQ (£)
HASTINGS RAPE PARISHES											
East Guldeford	1702	0.0	0.0	0.6	3.4	6.7	12.8	17.3	18.3	41.0	269.0
	1781	0.0	0.0	0.0	1.8	4.8	7.6	7.7	25.5	52.6	351.2
Iden	1702	0.7	1.2	5.1	3.9	3.1	6.8	3.3	30.7	45.2	275.0
	1781	0.9	0.9	3.5	5.0	5.9	6.8	3.1	19.8	54.0	277.1
Ninfield	1702	3.7	5.6	6.5	24.6	12.3	16.9	0.0	9.7	20.7	107.4
	1781	2.8	4.4	6.5	4.6	3.9	4.9	21.8	21.4	29.9	123.2
Ore	1702	1.5	3.1	14.4	16.2	5.1	0.0	20.8	0.0	39.0	78.0
	1781	1.2	0.0	10.3	18.4	4.9	10.3	0.0	26.1	28.9	99.0
Pett	1702	0.6	0.5	2.4	0.0	0.0	20.7	15.1	24.0	36.8	175.0
	1781	0.7	0.4	1.4	0.0	0.0	6.1	24.1	27.0	40.3	177.9
Playden	1702	2.2	3.5	12.6	13.1	10.9	13.9	10.4	33.4	0.0	80.8
	1781	1.4	3.4	9.4	6.0	4.8	31.0	0.0	15.4	28.6	83.2
Whatlington	1702	1.0	2.4	6.4	30.5	19.2	7.1	0.0	33.5	0.0	84.3
	1781	0.9	4.4	9.9	15.9	4.6	19.8	19.6	24.9	0.0	86.8
ST AUGUSTINE EAST PARISHES											
Adisham	1705	1.2	4.1	4.1	8.9	6.6	5.9	0.0	37.0	32.4	133.4
	1780	2.0	2.3	4.2	7.1	3.1	10.7	0.0	36.5	34.2	129.4
Guston	1705	2.3	0.0	4.7	13.5	0.0	0.0	11.7	28.7	39.2	68.4
	1780	3.0	0.9	3.6	3.9	7.2	0.0	12.0	0.0	69.5	66.8
Lydden	1705	4.3	3.0	11.1	20.4	0.0	14.5	17.0	29.8	0.0	47.0
	1780	4.7	6.0	15.1	10.7	0.0	0.0	0.0	63.5	0.0	46.6
Monkton	1705	1.9	1.3	1.5	6.8	2.4	3.1	4.2	11.3	67.4	199.4
	1780	0.8	4.4	6.4	4.7	2.0	2.8	0.0	18.4	60.6	199.6
Stonar	1705									100.0	54.0
	1780									100.0	36.0
Sutton	1705	3.5	2.7	2.3	35.2	7.8	0.0	15.6	32.8	0.0	51.2
	1780	1.6	4.0	0.0	34.1	0.0	0.0	34.9	25.4	0.0	50.4
Womenswold	1705	3.3	2.3	2.7	14.0	0.0	0.0	14.7	63.0	0.0	60.0
	1780	4.7	2.3	6.3	7.3	0.0	0.0	16.0	63.3	0.0	60.0
Worth	1705	0.5	0.8	5.4	2.5	3.4	6.3	0.0	31.5	49.7	365.6
	1780	0.7	1.6	3.2	4.9	6.0	3.1	7.4	19.8	53.7	372.4
TOTALS	1702 & 1705	1.2	1.6	4.5	8.5	4.8	8.2	7.2	25.2	38.7	2048.5
	1780 & 1781	1.2	1.8	4.2	6.0	4.0	6.8	8.5	24.0	43.7	2159.6

Size Groups: as for Table 3, none in Group 1

*Annual Tax Quota on landed property at four shillings in the pound

Sources: as for Table 1

Table 5: Numbers of Occupiers in Each Size Group

	Size Groups	2	3	4	5	6	7	8	9	10	Total
HASTINGS RAPE PARISHES											
East Guldeford	1702	0	0	2	2	0	8	5	9	2	28
	1781	0	0	0	2	2	5	3	7	6	25
Iden	1702	4	8	7	7	1	7	2	8	2	46
	1781	8	3	6	6	3	3	0	8	3	40
Ninfield	1702	11	6	11	8	4	2	2	1	0	45
	1781	11	7	5	5	1	5	2	3	0	39
Ore	1702	5	4	7	7	2	2	0	0	1	28
	1781	3	0	7	6	1	0	2	4	0	23
Pett	1702	5	2	3	3	3	8	4	4	0	32
	1781	3	1	2	0	1	4	5	4	2	22
Playden	1702	6	2	8	8	2	2	1	1	0	30
	1781	7	4	3	2	1	3	0	2	1	23
Whatlington	1702	3	3	6	10	3	1	2	1	0	29
	1781	8	3	3	6	0	3	2	2	0	27
ST AUGUSTINE EAST PARISHES											
Adisham	1705	6	6	7	4	2	1	1	5	0	32
	1780	8	7	4	2	1	2	2	3	1	30
Guston	1705	5	0	2	1	1	0	1	1	1	12
	1780	7	1	3	1	0	1	1	1	1	16
Lydden	1705	7	3	3	3	1	2	0	1	0	20
	1780	8	3	3	2	3	1	0	1	0	21
Monkton	1705	15	4	8	11	1	2	1	2	4	48
	1780	5	16	3	6	3	3	0	3	3	42
Stonar	1705								1	1	2
	1780									1	1
Sutton	1705	6	2	0	8	1	0	1	1	0	19
	1780	2	1	1	3	1	0	0	2	0	10
Womenswold	1705	7	4	2	2	0	0	1	3	0	19
	1780	18	4	3	2	0	0	2	2	0	31
Worth	1705	12	4	9	3	2	3	0	6	4	43
	1780	9	7	5	4	4	1	1	4	6	41
TOTALS	1702 & 1705	92	48	75	77	23	38	21	44	15	433
	1780 & 1781	97	57	48	47	21	31	20	46	24	391

Size Groups: as for Table 3, none in Group 1

Sources: as for Table 1

Table 6: Percentage of Tax Paid by Occupiers in Each Size Group

Size Groups		2	3	4	5	6	7	8	9	10	*ATQ (£)
HASTINGS RAPE PARISHES											
East	1702	0.0	0.0	0.9	2.4	0.0	20.6	17.1	40.9	18.1	269.0
Guldeford	1781	0.0	0.0	0.0	1.6	2.3	9.0	7.9	28.2	51.0	351.2
Iden	1702	0.4	2.0	3.7	6.6	1.5	16.6	6.1	42.3	20.7	275.0
**	1781	1.1	0.8	3.3	7.4	4.5	6.9	0.0	43.9	32.2	270.6
Ninfield	1702	3.2	4.1	13.4	22.2	16.0	13.2	15.8	12.1	0.0	107.4
	1781	2.8	3.9	6.3	9.9	3.7	26.1	13.8	33.4	0.0	123.2
Ore	1702	1.8	4.1	12.8	21.5	10.3	16.2	0.0	0.0	33.3	78.0
	1781	1.0	0.0	10.3	17.4	4.9	0.0	17.0	49.5	0.0	99.0
Pett	1702	0.6	0.9	2.5	5.5	7.4	28.1	20.3	34.6	0.0	175.0
	1781	0.7	0.4	1.5	0.0	2.2	13.9	24.1	29.1	28.1	177.9
Playden	1702	2.2	1.7	12.1	27.5	10.2	16.6	9.9	19.8	0.0	80.8
	1781	2.2	3.4	3.6	5.3	5.8	23.1	0.0	28.1	28.6	83.2
Whatlington	1702	1.4	2.4	9.5	30.5	14.5	7.1	19.5	15.2	0.0	84.3
	1781	2.8	2.5	5.1	18.2	0.0	21.2	20.8	29.5	0.0	86.8
ST AUGUSTINE EAST PARISHES											
Adisham	1705	1.5	3.0	6.7	10.0	6.6	5.9	6.0	60.3	0.0	133.4
	1780	2.3	4.0	3.7	5.3	3.4	11.9	13.0	39.7	16.7	129.4
Guston	1705	2.9	0.0	4.1	3.8	5.9	0.0	13.5	19.0	50.9	68.4
	1780	4.2	0.9	5.1	3.9	0.0	7.8	12.0	26.1	40.1	66.8
Lydden	1705	3.8	4.3	8.9	14.0	8.5	28.5	0.0	31.9	0.0	47.0
	1780	5.6	3.9	9.4	10.7	26.2	15.0	0.0	29.8	0.0	46.6
Monkton	1705	1.9	1.2	5.3	14.1	2.1	5.6	4.2	12.6	52.9	199.4
	1780	0.9	5.2	2.3	9.0	6.2	8.1	0.0	20.0	48.4	199.6
Stonar	1705								25.9	74.1	54.0
	1780									100.0	36.0
Sutton	1705	3.9	2.7	0.0	37.9	7.8	0.0	15.6	32.0	0.0	51.2
	1780	0.8	1.6	3.2	15.1	8.7	0.0	0.0	70.6	0.0	50.4
Womenswold	1705	3.7	4.0	4.0	10.7	0.0	0.0	14.7	63.0	0.0	60.0
	1780	7.3	4.3	6.7	7.3	0.0	0.0	31.3	43.0	0.0	60.0
Worth	1705	0.9	0.7	3.2	2.5	2.3	4.9	0.0	26.5	59.0	365.6
	1780	0.8	1.4	1.9	2.7	5.1	2.0	2.4	15.6	68.1	372.4
TOTALS	1702 & 1705	1.3	1.6	4.9	10.2	4.7	12.1	8.9	30.6	25.7	2048.5
	1780 & 1781	1.4	1.8	3.1	6.0	4.2	9.1	8.1	30.2	36.0	2153.1

Size Groups: as for Table 3, none in Group 1

*Annual Tax Quota on landed property at four shillings in the pound
**Property assessed at £6 5s per annum and occupied by Sewage Commissioners has been excluded

Sources: as for Table 1

The presentation of the results in this form implies that the sums of money paid as tax in the different parishes are in some sense comparable. Such an assumption was generally accepted until the 1960s when D.B. Grigg and G.E. Mingay drew attention to the wide differences in the tax per acre levied between parishes even within the same county.[14] Since then the authors of a number of studies have applied a tax/acreage ratio (often referred to as an acreage equivalent), calculated for each parish, to the tax payable on each property, and in this way have derived approximate areas of holdings. The tax payments from different parishes are thus reduced to a common denominator. For example, let us suppose that in 1798 Mr. A paid tax of one pound per annum on his property in parish Z and a further one pound on that in parish Y. In the absence of regular revaluations, the sums assessed are unlikely to bear a consistent relationship to the current rentals in the two parishes, and so are not directly comparable. However if the Land Tax was levied at an average rate of two shillings an acre in parish Z and at ten pence an acre in parish Y, we may estimate Mr. A's properties as being of ten and twenty four acres in size respectively and use these figures for comparison. However, as early chapters have shown, even this approach is not without its problems or its critics.

The area of a holding is in many respects not an ideal measure of its magnitude. Different agricultural enterprises have different optimal land inputs so that what may be a 'large' area for one enterprise is 'small' for another. Two examples serve to illustrate the problems of comparing the areas of holdings even within as small a geographical area as a division. The first example comes from the coastal parishes which had extensive marshland for fattening and grazing. As tables 3 and 5 illustrate, marshland parishes like Worth and East Guldeford contained larger estates and farms than the average in the divisions due to the distinctive enterprises found within them. As a second example the occupational structure differed between parishes so that in some a well-developed industrial and commercial base favoured small agricultural units worked on a part-time basis or as specialist enterprises catering directly for the retail market. Table 7 shows the occupational structure for Adisham and Ninfield. The former is based on an assessment made in 1705 for the duties on burials, marriages, and baptisms and the latter on a poll tax assessment for 1702.[15] As the poll tax exempted individuals in receipt of alms and those in households too poor to pay parochial rates,[16] the total number of households at Ninfield is underestimated. Whilst the two parishes had a similar number of resident farmers, there was a marked difference in the non-agricultural occupations found within them. Adisham had three different craft occupations present and these represented its total non-agricultural employment. Ninfield contained seven types of craftsman and a total of fourteen non-agricultural occupations. The data from the Land

Table 7

Occupational Structure of Adisham and Ninfield

Occupations	Numbers of Heads of Households	
	Adisham 1705	Ninfield 1702
Farmers	9	10
Labourers and Agricultural Craftsmen	7	7
Craftsmen	3	15
Agricultural Processing	0	7
Professions	0	2
Commerce	0	2
Unspecified	3	0
Totals	22	43

Craftsmen:	glover, weaver, wheelwright, carpenter, tailor, collier, brickmaker, shoemaker, cordwainer
Agricultural processing:	tanner, butcher, hopman, miller
Professions:	schoolmaster, civil servant
Commerce:	mercer

Sources: Kent Archives Office, duties on burials, marriages, and baptisms
East Sussex Record Office, poll tax assessments

Tax does not permit enterprises to be graded according to their standard labour inputs. However as the earlier date for the comparisons is 1702/5 when the assessed annual values should still have reflected current rentals, money values have been preferred to estimated areas as common denominator.

Overall the number of proprietors declined by three per cent between the two dates but there were significant variations both in the direction and the rate of change across the whole range of the size distribution. The number of proprietors in groups nine and ten actually increased by three per cent and those in groups two and three by five per cent. By contrast the intermediate groups paying between one and ten pounds per annum declined by eleven per cent. Those in groups two and three maintained their share of the tax at three per cent. The groups paying between one and ten pounds per annum experienced a decline in their share from thirty three to twenty nine per cent, whilst those paying twenty pounds or more increased their share from thirty nine to forty four per cent. The mean estate size increased by nine per cent.

The number of occupiers in the fifteen parishes fell by ten per cent between 1702/5 and 1780/1. All the parishes with the exceptions of Guston, Lydden, and Womenswold experienced a decline. However, as with the proprietors, this decline was not spread evenly throughout the size distribution. The smallest occupiers, those in the size groups two and three increased by ten per cent and the largest, those in groups nine and ten by nineteen per cent, and this was mainly due to an increase in those with the largest farms assessed at over twenty pounds per annum. The number of occupiers in groups four to eight declined by twenty-nine per cent, with a decline of thirty eight per cent being experienced amongst groups four and five. The largest units clearly prospered and one may hypothesise that those holdings which were capable of being worked on a part-time basis using family labour alone also survived. The decline was concentrated amongst the farms that were too large to be worked part-time but which were too small to enjoy the full economies of scale. The proportion of tax paid on farms in groups four to eight declined from forty one to thirty one per cent of the total. Farms in groups two and three paid three per cent of the tax at both dates whilst the proportion assessed on those in the largest group increased from twenty six to thirty six per cent. The changing size distribution of occupiers resulted in a sixteen per cent increase in the mean farm size between the two dates.

The trends amongst the proprietors were similar to those amongst the occupiers. The decline between the two dates was concentrated amongst the proprietors who seemed to specialise in providing the middle sized range of farms, but the trends amongst the proprietors were not as marked as amongst the occupiers. The explanation for this appears to have been due to the practice of renting land from more than one landlord so that a farm of the desired size could be assembled from components rented from different proprietors. On larger estates restrictive covenants in leases, such as banning the removal of manure, were imposed and these would have served to prevent land from being worked in conjunction with property rented from elsewhere or owner-occupied land.[17] However, permitting land to be farmed in conjunction with an owner-occupied unit or with property rented from another proprietor would offer a survival strategy for those landlords whose units were smaller than the optimal size or who possessed odd pieces of land. In 1702/5 sixteen per cent of the occupiers rented land from two or more land-lords, including those who worked a mixed-tenure unit of partially rented and partially owner-occupied land, and their holdings paid thirty-six per cent of the tax. Their numbers fell by eighteen per cent and the tax on their holdings by sixteen per cent by

1780/1, but they still numbered fifteen per cent of the occupiers and occupied land on which twenty nine per cent of the tax was paid.[18]

Owner-occupation increased in the fifteen parishes during the period. The number of owner occupiers grew by thirteen per cent and the tax paid on owner-occupied land by ninety per cent. Some twenty-nine per cent of the occupiers and thirty-three per cent of the proprietors were owner-occupiers in 1702/5, paying thirteen per cent of the tax. In 1780/1 thirty-six per cent of occupiers and thirty-eight per cent of proprietors were owner-occupiers, paying twenty-four per cent of the tax. However, the growth of owner-occupation had little to do with the survival of small cultivators. The increase in the numbers of owner-occupiers was due entirely to more proprietors retaining a part of their land for their own cultivation and to an increase in the number of mixed-tenure farms. The mean size of wholly owner-occupied farms, i.e., excluding the owner-occupied parts of mixed-tenure farms and estates, increased. The tax payable on owner-occupied farms increased by 118 per cent and the mean size unit by 120 per cent so that it grew from thirty one to fifty nine per cent of the size of the mean farm.

The survival of Assessments for the duties on marriages, burials, and baptisms for St. Augustine East for 1705 and of the poll tax assessments for Hastings Rape for 1702 means that, with the exceptions of Lydden and Ore, it is possible to identify those proprietors and occupiers who were resident in each parish. Residents owned little of the land. They formed fifteen per cent of the total of landowners in the thirteen parishes and paid five per cent of the tax. Their holdings were smaller than those of non-residents, the mean size of a resident proprietor's holding being twenty nine per cent of that of the non-resident. Some sixty per cent of the resident proprietors paid less than one pound per annum in tax compared with twenty-nine per cent for the non-residents. Resident occupiers amounted to forty four per cent of the total and occupied holdings assessed at fifty four per cent of the tax. Their holdings were larger than those of the outdwellers. The mean farm size of residents was fifty per cent larger than that of the non-residents, and seventeen per cent of residents occupied a holding assessed at ten pounds or more compared with eleven per cent for the non-residents. Residents were vulnerable to the subsequent changes in landownership and occupation. Some fifty two per cent of resident occupiers and thirty eight per cent of resident proprietors were in size groups four to eight where the decline in numbers was concentrated. The changes in the sizes of estates and farms could therefore have repercussions on the social structure of communities.

The evidence assembled here points to an adjustment in estate and farm sizes between 1702/5 and 1780/1. It indicates the vulnerability of a middle range of proprietors and occupiers but not to their wholesale demise. The picture which emerges is one of a polarisation in the size distribution of estates and farms, with the larger and smaller units increasing and the medium sized ones declining. In this respect the experience of these areas of Kent and Sussex was similar to one of the Cambridgeshire parishes and several of the Lincolnshire ones discussed in the previous chapter. The two chapters together have established the clear need for work to be done on early Assessments, wherever these can be seen to make a clear distinction between occupiers and proprietors. It is especially important that research should be done to indicate any fluctuations in landownership between the early eighteenth century and circa 1780. By such means it may be possible to impute the relative effects of changes in the seventeenth as opposed to the eighteenth century, the relative effects of the agricultural depression in the second quarter of the eighteenth century, and the consistency of such effects across the country at large.

These last two chapters have demonstrated some of the limitations as well as the usefulness of the Assessments. The context has been in terms of local studies based on a range of contemporary documents. By using the full available range, the shortcomings of one particular type of document can be minimised. Some of the ambiguities of the status of taxpayers can be resolved by cross reference to these other documents. Conversely the Assessments have the advantage that they are usually the nearest approximation to a cadastral survey available in the period before enclosure and tithe awards and have the advantage that the names of the proprietors and occupiers were regularly revised. The Assessments can act as a foundation on which to reconstitute communities, and to study the distribution of wealth in them.

NOTES

1 I am grateful for the helpful comments received from Dr. D.R. Mills and Dr. M.E. Turner.

2 Kent Archive Office (KAO) Q/CT1, Q/RP1; East Sussex Record Office (ESRO) D472, QD/E2. The St. Augustine East division is often also referred to as the Wingham division. All dates are New Style.

3 See Turner, M.E., 'Parliamentary Enclosure and Landownership Change in Buckinghamshire', *Economic History Review*, 2nd series, volume XXVIII, 1975, pp. 565–81; Walton, J.R., 'The Residential Mobility of Farmers and its relationship to the parliamentary enclosure movement in Oxfordshire' in A.D.M. Phillips & B.J. Turton (eds.), *Environment, Man and Economic Change*, London, 1975, pp. 238–52.

4 Clearly this would not apply to areas such as Cumberland where the introduction of the Land Tax did not result in new methods of tax assessment – Beckett, J.V., 'Local Custom and the 'New Taxation' in the Seventeenth and Eighteenth Centuries: The Example of Cumberland', *Northern History*, volume 12, 1976, pp. 105–26.

5 By using Assessments from this period one would not face the problem of using

valuations that no longer reflected current market values as was encountered by L. Soltow with Assessments from 1798 – 'The Distribution of Property Values in England and Wales in 1798', *EcHR*, 2nd series volume XXXIV, 1981, pp. 70–80; Ginter, D.E., 'A Wealth of Problems with the Land Tax' and Wilson, G.J., 'The Land Tax Problem', *EcHR*, 2nd series, volume XXXV, 1982, pp. 416–26. However there would still be the problem that the Assessments did not record all the property rights claimed for each property so that the net rent received by the proprietor would be less than the gross rental on which the Land Tax was assessed.

6 In 4 Wm. & Mary c.1, 1692, the annual value of a property was defined as 'what the premises are now worth to be leased if the same were truly and bona fide leased or demised at a rack rent and according to the full true yearly value thereof, without any respect being had to the present rents reserved for the same.' The Act instructed assessors how to treat fines, improvements, rates, and taxes in arriving at the annual value. Once quotas were imposed in 1697 the Land Tax acts reverted to the practice of the previous aids and enjoined the assessors to raise the quota as equally as possible, but without advising as to the method of assessment.

7 As an example Thomas Morris of Ashburnham in Hastings Rape was separately assessed in 1759 on real property and shop goods. In 1760 the two were joined in one assessment described as 'his own and shop goods'. From 1766 the distinction between the real and personal estates is lost with the property being described as 'his own and shop' and in subsequent years it was not described at all.

8 The sums assessed on certain of these are so low as to indicate that they may have been places for the manufacture of iron goods rather than for making iron itself.

9 The problem is explored in Wilson, G.J., 'West Derby Hundred and the Land Tax, 1780–1831', *Transactions of the Historic Society of Lancashire and Cheshire*, volume 129, 1980, pp. 63–91.

10 Obtaining relief when land ceased to be subject to double taxation proved difficult. As the sums assessed were not revalued, it became difficult to produce evidence that reapportionment of the double tax would result in a rate poundage in excess of the statutory rate on the then current rentals – Bourdin, M.A., *Exposition of the Land Tax*, 4th edition London, 1894, pp. 52–3. There were disputes amongst the commissioners for rival divisions over the sums that were abated. For example the commissioners for the St. Augustine West and Dartford divisions of Kent disputed between 1719 and 1729 as to whether an abatement in Kent's quota should be applied to relieve double taxation at Stourmouth or Swanscombe. KAO, Q/Ctc2, Q/CT1 Stourmouth, U410 L2.

11 H.J. Habakkuk notes that rents hardly rose between 1690 and 1720 after rising considerably between 1640 and 1690. Rack rents often decreased – 'English Landownership, 1680–1740', *EcHR*, 1st series, volume X, 1940, p. 13.

12 KAO, Sa/Z03.

13 For the Land Tax rates levied each year see p. 202, note 12 above.

14 Grigg, D.B., 'The Land Tax Returns', *Agricultural History Review*, volume 11, 1963, pp. 82–94; Mingay, G.E., 'The Land Tax Assessments and the Small Landowner', *EcHR*, 2nd series, volume XVII, 1964, pp. 381–8.

15 KAO, Q/CTz2; ESRO, D472.

16 1 Anne c 12, 1702.

17 For example when Daniel and John Swinford leased Minster Court Farm in Thanet in 1759 from Lord Conyngham, they agreed not to remove manure from the farm and also that all corn grown on the farm was to be threshed on the premises and the straw used only to feed livestock on the farm, KAO, U438 E45.

18 The scale of renting land from more than one landlord indicates that caution should be exercised in the interpretation of farm sizes derived from estate records or newspaper advertisements as these deal with letting rather than occupation units.

Appendix

Survival of Early Land Tax Assessments

DENNIS MILLS

The 1981 conference indicated two weak places in our understanding of Land Tax administration.[1] Little was known about the availability of Land Tax Assessments between the inception of the tax in 1692 and the start in 1780 of the main collections in Quarter Sessions records. Secondly, and following from this, questions concerning re-assessments, or the lack of them, to keep the tax burden equitable as between different properties in the same locality, could not be answered with any degree of confidence. The purpose of this appendix is to encourage research into these two areas.

With the support of conference members, I undertook to collect information on the availability of Assessments and related documents. A large team of volunteers was recruited and their detailed reports on the Assessments themselves have been published.[2] Schedule 1 in this appendix brings together, in a more-or-less standard format, such information as we have on the early, pre-1780 Assessments, while the second schedule summarises details of supplementary documents which might be used to gain insights into reassessment and related matters of land tax administration. I should like to take the opportunity of thanking all those who contributed to the survey and also to express our collective thanks to the staff of record offices across the length and breadth of England and Wales.

Schedule 1 indicates that an estimated 5,242 parishes (or townships, or urban wards, or tithings) possess an Assessment for at least one date before 1780. A round figure such as five thousand parishes is probably more appropriate, since the estimates remain subject to local verification in most cases. Those who took part in the survey were asked to give returns related to Hundreds (and other similar divisions), using the following conventions to indicate the extent of coverage within each Hundred during the dates specified: SP = Some Parishes MP = Many Parishes NC = Nearly Complete. Obviously relatively imprecise guidelines such as these will have been interpreted differently by the various surveyors and the amount of detailed information from which they worked must have varied, but to have asked for more precise figures would in some cases have involved calling for very large numbers of documents.

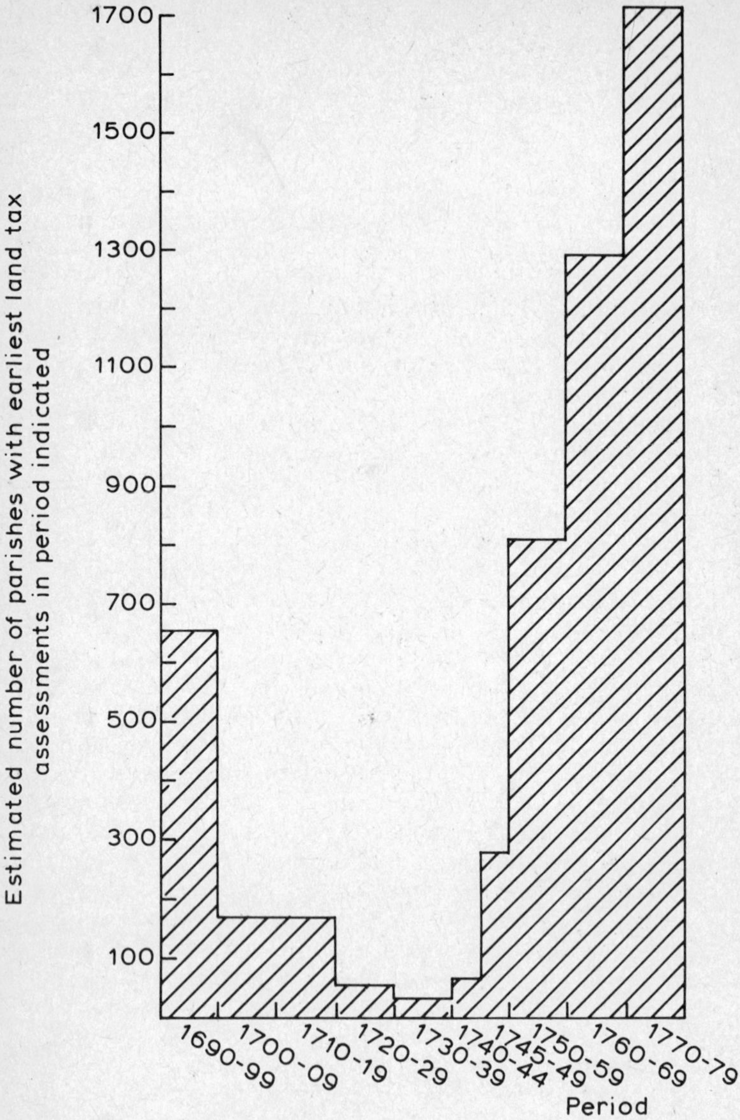

Figure 1. Distribution of Earliest Land Tax Assessments, 1690–1779.

On balance a total of 5,000 parishes may prove to be at least of the right order, moreover, there is no reason to suppose that inaccuracies apply to any greater or lesser extent in specific decades within the period 1690–1779. Therefore, the graph (Fig 1) showing the incidence of the earliest dates of survival may be taken as broadly reliable. Some inaccuracies will have crept in because the earliest date used for a group of parishes is the earliest date for only some unknown proportion of those parishes. There is no doubt, however, that the true distribution of earliest survivals must be U-shaped, with a very much larger population of first dates in the first decade of the tax's history than at any time until after the mid-point of the eighteenth century. From 1745 the distribution of survivals turns upwards again and would probably continue on that course if we could follow it into the Quarter Sessions period. Before making some historical commentary on this distribution, one last statistical caveat needs to be entered. As Schedule 1 indicates in detail, nearly all the earliest collections of Assessments are in broken series. Consequently, one could not rework the data in the graph to produce a cumulative frequency distribution of the availability of the documents. It seems, however, that the graph of earliest survival dates does have historical significance on its own.

It suggests that the quantity of survivals in the 1690s reflects the need for annual reassessments as a result of changes in legislative provisions. This need would slacken with the use of quotas from 1698 and one may suspect that parishes used the same assessment for several years running.[3] Moreover, some of these earliest Assessments are in collections which also contain other contemporary, or near-contemporary tax documents, such as those relating to poll taxes and to other taxes which fell by the wayside in the early eighteenth century. The late seventeenth century seems to have been a period when there were general reasons why those landowners who were involved in tax administration made a habit of keeping tax documents in secure places along with their estate papers. A significant but probably disproportionate number of the earliest Assessments relate to urban areas, especially corporate Boroughs, where the preservation of documents was probably a more regular habit than in the counties.

The Parliamentary Elections Act of 1745 may provide the vital explanation for the upturn in the graph at about that point. Section 3 of this Act provided that electors in a county election must be assessed to the Land Tax and section 4 required commissioners to transmit duplicates to the clerk of the peace.[4] Figure I suggests that this statute was not carried out by all clerks of the peace and/or that they were careless about ensuring the continued survival of the documents. They may only have sprung into action when elections were likely to be contested. Thirty five years later, it was felt necessary to remind them of this statutory duty in the

Parliamentary Elections Act of 1780.[5] This Act, which was supported by penalties for non-compliance, was the basis for the many collections which start in 1780 or thereabouts and finish about 1832. The Reform Act of 1832 removed the obligation to retain land tax duplicates for electoral purposes. However, it is also noteworthy that a significant number of these Quarter Sessions collections began *before* the 1780 Act had been passed, very frequently in the late sixties or in the seventies. Hence, we might provisionally conclude that the 1780 Act was confirming and enforcing existing best practice, itself based on the neglected Act of 1745.

Ward's study of Land Tax administration, which is based largely on central government documents, points to a decline in the efficiency in the tax system between *c.* 1710 and *c.* 1745, which is consistent with a poorer survival of Assessments. According to Ward, the Treasury and the Tax Office became seriously affected by patronage, and uninterested office holders occupied their places for longer periods. Ward is especially critical of the local tax commissioners, citing a reduction in the number of their meetings, a decline in their social standing and abuses by collectors and clerks which were insufficiently punished.[6]

Likewise there is some reason to think that changes in the central tax administration were responsible for the increase in the survival of Assessments after *c.* 1745. Reforms of the window tax in 1747, 1758 and 1761, the purging by Pelham of the receivers-general in 1747 and the transferral of the assessed taxes from the Excise and Stamp Office to the Tax Office in 1785 are again consistent with the improved rate of survival of Land Tax Assessments seen in Figure 1. After the American War of Independence started in 1776, the Tax Office staff was increased and attempts were made to enhance its efficiency, while Pitt's reforms of the taxes themselves and his use of the receivers-general are seen as important factors raising the standard of local administration.[7]

Subsequent studies show that it is necessary to be cautious about accepting Ward's interpretations, apart from the fact that he did not himself relate them to the survival rate of the Assessments. Beckett and Smith have shown that the 'mean return time' of land tax collection from local source to delivery in London lengthened from 1.095 years for the 1693 assessment to 1.461 for 1703 and 1.688 for 1743. However, it did not fall at that point, but reached a peak in 1773 of 1.953 years, before subsiding to 1.728 years for the 1793 collection. Therefore this analysis of return times gives only very general support to Ward's thesis as to improvements in the second half of the century, though other complications such as paying the militia out of the Land Tax from 1759, which could have slowed down returns of tax, need to be taken into account.[8]

A more serious criticism arises out of Brooks' comments on the evidence which Ward used. He has suggested that it is too much coloured by papers accumulating from atypical problems, leaving the long quiet periods of administration under-represented.[9] Probably the survival rate of the Assessments is too complex a subject to be explained in terms of one or two variables, except for the major change which occurred in response to the 1780 Act. Nevertheless this discussion may prompt other historians to consider the matter more fully in the light of local circumstances.

Schedule 2 contains examples of the kinds of documents which might throw light on the ways in which assessments and re-assessments were arrived at, how appeals against assessments were dealt with and how the Land Tax itself or its administration related to other taxes and their administration. This information was supplied to me by certain of the surveyors of Assessments who had the interest and time available to make enquiries beyond the survival of Assessments. It is, therefore, much more arbitrary than the contents of Schedule 1 and the absence from it of particular counties should not be taken as indicating the absence of relevant documents from their record offices. Indeed, one could go much further: our survey indicated that Land Tax documents in general are still turning up as deposits of estate papers are calendared and classified. Moreover, the Land Tax is not always recognised as a 'subject' and close study of record office guides, indexes and calendars is recommended to ensure that important documents are not missed.

NOTES

1 Mills, D.R., 'The Significance of the Land Tax Assessments', *Local Historian*, volume 15, 1982, pp. 161–5.

2 Gibson, J. and Mills, D. (eds) *Land Tax Assessments c. 1690–c. 1950*, Stourbridge, Federation of Family History Societies, 1983, reprinted 1984.

3 Dr John Beckett of the University of Nottingham offered this interpretation, in addition to other valuable comments.

4 I owe this observation to the kindness of Mr Philip Riden, University College, Cardiff.

5 Unwin, R.W., *Search Guide to the English Land Tax*, Wakefield, West Yorkshire County Record Office, 1982, p. 6. Parliamentary Elections Act 1745 = Act 18 Geo. II c. 18. Parliamentary Elections Act 1780 = Act 20 Geo. III c. 17.

6 Ward, W.R., *The English Land Tax in the Eighteenth Century*, Oxford, 1953, especially pp. 86, 90, 100; idem., 'The Office for Taxes, 1665–1798', *Bulletin of the Institute of Historical Research*, volume 25, 1952, pp. 204–12, especially pp. 206–7; and idem., 'The Administration of the Window and Assessed Taxes, 1696–1798', *English Historical Review*, volume 67, 1952, pp. 522–42, especially pp. 527–9.

7 ibid., *English Land Tax*, pp. 83 and 139–40, 'The Office for Taxes', pp. 208–9 and 'Administration', p. 533.

8 Beckett, J.V., and Smith, D.K., 'The Land Tax Returns as a Source for studying the English Economy in the Eighteenth Century', *Bulletin of the Institute of Historical Research*, volume 54, 1981, pp. 54–61, especially pp. 56 and 59.

9 Brooks, C., 'Public Finance and Political Stability: the Administration of the Land Tax, 1688–1720', *Historical Journal*, volume 17, 1974, pp. 281–300, especially p. 282 and pp. 287–96. I am much indebted to Mr Richard Grover of Portsmouth Polytechnic for providing the material for these last four paragraphs and for much other patient advice.

SCHEDULE I

Estimated Survival of pre-1780 Land Tax Assessments, by county, hundred, wapentake, division, etc.

Abbreviations: LTA - Land Tax Assessment M - Many NC - Nearly complete
Ps - Parishes S - Some Y - Years

ENGLISH COUNTIES

BEDFORDSHIRE

Hundred	Period	Ps	Hundred	Period	Ps
Barford	1720-58 SY	1	Redbornstoke	1765-6	1
Biggleswade	1765-70 SY SP	c.10	Stodden	1750 1765-7 (4 LTAs only)	2
Flitt	1750	1	Willey	1735-81 SY SP	c.10
Manshead	1750 NC	c.25		TOTAL	c.50

BERKSHIRE

First year of survival		Ps	First year of survival		Ps
	1692	1		1740	2
	1704	2		1743	2
	1716	26		1745	1
	1718	1		1773	1
	1728	1		1778	1
	1738	1		TOTAL	40

BUCKINGHAMSHIRE

Hundred	Period	Ps	Hundred	Period	Ps
Aylesbury	1777	1	Cottesloe	1753	42
Burnham	1718-43 3Y	1	Desborough	1700-12	1
	1765	1	Stoke	1773-81	1
				TOTAL	47

CAMBRIDGESHIRE (including the Isle of Ely)

Hundred	Period	Ps	Hundred	Period	Ps
Armingford	1699-1720	1	Whetherley	1707 1736 1767	5
Chilford	1694	1	Whittlesford	do. (3 LTAs only)	3
	1759-63 NC	10	Witchford, N	1755	1
Ely	1750-79	5	Witchford, S	1750-79	11
Papworth	1769	1		TOTAL	42
Radfield, S	1759-63	4			

CHESHIRE

Hundred	Period	Ps	Hundred	Period	Ps
Chester City	1704 NC 1764, 1767 and 1769 SP	10	Wirral	1778-9 NC	c.60
				TOTAL	c.70

CORNWALL

Division	Period	Ps	Division	Period	Ps
East Division	1710-53 (4 LTAs)	3	Pyder	1725, 1763 (2 LTAs)	2
Powder West	1709-62 (7 LTAs)	2	West Penwith	1690 onwards	1
				TOTAL	8

CUMBERLAND

Ward	Period	Ps	Ward	Period	Ps
Allerdale			Cumberland	1761-72 SY SP	c.25
Above	1762-79 SY NC	c.55		1779 NC	c.45
Allerdale			Eskdale	1761-67 SY NC	c.50
Below	1751-68 SY SP	c.30	Leath	1767-70 NC	c.50
	1762 NC	c.50		TOTAL	c.250

DERBYSHIRE

Hundred	Period	Ps	Hundred	Period	Ps
Appletree	1754	1	Scarsdale	1755	1
High Peak	1721	1	Wirksworth	1693	1
	1778-79 NC	c.60		TOTAL	c.64

DEVON

Hundred	Period	Ps	Hundred	Period	Ps
Coleridge	1747 1751 NC	c.15	Stanborough	1747 1751 NC	c.15
Exeter City	1730-67 16Y	c.15		TOTAL	c.50
Plymouth Boro	Pre-1780	A few LTAs			

(Reference to the Devon RO index may turn up other pre-1780 LTAs)

DORSET

1715 1738 Alton Pancras parish

DURHAM

1735 1744 Elwick Hall parish
1759-70 Most of tne county has at least one LTA per parish: TOTAL c.250 Ps.

ESSEX

Hundred	Period	Ps	Hundred	Period	Ps
Becontree	1698	14	Tendring	1742 1743 1775	
Chafford	1698	17		(3 LTAs)	3
Dengie	1705-15 SY	1	Uttlesford	1773-7	1
Freshwell	1762-79 SY MP	c.7	Waltham	1738 1740-42	1
Havering	1698	7	Colchester Borough	1778	1
Hinckford	1762-79 SY MP	c.35		TOTAL	c.87

GLOUCESTERSHIRE

Pre-1775: ten scattered parishes with one or two LTAs each, dates ranging from 1701 to 1774.
1775-79: all Hundreds except Gloucester Borough NC from either 1775 or 1776.
TOTAL c.400 parishes.

HAMPSHIRE

Division	Period	Ps	Division	Period	Ps
Alton North	1692-1720 SY	1	Southampton	1711-78 MY MP	8*
Andover	1708-16 SY	4	Winchester	1703-30 1757-74	1*
New Forest W	1774-75 MP	c.5		TOTAL	c.23
Portsdown	1703-16	4	*Soton and Winchester all urban		

HEREFORDSHIRE

Hundred	Period	Ps	Hundred	Period	Ps
Broxash	1777-79 SP SY	c.15	Stretford	1776-79 SY	1
Greytree	1747-79 MP SY	c.15	Webtree	1777-79 SY	30
Grimsworth	1777-79	1	Wormelow	1774-79 SY	31
				TOTAL	c.93

HERTFORDSHIRE

Hundred	Period	Ps	Hundred	Period	Ps
Braughin	1711-67 MP SY	c.10	Hertford	1711-67 MY MP	c.15
Broadwater	1711-67 MP MY	c.20	Hitchin	1753 NC	c.10
Cashio	1690		Odsey	1753 MP	c.15
	1711-67 MP SY	c.20	St Albans		
Dacorum	1690 1753 MP	c.25	Borough	1753	1
Edwintree	1753 MP	c.5		TOTAL	c.131

HUNTINGDONSHIRE

Hundred	Period	Ps	Hundred	Period	Ps
Hurstingstone	1732	1	Normancross	1767 NC	c.25
	1767	24	Tozeland	1705-10	1
Leightonstone	1767	30		1767	25
				TOTAL	c.105

KENT

Division	Period	Ps	Division	Period	Ps
Aylesford E	1744-79 SY MP	c.5	Scray Lower	1756 1759 MP	c.5
Aylesford W	1754 1764 1769		Shepway Lower	1746 MP	c.50
	Burham only	1	Shepway Upper	1753	
St Augustine	1698-99 1704-79			Folkestone only	1
East	MY MP	c.50	Sutton at Hone	1729-71 18Y	
St Augustine				Upper Bromley only	1
West	1723-79 MY MP	c.25	Greenwich	1707-75 35Y	
Sandwich	1718-71 SY	1		SY SP	c.5
Romney Port	1692-1779 60Y	1		TOTAL	c.145

LANCASHIRE

No pre-1780 survivals reported

LEICESTERSHIRE

1773-4 complete for most of the county, part for 1775-6. TOTAL c.300 Ps.

LINCOLNSHIRE

HOLLAND

Wapentake	Period	Ps
Elloe	1777-79	15
North Holland (ie Skirbeck and Kirton Wap'takes)	1724-79 SY SP	c.10
Spalding	1743 Town only	1
Skirbeck	1777-79	8

LINDSEY

Wapentake	Period	Ps
Bolingbroke	1759-79 NC SY	c.20
Candleshoe	1695-1747 NC SY	c.20
None in Kesteven		
	TOTAL	c.74

LONDON

From 1692 there are assessments, including LTAs, for very substantial parts of the City of London.

MIDDLESEX

Division	Period	Ps
Brentford	1693-94 MP	c.5
	1767 NC	c.6
Edmonton	1693-94	c.3
	1767 NC	c.4
Finsbury	1767	12
Gore	1693-94 SP	c.4
Holborn	1767 NC	c.5
Kensington	Fulham 1755-56	1
	Paddington 1730 1733 1746-48	1
St Anne	1767	at least 1
St Giles	1767	c.2
St Margaret	1767	c.2
St Martin's in the Field	1767	c.6
St Paul, Covent Garden	1767	2
Staines	1693-94 SP	c.6
	1767 NC	c.12
Tower	1705-79 MP SY	c.18
Uxbridge	1693-94 1767 NC	c.10

TOTALS 1693-94 c.34. Various dates 1705-79 c.20. The whole county lacks only 24 parishes for 1767. There could be as many as 200 LTAs for this date, but a conservative estimate is about 80.

NORFOLK

Division	Period	Ps
Clackclose	1767	32
Flegg, E & W	1695	22
Forehoe	1767	32
Freebridge Lynn	1767 NC 1777	c.30
Greenhoe, S	1778	23
Guiltcross	1767	12
Happing	1702-14	16
Holt	1767 MP	c.20
Launditch	Stanfield 1767	1
Norwich	1710-79 SY SP	c.20
Shropham	1767	20
Smithdon Brothercross	1777 NC	c.16
Tunstead	1702-14	26
Yarmouth	1750 1777	some wards
	TOTAL	c.270

NORTHAMPTONSHIRE

Hundred	Period	Ps	Hundred	Period	Ps
Cleley	1774-75 1778 NC	c.10	Nobottle		
Corby	1752-55 1774 NC	c.25	Grove	1771-79 NC	c.15
Fawsley	1752-75 NC	c.20	Orlingbury	1753-79 14Y NC	c.12
Guilsborough	1752-75 NC	c.15	Polebrook	1775-79 NC	c.6
Hamsfordhoe	1751-79 15Y NC	c.6	Rothwell	1752-55 1774 NC	c.20
Higham			Spelhoe	1772-79 NC	c.10
Ferrers	1751-79 15Y NC	c.12	Towcester	1774-75 1778 NC	c.5
Huxloe	1752-55 1774 NC	c.15	Willibrook	1775-79 NC	c.12
Nassaburgh	1767	2	Wymersley	1771-79 NC	c.18
Navisford	1775-79 NC	c.5		TOTAL	c.208

NORTHUMBERLAND

Ward	Period	Ps	Ward	Period	Ps
Bamburgh	1748-79 15Y NC	c.5	Glendale	1748-79 14Y NC	c.8
Castle	1748-79 13Y NC	c.15	Morpeth	1748-79 15Y NC	c.12
Coquetdale	1748-79 15Y NC	c.12	Tynedale	1748-79 13Y NC	c.25
				TOTAL	c.77

NOTTINGHAMSHIRE

Wapentake	Period	Ps	Wapentake	Period	Ps
Bassetlaw			Broxtowe S	1737 1750-80	1
Hatfield	1752-53 NC	c.35	Newark	1700 MP	c.20
Bass'w N Clay	1752-53 NC	c.20	Nottingham		
Bass'w S Clay	1704 1752-53 NC	1	Town	1753 1758-59	1
Bingham	1731 1761-80	1	Rushcliffe	1770-79	1
Broxtowe N	1740	1		TOTAL	c.103

OXFORDSHIRE

1760 Ploughley and Wootton Hundreds: 80 parishes. 1762 Ploughley only.

RUTLAND

1716 Whole county: 56 parishes. 1722: 3 parishes. 1760: one parish.

SHROPSHIRE

1765 1771-74 one township, Soughton.

SOMERSET

Storage and calendaring are such that estimates are difficult, but:
1694-99 Bristol: SP SY
1700-79 Bristol: All 19 parishes SY
1759 Hartcliffe cum Bedminster and Portbury Hundreds: 20 parishes
1766-67 All Hundreds have some parishes, say, 200 parishes

STAFFORDSHIRE

1772 Offlow Hundred 76 parishes

SUFFOLK

Hundred	Period	Ps	Hundred	Period	Ps
Bury St Ed	1769-79 SY	2	Ipswich Boro	1721-79 MY SP	c.8
Carlford	1707 SP	c.10	Plomesgate	1737	1
Colneis	1707 SP	c.5	Wilford	1707 SP	c.8
Cosford	1707 SP	c.10		TOTAL	c.46

SURREY

Division	Period	Ps	Division	Period	Ps
Elmbridge	1751 1754 SP	c.5	Reigate	1760	1
Kingston	1751 SP	c.5		1766	1
	Malden 1751-73 SY	1		TOTAL	c.12

SUSSEX

Division	Period	Ps	Division	Period	Ps
Hastings Rape	1693-1779 SY MP	c.30	Pevensey		
Lewes Upper	1703 1743	1	Liberty	1746 1771-73	1
Pevensey Rape	1750-79 MY MP	c.40	Rye	1711-23 5Y	1
				TOTAL	c.78

WARWICKSHIRE

1775-79 Whole county has good coverage, say, 250 parishes

WESTMORLAND

Ward	Period	Ps	Ward	Period	Ps
East	1765 1773 MP	c.30	Kendal and		
West	1765 MP	c.20	Lonsdale	1773	50
				TOTAL	c.100

WILTSHIRE

Hundred	Period	Ps	Hundred	Period	Ps
Bradford	1773-74 MP	c.8	Melksham	1773-74	c.12
Chalke	1740-79 MY	1	Trowbridge	1773-74	1
Chippenham	1761 1773	1	Underditch	1739	1
Downton	1740-79 SP SY	c.6	Warminster	1773 MP	c.10
Heytesbury	1773 NC	c.15	Westbury	1773-74 SP	c.8
Highworth	1700 1750 SP	c.15		TOTAL	c.78

WORCESTERSHIRE and YORKSHIRE, EAST RIDING and YORK

No pre-1780 survivals reported

YORKSHIRE: NORTH RIDING

Wapentake	Period	Ps	Wapentake	Period	Ps
Allertonshire	1774 NC	c.30	Gilling West	1769-74 1778 NC	c.30
Birdforth	1692-95 1699		Hang East	1769	30
	1712-65 NC	c.40	Hang West	1759-60 1769 NC	c.30
Gilling East	1770-76 NC	c.25	Richmond Boro	1700-79 SY	1
				TOTAL	c.186

YORKSHIRE: WEST RIDING

1698 Whole Riding, say, 350 parishes
Also 1695, 1700-28 Staincross Wapentake, 40 parishes
1752-80 (23 years) townships of Wakefield parish

WELSH COUNTIES

The following counties have no known survivals from before 1780:
Cardigan, Carmarthen, Flint, Pembroke, Radnor

ANGLESEY

Hundred	Earliest Dates pre-1745	Ps	Earliest Dates 1745-79	Ps
Llifon	1744	11	1745-50	4
Malltraeth	1732-44	4	1745-46	7
Menai			1745-50	14
Talybolion	1693	12	1745-53	4
Tindaethwy	1712-44	9	1745-53	8
Twrcelyn	1744	3	1745-60	6
	TOTAL	39	TOTAL	43

BRECONSHIRE

1743-78 (12Y) 18 parishes mainly in the Hundreds of Merthyr and Defynnog

CAERNARVONSHIRE

Hundred	Period	Ps	Hundred	Period	Ps
Arllechwedd			Dinlläen	1767	1
Isaf	1746-76 8Y NC	c.6	Eifionydd	1769-71 MP	c.8
Arllechwedd			Is-gwyrfai	1761	1
Ushaf	1746-76 8Y NC	c.4		1770-79 NC	c.8
Creuddyn	1746-76 8Y NC	c.4	Uwchgwyrfai	1770-79 NC	c.4
Nantconwy	1746-76 8Y NC	c.6		TOTAL	c.41

DENBIGHSHIRE

Hundred	Period	Ps	Hundred	Period	Ps
Bromfield	1759-60	c.20	Isdulas	1747-61 SP SY	c.4
	1778-79 NC	c.40	Ruthin Boro	1760-61	1
Chirk	1758-59 SP	c.10	Yale	1759-61 SP	c.2
Isaled	1754 1760 SP	c.4		TOTAL	c.61

GLAMORGAN

Hundred	Period	Ps	Hundred	Period	Ps
Cowbridge			Ogmore	1692-1707	1
Borough	1773	1		1707	1
Langyfelach	1772-79 NC MY	c.12	Swansea	1766-67	
Newcastle	1704	2		1771-79 NC	c.25
				TOTAL	c.42

MONMOUTHSHIRE

1716-35 Itton parish

MONTGOMERYSHIRE

1710 Churchstoke parish
1762-79 Berriew parish
1765 1771-74 Most of the county, especially the later dates, say, 120 Ps

For a complete survey of surviving Land Tax Assessments see:
Gibson, J. and Mills, D., Land Tax Assessments c.1690-c.1950, Stourbridge, Federation of Family History Societies, 1983, reprinted 1984.
Available from J.S.W.Gibson, Harts Cottage, Church Hanborough, Oxford, OX7 2AB; price in 1984 £1.00, plus 20p postage in UK, or 75p for airmail overseas.

SCHEDULE II

Abstract of certain Administrative/Background Documents related to the Land Tax Assessments

Bedfordshire

Dissertation on Land Tax by Richard How of Aspley Guise, 1770–1. BRO HW 45, 48.

Berkshire

Abstracts of the Assessments of the whole County down to parish totals. BRO D/Est 07/4 and /5.
Abstract for Theale Hundred 1693 and 1704 by parishes. D/Ewi E14. Survey for Land Tax 1693 for Berkshire down to parish level with one figure for real property, one for personal. D/EBy 04. Minutes of the Commissioners for Land and Window Taxes, Abingdon Division 1722–71. D/EP4 08/1–4. Proceedings of the Commissioners of the land and other taxes within the Forest Division, beginning 1791. D/P 154/28/1.

Buckinghamshire

Burnham Hundred Proceedings of Land Tax Commissioners 1699–1869. AR33/73/1–5

Derbyshire

Appointment of assessors in liberty of Ripley, with detailed instructions 1707. DRO, D895 B/Z1. Abstract of parish totals 1740 for Repton and Gresley Hundred, D1222 Z/Z2 Dethick Lea and Holloway Assessment 1693 is accompanied by other minor papers 1723–34 D1088 M/R 10–19.

Essex

Papers, mostly counsel's opinions 1699–1714, re Land Tax on Lord Petre's estates. ERO D/DP L91. Petition 1707 for exemption from Land Tax upon lands flooded by breach. D/DSa vol. II, p 482. Assessment down to parish totals for whole county 1692–3 D/DKW 06/1. Becontree half-Hundred parish totals 1712–13 D/DB E59. Lexden, Thurstable and Witham Hundreds, 1734. Duplicate assessments down to parish totals D/DSq 07. Minutes of Commissioners for various areas, some with detail re appeals against over-assessment, eg DZ 2/8/1. Dispute at Dagenham 1750 and 1756, D/D St El, D/DBy 29/2.

Hampshire

Minute books for Winchester 1691–1740 and Minute books and other papers for Southampton 1696–1778.

Hertfordshire

Miscellaneous LT section 1/80 includes considerable early administrative material eg minutes and notes of appeals c1712–67.

Huntingdonshire

The Norris Museum and Library, The Broadway, St Ives, nr Huntingdon contains the survey of St Ives conducted by Edmund Pettis in 1732, which gives Land Tax Assessments, some amended, and much other information relating to property; also county and town LT quotas for whole county.

Kent

Minutes and other papers are available (a) at County level 1702–1812 (b) for the following areas:– Aylesford South, Faversham Town, St Augustine East, Sandwich, Lydd Town, Romney Port, Sutton at Hone Lower* and Scray Upper*

*In petty session minute book

Receivers Generals' Accounts and Papers: Sir Brooke Bridges 1784–91, Richard James 1792–1805, Sir William Twysden 1806–20.

Leicestershire

Parish totals for East Goscote Hundred 1700–49 in LRO DE565, Box 4911–Pochin MSS. Other miscellanea in LRO Subject Index.

Lincolnshire

LAO, Lindsey Deposit 35/2 contains a wide variety of papers for Candleshoe Wapentake 1692–1711 and Assessments by townships for Lincoln City and most of Lindsey 1692–3. Horncastle valuation to equalise Land Tax 1813 LAO/CHAT/5/16.

Middlesex

Uxbridge Division Commissioners Minutes, including appeals, 1745–85.

Montgomeryshire

In the National Library of Wales the Powis Castle Deeds and Documents contain a Canvass Book with names of the freeholders qualified to vote . . . with their places of abode, the names of their estates . . . how their estates are assessed and for whom they vote, 1774.

Nottinghamshire

Some supplementary material including redemption certificates for Rempstone (1725–35), Teversal (1814–38), Tiln (1738–48) Thorpe-next-Newarke (1691–1824) and Warsop (1689–1845).

Suffolk (East)

Various Land Tax documents re administration 1704–30 including re-assessment warrants for Hartismere Hundred 1711.

Surrey

Minute Book etc for Kingston and Elmbridge 1723–57.

Sussex

Minute Books : Rye 1688–1838, Winchelsea 1769–94 (correspondence 1801–18), Pevensey Liberty 1771–98, Bramber Upper 1803–20, 1837–43.

Wiltshire

Land Tax roll for Ramsbury Hundred 1661 (sic) in Berkshire (sic) Record Office, D/EB n 05.

Worcestershire

Assessment totals for 1751 by parish, HWRO 705 : 73 BA 2007 (ii)
Minutes 1814–45, Worcester Division HWRO 899: 599 BA 7442.

Yorkshire WR

See R W Unwin, *Search Guide to the English Land Tax*, West Yorkshire County Record Office 1982.

Index

Readers should note that the Land Tax itself has not been used as an entry, although a few topics are to be found under Tax, eg amounts of tax paid. Similarly, Land Tax Assessments has not been used as an entry, but early Land Tax Assessments, and other related Assessments may be found under Assessments.